S0-ADL-509

Sweetieapplepie_89@hotmail.com (Kimkim)

DICTIONARY
OF PROVERBS

Linda Flavell completed a first degree in modern languages and has subsequent qualifications in both secondary and primary teaching. She has written three simplified readers for overseas students and co-authored, with her husband, *Current English Usage* for Papermac and *Dictionary of Idioms*, *Dictionary of Proverbs* and *Dictionary of Word Origins* for Kyle Cathie Limited.

Roger Flavell's Masters thesis was on the nature of idiomaticity and his doctoral research on idioms and their teaching in several European languages. He is currently chairman of the Department of English for Speakers of Other Languages at the University of London Institute of Education.

Linda and Roger Flavell live in Sussex and have a son and a daughter.

DICTIONARY
OF PROVERBS
and their Origins

LINDA AND ROGER FLAVELL

HIPPOCRENE BOOKS
New York

First published in Great Britain in 1993 by
Kyle Cathie Limited
7/8 Hatherley Street, London SWIP 2 QT

All rights reserved. No reproduction, copy or transmission of this
publication may be made without written permission. No paragraph of
this publication may be reproduced, copied or transmitted save with
written permission or in accordance with the provisions of the Copyright
Act 1956 (as amended). Any person who does any unauthorized act in
relation to this publication may be liable to criminal prosecution and civil
claims for damages.

Copyright© 1993 by Linda and Roger Flavell.

Hippocrene edition, 1997, published by arrangement with Barnes & Noble, Inc.

Library of Congress Cataloging-in-Publication Data
Flavell, Linda.
        Dictionary of proverbs and their origins / Linda and Roger
    Flavell.
            p.   cm.
        Originally published: London : K. Cathie, 1993.
        Includes bibliographical references and index.
        ISBN 0-7818-0591-0
        1. Proverbs, English. I. Flavell, Roger. II. Title.
    PN6405.F53   1997
    398.9'21--dc21   97-15514
                                                              CIP

Printed in the United States of America.

INTRODUCTION

A proverb has three characteristics: few words, good sense, and a fine image
(Moses Ibn Ezra, SHIRAT YISRAEL, 1924)

For thousands of years proverbs have been amongst us. For example, a major early collection is the BOOK OF PROVERBS in the OLD TESTAMENT. It is in fact a collection of collections, which reached its final edited form in about the fifth century BC. However, many of the individual sayings within it date, according to scholars, to at least the seventh century BC. From this and other early beginnings, proverbs have always had a strong hold on cultures throughout the world. Each language has its own treasuries of folk sayings. For British collections, see **An accumulation of wisdom** (page 108); and for one of the greatest and most influential collections, see **Erasmus's Adagia** (page 8).

Why is it that proverbs have exercised such a fascination over millennia? Moses Ibn Ezra's definition provides an explanation. Above all, they offer good sense. Proverbs are guidelines for life, based on the collective folk wisdom of the people. Such riches are eagerly sought after at any age in mankind's development. They are also pithily, even wittily, and always memorably phrased, as a result of a refining process that often takes them through various versions before they reach their polished final form. They are *The wisdom of many and the wit of one*. Many have tried to define a proverb; some of their efforts are gathered in **What is a proverb?** (page 3).

This book responds to the interest in proverbs by providing information both for reference purposes and for the browser.

BROWSING

It might be Ezra's 'fine image' of the language, it might be a fascination with customs of past ages, it might be a love of life and of wisdom – whatever the attraction to a book on proverbs, we have taken great pains to please the browser.

The entries have been selected because they have a tale to tell. There are many more that could have been included but we hope that we have provided a satisfying cross-section of the vast range of proverbs that occur in English, even if we cannot claim it to be a comprehensive list.

The etymology (or etymologies, since there are sometimes alternative accounts) tries to go back to the earliest origins. We endeavour to give dates, although it is often impossible to do this with any confidence. As proverbs are folk wisdom, passed down in the oral tradition from generation to generation, the first written record (even if we can specify *that* with any certainty) is likely to be a poor indication of the saying's actual origin. This is an important reservation to bear in mind when for brevity in an entry we say something like 'This is the earliest use'. What we do have sometimes is *the wit of one* that reflects the previous *wisdom of many*, such as Shakespeare's *Neither a borrower nor a lender be*, Pope's *To err is human, to forgive divine*, and so on. We have done our utmost to be precise about the dates of quotations, both in the etymology and in the quotation sections, in order to show the development of the saying, in form, meaning and use. There are real difficulties with many works, and in each case we have chosen what seems to be an appropriate solution. For example, we have followed the OXFORD ENGLISH DICTIONARY dates for Shakespeare's plays; given the last edition (1536) that Erasmus himself produced of his ADAGIA; used one date for the CANTERBURY TALES, even though they were written over fourteen years or so; and so on.

Proverbs mainly come from worlds that are far removed from our contemporary civilisation. Where necessary, we have offered information on the context of the saying, within the entry itself or within one of the boxes or essays throughout the book. For example, an explanation of the unpopularity of the medieval baker comes in *Pull devil, pull baker;* the place of the devil in the popular mind is developed more fully in **The devil to pay** (page 66). On occasions we have gone beyond the general cultural context to events surrounding the use of proverbs. For a tale of skulduggery in the highest places, follow the sad tale of Sir Thomas Overbury and the dubious activities of James I in *No news is good news* and *Beauty is only skin deep*.

The essays and boxes strategically situated throughout the book (usually near entries on a connected theme) are of various kinds – cultural, linguistic or just plain curious. They are designed to reflect the riches and diversity of proverb lore.

REFERENCE

Each saying dealt with in the body of the book is listed alphabetically in relation to a key word within it. As proverbs are usually whole sentences and not single words, there is necessarily a choice to be made regarding the main word. We have exercised our judgement as to which is the key word (normally a noun or a verb) but, in case our intuitions do not coincide with the reader's, we have provided an index of all the important words in each saying at the back of the book.

The proverb itself is followed by a definition, giving the contemporary meaning. This is often necessary because the sense, after a long history of slowly changing use, may not be immediately clear. Common variants are given in another section, and occasional notes on formality and informality, connotations, grammatical peculiarities and so on are found under *Usage*.

Many entries are complete with one or more illustrative quotations – a further guide to usage, as well as an illustration of the proverb's development. Quotations are listed in chronological order and the more recent provide a taste of modern authors. Their mainly allusive reference to proverbs, presuming that the reader will recognise the reference to the expression, is rather different from the direct quoting of the full saying in earlier times. We have drawn on a very wide range of sources for the quotations, but the great majority of the contemporary illustrations are from our eclectic reading – a genuine serendipity, with no claims to be systematic or comprehensive!

The bibliography is there both to show our sources and to provide a point of extended reference. It is only a selective list. To have included all the thousands of sources we referred to would have made the bibliography unmanageable. In the text of the book we usually refer to an author just by name (e.g. Walsh). Full details are in the Bibliography. If there is the possibility of confusion because the author has more than one entry, the name is followed by the date of publication of the relevant book.

Our thanks are due to the various libraries we have extensively consulted: our local library in Sussex, The University of London Library and, above all, the British Library, without which it would not have been possible to write a book like this. Our indebtedness is even greater to scholars who have preceded us in the field. The subject of the proverbs has benefited from the herculean labours of many. Lean, for example, devoted over fifty years of his life to his monumental collection of 1902–4. We would like to acknowledge our appreciation of the pioneering work of William Shepard Walsh, whose aims, approach and spirit are very much our own. We stand in awe of the erudition and immense scholarship and diligence of Burton Egbert Stevenson. We are very grateful for the comprehensive bibliographical endeavours of Wolfgang Mieder. We hope that where we follow their lead they will indeed recognise that *Imitation is the sincerest form of flattery.*

Inevitably we have made mistakes, for which we bear sole responsibility. We would welcome comments and corrections.

In short, our aim has been to inform and entertain, to provide a balance of reference material and a rich and varied diet for the curious; we have striven for scholarly accuracy without falling into academic pedantry. Now it is for you to judge for, after all, *The proof of the pudding is in the eating.*

How to find a proverb: Each proverb is listed under a key word. For example, *An apple a day keeps the doctor away* is under **Apple**. However, there is often a choice of keyword, so the index at the back of the book lists all the significant words within an expression. You could look up **Apple**, **Day** or **Doctor** and immediately be guided to the right page.

MAIN ESSAYS

ABSENCE

■ **Absence makes the heart grow fonder**

Our feeling for those we love increases when we are apart from them

This is a line from a song ISLE OF BEAUTY (before 1839) by Thomas Haynes Bayly. It was Bayly who popularised the words but Stevenson says they are not of his inspiration, being originally the first line of an anonymous poem which appeared in Davison's POETICAL RAPSODY of 1602.

The sentiment is endorsed in literature. In Shakespeare's OTHELLO (1604), Desdemona confesses *I dote upon his very absence* (Act 1, scene ii); in FAMILIAR LETTERS (1650) James Howell discloses that *Distance sometimes endears friendship, and absence sweeteneth it.* La Rochfoucauld quotes a French proverb which says that *Friends agree best at a distance* (MAXIMES, 1665) while Roger de Bussy-Rabutin writes: *Absence is to love what wind is to fire; it puts out the little, it kindles the great* (MAXIMES D'AMOUR, 1666).

Proverbs from other countries also find virtue in separation and absence:

A little absence does much good (French)
Love your neighbour but do not pull down the hedge (German)
Go to your brother's house, but not every day (Spanish)

The other side of the coin is *Out of sight, out of mind.* Psychologists say that many people are lazy about personal relationships and find it quite easy to put them aside when separated. But, for those who are parted from a loved-one and concerned that absence might not be having its intensifying effect, Charles Lamb in his DISSERTATION ON A ROAST PIG (1823) offers this timely advice: *Presents, I often say, endear absents.*

ACCIDENTS

■ **Accidents will happen in the best regulated families**

No one is immune from the unforeseen

Variant: Accidents will happen even in the best circles

Every copy of the book was paid for in full by the insurance company, and my friend was as much in pocket as if he had sold an edition to the book-sellers. Poets, however, cannot expect always to be so fortunate as this. Accidents of the desired kind simply will not happen to their verse.
(Robert Lynd, THE BLUE LION, 'OUT OF PRINT', 1923)

And because accidents will happen, at Audi we haven't ignored 'passive safety' either.
(Advertisement for Audi, OBSERVER, 25 August 1991)

The modern ear is probably more accustomed to *Accidents will happen* than to the longer proverb alluded to by Sir Walter Scott in PEVEREL OF THE PEAK (1823): *Nay, my lady, . . . such things will befall in the best regulated families.* In the nineteenth century the words were a balm to soothe away the agitation or shame felt by good families when circumstance or the family black sheep dealt them a severe blow. A frequent reference was, and still is, to an unwanted pregnancy. In the first half of the twentieth century the proverb was much loved by popular crime writers when an unsavoury piece of information had come to light.

Usage: The abbreviated form *accidents will happen . . .* is often left hanging in the air as a comment on a situation. The tone implicit can range from the commiserating through to the delighted.

ACTIONS

■ **Actions speak louder than words**

What people do reveals more about them than what they say

See also: Handsome is as handsome does; Fine words butter no parsnips

The gallant foreigner, who could not tell them how he sympathized with them, but whose actions spoke louder than words.
(F McCullagh, WITH THE COSSACKS, 1906)

In fact he told everyone he had masterminded the whole move. 'Council just 'ad to give in, because wi' me, actions speak worder than louds,' he said defiantly, thumping the arm of his chair to show he meant business.
(Michele Guinness, PROMISED LAND, 1987)

An abundance of proverbial literature exhorts the reader to relate his words to his deeds. *Deeds are fruits, words are but leaves,* declares Thomas Draxe (BIBLIOTHECA, 1633). The Bible's message *by their fruits ye shall know them* (MATTHEW 7:20) supports his analogy, exhorting us to judge people on the quality of their lives rather than the persuasiveness of their speech. Another old saying on a horticultural theme compares a person whose words are more forthcoming than his actions to a garden:

*A man of words and not of deeds
Is like a garden full of weeds.*
(James Howell, ENGLISH PROVERBS, 1659)

The Roman poet Ovid is quite blunt about the criterion for assessing others.

What is a proverb?

The wisdom of the street

Daughters of daily experience

A short pithy saying in common and recognized use
(OXFORD ENGLISH DICTIONARY)

A concise sentence, often metaphorical or alliterative in form, which is held to express some truth ascertained by experience or observation and familiar to all
(OXFORD ENGLISH DICTIONARY)

A brief epigrammatic saying that is a popular byword
(WEBSTER'S NEW INTERNATIONAL DICTIONARY)

Proverbs are short sentences drawn from long experience
(Cervantes, DON QUIXOTE, 1605)

The People's Voice
(James Howell, 1594-1666)

Proverbs may not improperly be called the Philosophy of the Common People, or, according to Aristotle, the truest Reliques of old Philosophy
(Howell, LEXICON, PROVERBS, 1659)

Much matter decocted into a few words
(Thomas Fuller, THE WORTHIES OF ENGLAND, 1662)

What is a proverb, but the experience and observation of several ages, gathered and summed up into one expression?
(Robert South, SERMONS, 1692)

Notable measures and directions for human life
(William Penn, ADVICE TO HIS CHILDREN, 1699)

The wit of one man and the wisdom of many
(Lord John Russell, QUARTERLY REVIEW, 1850)

A proverb has three characteristics: few words, good sense, and a fine image
(Moses Ibn Ezra, SHIRAT YISRAEL, 1924)

No need of words, trust deeds, he urges (FASTI, c AD 8). George Herbert concurs: *The effect speaks, the tongue need not*, (JACULA PRUDENTUM, 1640). It would seem to be a precursor of our present-day proverb *Actions speak louder than words*, which, though relatively recent in coinage, expresses the ancient wisdom that the way a person conducts his life proclaims his character better than any words can.

APPEARANCES

■ **Appearances are deceptive**

Outward show is misleading; internal reality is often different from external looks

Variant: Appearances are deceitful

See also: All that glitters is not gold; Never judge by appearances; Beauty is only skin deep

With his white beard, his long and curly white hair, his large dark liquid eyes, his smooth broad forehead and aquiline nose, he had the air of a minor prophet. Nor were appearances deceptive. In another age, in other surroundings Mr Falx would in all probability have been a minor prophet.
(Aldous Huxley, THOSE BARREN LEAVES, 1925)

Appearances can be deceptive, the North Yorkshire training centre Middleham is living proof. Simply being a picturesque Wensleydale town, set in holiday brochure countryside, makes it unexceptional. This is

Herriot country, embarrassingly rich in natural beauty. But behind the façade of pubs and coffee shops that line Middleham's cobbled market square lies enough history to fill a few lessons in the national curriculum.
(DAILY MAIL, 8 February 1993)

The cautionary note sounded by this proverb is an ancient one. In his fable THE WOLF IN SHEEP'S CLOTHING (c 570 BC) Aesop tells of a wolf who pulls a sheepskin over his back and joins a flock so that he can enjoy a meal when the fancy takes him. *Appearances are deceptive.*

The adage came into English in the eighteenth century. Walsh quotes the interesting entry of Judge Haliburton in his MAXIMS OF AN OLD STAGER for this proverb:

Always judge your fellow-passengers to be the opposite of what they appear to be. For instance, a military man is not quarrelsome, for no man doubts his courage, but a snob is. A clergyman is not over strait-laced, for his piety is not questioned, but a cheat is. A lawyer is not apt to be argumentative, but an actor is. A woman that is all smiles and graces is a vixen at heart; snakes fascinate. A stranger that is obsequious and over-civil without apparent cause is treacherous; cats that purr are apt to bite and scratch. Pride is one thing, assumption is another; the latter must always get the cold shoulder, for whoever shows it is no gentleman: men never affect to be what they are, but what they are not. The only man who really is what he appears to be is – a gentleman.

■ Never judge by appearances

Looks should never be used as a criterion for assessment

Variant: You can't judge by appearances

See also: Appearances are deceptive; The cowl does not make the monk; Fine feathers make fine birds

She wore . . . every appearance of innocence, but in her person she illustrated the truth of the old adage that one should not judge by appearances.
(M. Williams, LEAVES OF A LIFE, 1890)

Don't judge by appearances, but by his actions more,
You never know when you may drive a good man from your door;
Clothes don't make the man, you know, some wise person wrote,
For many an honest heart may beat beneath a ragged coat.
(Hawley Franck, MANY AN HONEST HEART MAY BEAT BENEATH A RAGGED COAT, 1901)

Why should one *never judge by appearances?* Because, to quote another proverb, *Appearances are deceptive.* Not surprisingly, this thought finds expression in both Old and New Testaments. When Samuel searches amongst the sons of Jesse for God's intended king over Israel, he is tempted to choose the brother with the most striking appearance. God, however, rejects him saying, *Look not on his countenance, or on the height of his stature, because I have refused him; for the Lord seeth not as man seeth, for man looketh on the outward appearance, but the Lord looketh on the heart* (I SAMUEL 16:7). God's choice is David.

In John's gospel Jesus commanded his followers *Judge not according to the appearance, but judge righteous judgement* (JOHN 7:24) when he was criticised for healing a man on the sabbath day.

The latter reference is the probable source of the proverb which came into use in the eighteenth century. Its accepted wisdom is not unchallenged. Oscar Wilde declared that *it is only the shallow people who do not judge by appearances* (THE PICTURE OF DORIAN GRAY, 1891), presumably assuming that such people did not have the wit to form a shrewd opinion of what they saw.

APPLE

■ **An apple a day keeps the doctor away**

Eating an apple every day will keep you in good health

At Tesco, it's the doctor that keeps the apples away. This is the doctor in charge of quality control at Tesco. With the aid of his penetrometer he's about to test an apple for crunchiness. Too soft and he'll be very hard on it. The entire load will be rejected.
(Advertisement for Tesco in GOOD HOUSEKEEPING, November 1992)

Apples were originally cultivated from wild crab-apples. When the Romans occupied Britain they brought several different varieties with them. The fruit has had special significance in many cultures and is central to several Greek, Roman, Celtic and Norse legends.

In England, over the centuries, a number of charms and omens have sprung up about the apple. Apple pips cast into a fire or pressed to the cheek are a test of true love. Apple peel cast over the shoulder will form the initial of one's future sweetheart and a good crop of apples signifies a good year for twins.

In THE HAVEN OF HEALTH (1612), Thomas Cogan writes that *apples are thought to quench the flame of Venus* and he quotes the rhyme:

He that will not a wife wed,
Must eat a cold apple when he goeth to bed.

An apple before retiring recurs in what is quoted by some as 'an old English verse':

Ate an apfel
avore gwain bed
makes the doctor
beg his bread.

Appearances flatter to deceive, however. In fact, the verse is first found as late as E M Wright's RUSTIC SPEECH (1913), where it is an attempt to give the nineteenth century proverb *An apple a day keeps the doctor away* some rural roots.

But is there any truth in the proverb? It is certainly possible to eat an apple a day, for the fruit has excellent keeping qualities if stored in a cool, dry place. Nutritionally the apple contains no harmful sodium or fat to make a doctor frown. On the contrary it provides vitamins, fibre and boron, an ingredient which aids the body's absorption of calcium, so promoting strong teeth and bones and guarding against osteoporosis.

It seems that our ancestors were wise indeed; a daily apple can do us nothing but good – unlike some other things we might eat. Robert Reisner records this 'anti-proverb' in GRAFFITI: TWO THOUSAND YEARS OF WALL WRITING (1971): *An apple a day keeps the doctor away, but an onion a day keeps everybody away.*

■ **How we apples swim**

How well you think you've done

And even this, little as it is, gives him so much self-importance in his own eyes that he assumes a consequential air, sets his arms akimbo, and, strutting among the historical artists, cries, 'How we apples swim!'
(Hogarth, WORKS, 1768)

This proverb is applied to a person, usually pompous and overbearing, who is indulging in a spot of self-aggrandisement. It alludes to the fable of the apples and the horse's dung. Following a heavy fall of rain, a rush of water swept away a large pile of apples and a nearby dunghill. As they bobbed along together in the flood, the balls of dung cried out to the apples, 'How we apples swim.' In BROTHER PROTESTANTS (1733), Swift puts the fable into verse:

A Ball of new-dropt Horse's Dung,
Mingling with Apples in the Throng,
Said to the Pippin, plump and prim,
See, Brother, how we Apples swim.

Usage: Dated

ART

■ **Art is long, life is short**

There are so many skills and so much knowledge to acquire that a lifetime is not long enough to do it

Art is long, and Time is fleeting,
And our hearts, though stout and brave,
Still, like muffled drums, are beating
Funeral marches to the grave.
(Henry Wadsworth Longfellow,
A PSALM OF LIFE, 1839)

Hippocrates was the most well-known and highly acclaimed physician of ancient Greece. His work consists of a collection of his own writings on the art of healing together with those of other Greek physicians. (See also *Desperate diseases call for desperate remedies.*) Of particular interest is the Hippocratic Oath which provides the ethical framework of modern day medical practice. In APHORISMS (c 400 BC) Hippocrates expresses the frustration of the physician thus: *Life is short, the art long, opportunity fleeting, experience treacherous, judgment difficult.*

The influence of the phrase was greatly helped by its formulation in Latin (c AD 49) by Seneca in his appropriately entitled DE BREVITATE VITAE (On the Shortness of Life). Seneca's original *Vita brevis est, ars longa* was recast in subsequent centuries to *Ars longa, vita brevis,* which is still quoted on occasion in Latin today.

In English, the earliest reference is in Chaucer's PARLEMENT OF FOULES (c 1374):

The lyf so short, the craft so long to lerne,
Th'assay so hard, so sharp the conqueriynge

And two centuries later Sir John Davies encapsulates the full meaning of the emergent proverb in these words:

Skill comes so slow, and life so fast doth fly,
We learn so little and forget so much.
(NOSCE TEIPSUM, 1599)

Hippocrates was, of course, referring to medical skill but it has since pleased many writers to apply his words to their own particular craft. In AN ESSAY ON CRITICISM (1711), Pope uses them to refer to critics who, he argues, should know themselves, their abilities and their limitations. It is one of life's frustrations that any one person can only aspire to so much:

One science only will one genius fit;
So vast is art, so narrow human wit:
Not only bounded to peculiar arts,
But oft' in those confin'd to single parts.

Many other famous writers, in the nineteenth century in particular, have echoed similar themes. Goethe, Baudelaire, Longfellow and Browning all used the saying, thereby adding to its popularity.

Usage: The phrase is sometimes misused to mean that art lives beyond the end of the (short) life of its creator, providing a kind of immortality

BABY

■ **Don't throw the baby out with the bathwater**

When making changes be careful that you don't sweep away the good things along with the bad

Variant: Don't empty the baby out with the bathwater

When changing we must be careful not to empty the baby with the bath in mere reaction against the past.
(George Bernard Shaw, EVERYBODY'S POLITICAL WHAT'S WHAT, 1944)

Q. *How can I make sure I continue to receive Business News? I have seen copies of two issues recently which have not been sent to my office, though I always used to get it. Was it something I said?*
A. *Nothing personal. BT is continually refining its database to make sure Business News is only mailed to people who are actually interested in reading it regularly. Sometimes, inevitably, the baby goes out with the bathwater.*
(BRITISH TELECOM BUSINESS NEWS, Spring 1993)

British aid officials agree: 'There have been some problems with Lome and improvements are needed, but over 15 years and four renegotiations, Lome has proved a fairly good development instrument. Marin wants to throw the baby out with the bathwater, said one.
(DAILY TELEGRAPH, 18 March 1993)

Some authorities claim that this was of German origin, a translation of *Das Kind mit dem Bade ausschütten.* The English saying has been traced back to a first use by Thomas Carlyle in 1853. Since Carlyle was a considerable author on the subject of German culture, language and literature, it is probable that this theory is correct. It is all the more likely because in the early 1850s Carlyle was heavily engaged in research into his monumental treatise THE HISTORY OF FREDERICK THE GREAT.

The phrase has gradually taken on the status of a modern day proverb, in that it offers popular advice and guidance. It was a favourite of George Bernard Shaw, appearing in several different forms in a number of his books, before it assumed the familiar shape we know today.

Usage : Informal

BACK

■ **You scratch my back, and I'll scratch yours**

If you help me, I'll help you

See also: One good turn deserves another

Mutuum muli scabunt (Mules scratch each other) is a Latin adage quoted by Erasmus in ADAGIA (1536). Thomas Coryat explains it thus: *Mulus mulum scabit; by which the Ancients signified, the courtesies done unto friends, ought to be requited with reciprocal offices of friendship* (ENGLISH WITS, 1616).

Erasmus's Adagia

Desiderius Erasmus (1466–1536) was one of the greatest scholars of his age. He was born in Rotterdam, subsequently travelling widely throughout Europe. He had strong links with England. For example, he was the Lady Margaret Reader in Greek at Cambridge from 1511–14. His output was prodigious and immensely influential. In the evenings, it seems, he would turn from the labours of the day to the development of his collection of proverbs, an enterprise that occupied him for some forty years. The very first edition, the COLLECTANEA, was published in 1500 and contained 818 sayings, traced to their Latin and Greek origins and illuminated by Erasmus's own commentary. The second edition, the CHILIADES, was published in 1508 in Venice and contained 3260 adages. The collection grew in the various later editions in Erasmus's lifetime (1515, 1517–8, 1520, 1526, 1528, 1533 and 1536), mostly published in Basle.

John Ray puts it rather more bluntly: *Scratch my breech and I'll claw your elbow. Mutuum muli scabunt. Ka me and I'll ka thee. When undeserving persons commend one another* (ENGLISH PROVERBS, 1670).

The expression has been variously expressed over the centuries with no particular fixed form. *You scratch my back and I'll scratch yours* seems to be from the nineteenth century.

A literary instance of mutual back-scratching in the form of flattery took place between Sir Edward Bulwer and Dickens. In July 1865 both authors were present at the inauguration of the Guild of Literature and Art. Bulwer referred to Dickens as 'a resplendent ornament of literature'. Dickens, in return, praised Bulwer as 'the brightest ornament of the literary class'. Bulwer then pronounced Hertfordshire fortunate in welcoming such a famous man while Dickens declared that county 'the envy of every other county in England' because Bulwer lived there. Dickens then went on to counter Bulwer's fulsome praise of his literary mastery by pronouncing that 'when the health, life, and beauty now overflowing these halls shall have fled, crowds of people will come to see the place where our distinguished host lived and wrote'. Commenting on the occasion, the SATURDAY REVIEW called it 'a wonderful match of mutual admiration and laudation' and looked forward to more back-scratching for it supposed 'that a Guild of Literature and Art means an institution where, on paying your subscription punctually, you are entitled to be called by the others who have also paid their subscriptions "a resplendent ornament", or any other complimentary name to which you have a mind.'

Usage: The saying always has negative connotations. It might be at the level of the relatively harmless mutual congratulation of Dickens and Bulwer; it may well refer to insider dealing in the City or corrupt practices for contracts at the Town Hall.

BEAUTY

■ **Beauty is in the eye of the beholder**

One person's aesthetic sensibilities may differ from another's

Variant: Beauty lies in the eye of the beholder

See also: One man's meat is another man's poison

'One moment, Marcia. Many people come yet?' . . .
  'My cousin, Eleanor Massereene.'
  'The cousin! I am so glad. Anything new is such a relief. And I have heard she is beautiful – is she?'
  'Beauty is in the eye of the beholder,' quotes Marcia in a low tone, and with a motion of her hand towards the open door inside which sits Molly, that sends Lady Stafford upstairs without further parley.
(Margaret Hungerford, MOLLY BAWN, 1878)

About noon he was interrupted.
  'My father.'
  Recognizing the voice, he pushed the proofs of labor from him almost to the other side of the table, turned in his seat, and replied, his face suffused with pleasure:

'Thou enemy to labor! Did not some one tell thee of what I have on hand, and how I am working to finish it in time to take the water with thee this afternoon? Answer, O my Gul-Bahar, more beautiful growing as the days multiply!'

'Thou flatterer! Do I not know beauty is altogether in the eye of the beholder, and that all persons do not see alike?'

(Lewis Wallace, PRINCE OF INDIA, 1893)

Is beauty absolute or is it relative? If the latter, is it to be decided on the statement of one perceiver, or is more evidence needed? David Hume, the philosopher, certainly took the view that it was relative: *Beauty in things exists merely in the mind which contemplates them.* (ESSAYS MORAL AND POLITICAL, 1742).

In more popular form Benjamin Franklin expressed the same view at the same period:

Beauty, like supreme dominion,
Is but supported by opinion
(POOR RICHARD'S ALMANACK, 1741)

A hundred years earlier, a proverb which looked to the farmyard for expression, encapsulated a similar thought: *An ass is beautiful to an ass, and a pig to a pig.* (John Ray, ENGLISH PROVERBS, 1670)

Over many centuries, then, a popular view has been that *beauty is in the eye of the beholder*, although this precise formulation is not recorded before the last quarter of the nineteenth century. The tradition continues, sometimes with the highest level of aesthetic support. Henry Moore, perhaps England's greatest twentieth century sculptor, speaks with some authority: *Too many people say 'beautiful' when they really mean 'pretty'. To me, a hippopotamus is beautiful. I much prefer them to swans!*

■ Beauty is only skin deep

A good looking woman does not necessarily have an attractive character, so don't judge by appearance

See also: Handsome is as handsome does; Never judge by appearances

I'm tired of all this nonsense about beauty being only skin-deep. That's deep enough. What do you want – an adorable pancreas? (Jean Kerr, THE SNAKE HAS ALL THE LINES, 1960)

'Handsome is as handsome does,' my father was rather given to saying; 'beauty is only skin deep,' my mother would echo . . . and while beauty does indeed hover just above the epidermis, it's a touch more useful there than below it.
(GOOD HOUSEKEEPING, November 1992)

Behind the aged face of a long-time Christian are memories of family and friends. Wrinkles stand for earnest times of prayer, loving care, and decades of useful work. The beauty is no longer the skin-deep charm of youth but the time-honoured loveliness of a life well-lived.
(J David Branon, OUR DAILY BREAD, December 1992)

THIS CARBON COPY CUTIE IS SKIN-DEEP. Macaulay Culkin is an infant prodigy to bring out the Herod in me. He has widened his eyes in wonderment just once too often.

From a small innocent, . . . he's become an old pro who thinks he can get away with the same tricks of gaucherie.
(MAIL ON SUNDAY, 13 December 1992)

Beauty is more than skin deep. Considerably more goes into a Nigel Gilks kitchen than is first apparent.
(Advertisement, KITCHENS, BEDROOMS AND BATHROOMS, January/February 1993)

Two of the earliest references to beauty being only skin deep are connected with Sir Thomas Overbury. For a full account of the skulduggery surrounding his murder, see *No news is good news*. The first reference comes from his poem, A WIFE, written in 1613 but published posthumously in 1614:

All the carnall beauty of my wife
Is but skin-deep, but to two senses known.

The next reference to *beauty being only skin deep* is by the Hereford poet John Davies in A SELECT SECOND HUSBAND FOR SIR THOMAS OVERBURIE'S WIFE, which was published in 1616, three years after Overbury's murder:

Beauty's but skin-deepe; nay, it is not so;
It floates but on the skin beneath the skin,
That (like pure Aire) Cerce hides her fullest flow;
It is so subtill, vading, fraile, and thin:
Were the skin-deepe, she could not be so shallow,
To win but fooles her puritie to hallow.

But if 'carnal beauty' is only skin deep, what lies beneath the surface? Contrasting the fine externals with the 'loathesomeness' within, goes back at least to the early Church Fathers. Centuries later Thomas Fuller echoes their sentiments: *Beauty is but Skin deep; within is Filth and Putrefaction* (GNOMOLOGIA, 1732). Stevenson records a Leicestershire proverb noted in the form of an old jingle which has much the same message:

Beauty is but skin deep, ugly lies the bone;
Beauty dies and fades away, but ugly holds its own.

And a Moroccan proverb has this to say about a woman's appearance: *My daughter-in-law is beautiful! But don't look any deeper.*

But although many recognise truth behind the proverb others consider that its use is a weapon in the armoury of the plain woman and not to be taken too seriously. In ADVICE TO YOUNG MEN (1829) Cobbett has this to say: *The less favoured part of the sex say, that 'beauty is but skin deep':. . . but it is very agreeable, though, for all that.*

Perhaps Mr Cobbett should be more careful how he encourages his young charges for, as the French say, *Beauty without virtue is a flower without perfume.*

Georg Philipp Harsdörffer (1607–58) managed to write two satirical love letters entirely in proverbs. His ability to do so, he claimed, was a sign of the richness of German folk speech.

BED

■ **As you make your bed, so you must lie in it**

You must accept the consequences of unwise actions and decisions

See also: You reap what you sow

She felt that she must not yield, she must go on leading her straitened, humdrum life. This was her punishment for having made a mistake. She had made her bed, and she must lie on it.
(Theodore Dreiser, JENNIE GERHARDT, 1911)

But I did hear from Robin, who'd got it from those relations of Marie Helene's, that she had a sort of stroke after Christmas. Of course, she's made her bed and she's got to lie on it.
(Angus Wilson, ANGLO-SAXON ATTITUDES, 1956)

Rose once left Joe Kennedy, but her father sent her back. It was the duty of a Roman Catholic wife to lie in the bed she had made.
(DAILY TELEGRAPH, 7 November 1992)

Bed for the sixteenth century cottager or servant would be no more than a straw palliasse and rough sheeting made of hemp. Furniture was very expensive and even the well-to-do family of the yeoman farmer would probably own no more than three beds, mostly simple trestle affairs, the more substantial bedstead, complete with a feather mattress, linen sheets and a coverlet, being for the head of the household. Nights were guaranteed to be more restful if wormwood were tucked under the mattress to guard against fleas and the bedstaff were to hand to keep the bed covering in place.

The proverb draws on these practical contemporary difficulties of getting a good night's sleep and metaphorically extends the field of application. An early form of *As you make your bed, so you must lie in it* was known in the sixteenth century. Gabriel Harvey refers to it in MARGINALIA (c 1590): *Lett them . . . go to there bed, as themselves shall make it.* In the following century *He that makes his bed ill, lies there* is quoted by George Herbert (JACULA PRUDENTUM, 1640) and John Ray (ENGLISH PROVERBS, 1670). The proverb in the form we know it today emerged in the nineteenth century.

In most uses of the proverb the implication is that the person addressed has mismanaged his affairs and now must suffer the consequences. There are a number of proverbs from Latin, Greek, German, French and Arabic that make this idea quite explicit. Terence in PHORMIO (161 BC) puts it well: *You have mixed the mess and you must eat it.* Similarly this example in English from John Gower's CONFESSIO AMANTIS (c 1390):

And who so wicked ale breweth
Full ofte he mot the worse drinke.

■ **Early to bed and early to rise, Makes a man healthy, wealthy and wise**

The well-balanced individual leads a life of self-discipline and hard work and reaps the benefits

See also: The early bird catches the worm

This proverb is sometimes erroneously attributed to Benjamin Franklin who included it in more than one edition of POOR RICHARD'S ALMANACK. In fact the wisdom of the adage was already established in both England and Europe by the time John Fitzherbert wrote his BOKE OF HUSBANDRY in 1523. In it Fitzherbert tells us how he learnt at school that *erly rysyng maketh a man hole in body, holer in soule, and rycher in goodes.* Indeed the proverb must have been heard in many a schoolroom over the centuries. In the seventeenth century its edifying message could be found between the pages of reading primers and Latin grammars. In the eighteenth century it appeared in the children's book GOODY TWO-SHOES (1766) where Ralph, the raven, refers to it as a verse which *every little good Boy and Girl should get by heart.* In the nineteenth century it was often coupled with another rhyming adage of the day:

The cock doth crow,
To let you know,
If you be wise,
'Tis time to rise.

This verse, describing the dire fate of the child who does not heed the proverb's collective wisdom, comes from LITTLE RHYMES FOR LITTLE FOLKS (c 1812):

The cock crows in the morn,
To tell us to rise,
And that he who lies late
Will never be wise:
For heavy and stupid,
He can't learn his book:

So as long as he lives,
Like a Dunce he must look.

The emphasis on early rising throughout these centuries is not surprising. The productive part of the day was when the sun was up. Only those who could afford candles or gaslight stayed up beyond sunset. In the morning it was essential to rise with the dawn or dawn chorus (we still say *up with the lark*) and get down to work while there was natural light.

Later, in the twentieth century, the proverb became a favourite with humourists. George Ade couldn't help feeling that to obey the proverb would be to miss out on something:

Early to bed and early to rise
Will make you miss all the regular guys.
(EARLY TO BED, c 1900)

The great Spanish dramatists of the Spanish Golden Age, such as Lope de Rueda (1510?–65) and Tirso de Molina (1584?–1648), used proverbs widely in their short one act farces. One of the greatest of them all, Lope de Vega Carpio (1562–1635), was well aware of the genre and in LA DOROTEA parodied the literary vogue for proverbs. He managed to introduce 153 sayings into the play.

All the regular guys are obviously taking advantage of the recent invention of electricity to light up their nocturnal activities. It was just a few years before, in 1881, that Sir William Armstrong had installed the first domestic electric light in his Northumberland home, Cragside.

By the middle of the century, the rot had clearly set in. Humourist James Thurber points to the enlivening effects of a neon-lit night life:

Early to rise and early to bed
Makes a male healthy and wealthy and dead.
(FABLES FOR OUR TIME: THE SHRIKE AND THE CHIPMUNKS, 1940)

Perhaps the regular guys would feel happier with a proverb of equal wisdom, *All work and no play makes Jack a dull boy.*

BEES

■ **A swarm of bees in May is worth a load of hay**

Activity at the proper season produces good fruit; lateness reduces the yields

In the first week of August, a swarm of bees came to stay with me in Derbyshire. It was too late for them to make much honey. The tedious English proverb says:

A swarm of bees in May
Is worth a load of hay.
A swarm of bees in June
Is worth a silver spoon.
A swarm of bees in July
Is not worth a fly.

But I was honoured that the swarm should have chosen my door above which to hang, though to enter my office you had to duck. A dark night, a moment of absentmindedness . . . it didn't bear thinking about. Still, I thought, the bees, like new age travellers, would soon move on.

The days passed. The swarm grew. Worker bees returned with full pollen sacs. They were making honeycombs. Plainly there had been a misunderstanding. Overnight hospitality is one thing; permanent houseguests, another. Yet dispersing them now, with autumn approaching, would be heartless. And besides, this was the week of my birthday. To kill or scatter them could anger the gods.
(THE TIMES, 12 August 1992)

Earliest written records of the proverb date back to the mid-seventeenth century but it must have been a pearl of household management long before. Honey was the main ingredient used to sweeten food, so the productivity of the bees was of prime importance. No farmhouse would have been without a cluster of plaited straw hives. The repair of the hives, the well-being of the bees and collecting the honey were all the responsibility of the busy housewife. Some of the honey would be kept for her own household's use, the surplus would be sold.

The unknown author of REFORMED COMMONWEALTH OF BEES (1655) records the rhyme thus: . . . *a swarm of bees in May is worth a cow and a bottle (bale) of hay, whereas a swarm in July is not worth a fly.*

John Ray has:

A swarm of bees in May is worth a load of hay,
But a swarm in July is not worth a fly.
(ENGLISH PROVERBS, 1670)

The line *A swarm in June is worth a silver spoon* is a later addition, possibly nineteenth century. A correspondent of NOTES AND QUERIES of 1864 gives this fuller version: *A swarm of bees in May/Is worth a load of hay./A swarm of bees in June/Is worth a silver spoon./A swarm of bees in July/Is not worth a butterfly.*

The proverb is still true since honey is a natural and seasonal product. By July it is too late in the year for the bees to store up honey before the flowers fade.

BEGGARS

■ **Beggars can't be choosers**

A person in need should gratefully accept what is offered rather than complain that it is not exactly what is wanted

See also: Never look a gift horse in the mouth

Gordon accepted promptly. Mr Cheeseman was perhaps faintly disappointed. He had expected an argument, and would have enjoyed crushing Gordon by reminding him that beggars can't be choosers.
(George Orwell, KEEP THE ASPIDISTRA FLYING, 1936)

'For a few years undoubtedly you'll have to feed them mostly on mashed triffids – there won't be any shortage of that raw material by the look of it.'
'Cattle food!' I said.
'But sustaining – rich in the important vitamins, I'm told. And beggars – particularly blind beggars – can't be choosers.'
(John Wyndham, THE DAY OF THE TRIFFIDS, 1951)

The problem of vagabondage in the sixteenth century was dire. Town populations, especially that of London, were increasing rapidly as hungry vagrants flooded in to find casual work or make a living begging and stealing. An old rhyme, thought by one eminent historian to describe the vagrancy of the period, sets the scene:

Hark, hark,
The dogs do bark,
The beggars are coming to town;
Some in rags,
And some in jags,
And one in a velvet gown.

Apart from society's natural misfits, other factors contributed to the growing problem of homelessness. Much of the misery was caused by agrarian change. During the late fifteenth century the old feudal system, where the medieval villein was cared for by his lord, gradually gave way under economic pressure. The sixteenth century saw a steady increase in population and subsequent rise in the demand for food. Landlords, realising that larger units could be farmed more profitably, sometimes squeezed out their small tenants. There was also new wealth to be made by enclosing cultivated land and grazing sheep, a much less labour intensive industry than arable farming. Characters in John Hales' DISCOURSE OF THE COMMON WEAL OF THIS REALM OF ENGLAND (1549) complain, . . . *these enclosures do undo us all, . . . all is taken up for pastures either for sheep or for grazing of cattle. So that I have known of late a dozen ploughs within less compass than six miles about me laid down within these seven years; and where forty persons had their livings, now one man and his shepherd hath all.*

A further factor influencing the increase in vagrancy was a reduction in warfare. Fewer wars, at home and abroad, set large numbers of retainers at liberty with little chance of finding alternative employment. The dissolution of the monastries under Henry VIII removed the very institutions which supported the dispossessed with alms, further exacerbating the crisis.

In spite of these obvious social and economic difficulties, popular and state opinion worked on the assumption that there was enough employment for those with a mind to do it and that vagrancy had its roots in idleness. Distinctions, however, were made between the 'impotent poor', the aged and crippled who might expect to survive on charitable alms supplied by their own parishes, and the 'sturdy beggars', who received brutal treatment, hence the proverb *A sturdy beggar should have a stout naysayer.*

Beggars can't be choosers emerges against this background. Its tone is uncompromising. John Heywood records it as: *Folke saie alwaie, beggers should be no choosers* (PROVERBS, 1546), and the form *Beggars must not be choosers* was current from the sixteenth until the twentieth century.

BIG

■ **Big is beautiful**

Large size and scale has inherent advantages

See also: Small is beautiful

Big is beautiful. But big can also be expensive – one reason why parents-of-five Robert and Jane Blow started The Big Family Club . . . 'Most large families spend at least £100 a week in supermarkets,' they say, so by joining forces with similar families, they hope to push for discounts.
(GOOD HOUSEKEEPING, November 1992)

Do you remember a chap called Dr E F Schumacher who preached that small is beautiful? These blokes believe that big is beautiful. But it ain't. Big is broke. Ask the late Cap'n Bob [Robert Maxwell]. Ask some of the international tycoons who owe more to the banks than the Third World.
(DAILY MAIL, 21 January 1993)

The way to tell a bad bulb, he advised, was not just by price but by size. Big is beautiful; cheap bulbs are small, and produce small flowers.
(WEEKEND TELEGRAPH, 30 January 1993)

American big business was appropriately so named in the 1950s, 60s and 70s. The belief was that size created economies of scale, cheaper prices, more sales and more profits. Vast conglomerates arose that spread their tentacles across the world as multinationals. Working practices involved shifts on conveyor belts, with endless repetition of the same limited, boring tasks. *Big was beautiful.*

The pendulum swung back the other way in the 1970s, heralded by Schumacher's phrase and book *Small is beautiful* (see the entry for details). Since then, both philosophies have their advocates and their respective slogans have an acknowledged presence in the language.

BIRD

- **A bird in the hand is worth two in the bush**

A small, certain gain is of greater value than a larger, speculative one. Don't trade a certainty for an uncertainty.

'Did they agree to the four thousand dollars?'

'Shelby wouldn't listen to it. He insisted on going after something big.'

'I was afraid he might do that. Personally, I'd rather have had the bird in the hand than gone chasing round after the two in the bush.'

(Erle Stanley Gardner, THE CASE OF THE HALF-WAKENED WIFE, 1945)

You have two business options to choose from. One will get you a guaranteed £30,000. The other gives you an 80 per cent chance of a £40,000 payoff, set against a

one-in-five chance of making no profit at all. Which do you choose?

That's right. You go for the bird in the hand. Take the £30,000 and thank you very much.

(BT BUSINESS NEWS, Summer, 1992)

The general wisdom of the proverb is ancient. It was taught by Aesop in the sixth century BC in fables such as THE LION AND THE HARE and THE FISHERMAN AND THE LITTLE FISH. In THE NIGHTINGALE AND THE HAWK the nightingale, who has fallen prey to the hawk, protests that she will make a meagre meal. The hawk, however, refuses to release her, saying that he would be foolish to let go of a bird he already held in his talons simply to hunt another.

In the early middle ages the proverb was known in a popular Latin form (for another instance see *The devil sick would be a monk*) coined from an existing hunting expression, but in the fifteenth century it was recorded in English: *'Betyr ys a byrd in the hond than tweye in the wode'* (HARLEIAN MS, c 1470). 'Wood' gave way to 'bush' in the wording in the following century, around the time of a well-known anecdote concerning Henry VIII's jester, Will Somers. Lord Surrey had given him a kingfisher from his aviary. Shortly afterwards, Lord Northampton asked Lord Surrey for this fine bird as a gift for a lady friend. To console him on discovering that the bird had already been given away, Lord Surrey assured him that Will Somers would surely give it up on the promise of two birds on some future occasion. The jester was not so to be taken in.

'Sirrah,' he is reputed to have said to the messenger, 'tell your master that I am much obliged for his liberal offer of two for one, but that I prefer one bird in hand to two in the bush.'

The proverb, in one form or another, is found throughout Europe from Sweden to Romania: the Romanians say *Better a bird in the hand than a thousand on the house;* the French, *A bird in the hand is better than two in the hedge;* and the Italians have a number of variants, amongst them, *Better a sparrow in the pan than a hundred chickens in the priest's yard.*

Another European adage came into use in the sixteenth century and bore the same message as *A bird in the hand is worth two in the bush.* This alternative expression *A Sparrow in Hand is worth a Pheasant that flyeth by,* recorded in Thomas Fuller's GNOMOLOGIA of 1732, is no longer used in England, though still heard, for instance, in France. It compares the great value of a small bird (a sparrow) held in the hand with the dubious worth of a large uncaptured bird (a goose, a crane, a pigeon, a heron or a bittern, depending on the language). The proverb reflects the hunting interests and eating habits of past centuries when swans, cranes, herons, peacocks, and even gulls made acceptable meat for the dinner table. The BOKE OF KERVYNGE, published by Wynkyn de Worde in 1508, gives these directions: . . . *lift a swan, sauce a capon, frusshe a chicken, spoyle a hen, unbrace a mallard, dismember a heron, display a crane, disfigure a peacock, unjoint a bittern, untach a curlew, allay a pheasant, wing a partridge, wing a quail, mince a plover and thigh a pigeon and other small birds.*

Archbishop Neville of York gave a banquet in 1465 which included amongst other delicacies: 4000 teals and mallards, 1000 egrets, 204 cranes, 204 bitterns, 400 swans, 400 heron-storks, 400 curlews and 104 peacocks. Conservationists and gourmets alike might object to such slaughter today!

■ **Birds of a feather flock together**

People of the same sort seek out each other's company

See also: A man is known by the company he keeps

His expenses were twopence a day for food and fourpence for his bed in a café full of the birds of his feather.
(John Galsworthy, CARAVAN, 'COMPENSATION', 1925)

. . . I noticed a white Ford saloon, about three cars off. Its front offside wing was badly damaged, as though it had run into a wall somewhere. I went and had a peer at it. Maybe it really was the one which had been parked next to Michael Fenner's grand posh Rover outside his bookseller's place. So it hadn't been Jason driving after all. Well, birds of a feather and all that.
(Jonathan Gash, THE SLEEPERS OF ERIN, 1983)

Some birds are, of course, solitary but those which habitually gather together to fly or feed do so with their own kind. The proverb has been current since the sixteenth century. Although it may mean that people with similar backgrounds or interests move in the same circles, the proverb is more often used to register disapproval of another group or individual. Thus, in NONSUCH PROFESSOR (1660) Thomas Secker uses the expression to warn against keeping bad company: *We say, 'That birds of a feather will flock together.' To be too intimate with sinners is to intimate that we are sinners.* And, in PELHAM (1828) Lord Lytton describes the London underworld in the same terms: *It is literally true in the systematised roguery of London, that 'birds of a feather flock together.'*

Usage: The sense is usually that wrongdoers seek out others of their own kind, rather than any group of like-minded people

■ **The early bird catches the worm**

The first in line gets the pick of the opportunities. To delay in taking action may end in disappointment

See also: Early to bed and early to rise, Makes a man healthy, wealthy and wise

'You're very skittish this morning, superintendent. I shall always know now what the early bird looks like when it has caught the worm.'
'Well, sir, mustn't waste any more time. Got the warrant here; going to arrest them now and get it over.'
(Nicholas Blake, A QUESTION OF PROOF, 1935)

THE EARLY BIRD CATCHES AN EARFUL
We are not on speaking terms at the moment, my daughter and I. Laura, being only nine months old, is still at the 'ba' and 'ho' stage, and I'm sulking until she stops *waking me up at 5.30 every morning.*
(DAILY TELEGRAPH, 27 November 1992)

HOW TO DO YOUR BIDDING
Early birds: You can make an offer for a home before the auction. If you put in a bid in advance, you will normally pay more than the likely auction price, but less than if you had bought through an estate agent.
(DAILY EXPRESS, 3 March 1993)

THE EARLY WORM GETS THE RUBBISH
Worms are turning, or at any rate recycling, in a London council's attempts to cut down domestic rubbish.
Tomorrow Sutton begins a major experiment in which householders will be encouraged to put their waste food, tea bags and other organic refuse into 'wormeries' – plastic containers holding a colony of Tiger worms.
(SUNDAY TELEGRAPH, 17 May 1992)

In BEAST AND MAN IN INDIA (1891), John Lockwood Kipling noted a Hindu version of the expression: *Where we would say 'The early bird catches the worm' the Indian rustic says, 'who sleeps late gets the bull-calf, he who rises early the cow-calf'* – which is more valuable.

The English adage which praises and rewards the bird for his early rising has been recorded in collections of proverbs since the seventeenth century. It is not the only perspective from which to see things. J G Saxe challenges the accepted wisdom and looks upon the incident from a worm's-eye view. *The worm*, he states, *was punished for early rising* (EARLY RISING, 1860). Similarly, Walsh quotes a joke book of the same period:

A father exhorting his son to rise early in the morning reminded him of the old adage, 'It's the early bird that picks up the worm.'

'Ah,' replied the son, 'but the worm gets up earlier than the bird.'

BITTEN

■ **Once bitten, twice shy**

We learn from experience to avoid things which have caused us trouble and pain in the past

See also: A burnt child dreads the fire

Hardly a week goes by without one or the other proposing that they formalise their relationship. But, so far, they have never managed to arrive at that idea on the same day. 'Once bitten, twice shy,' says Richard, who has been married once. 'Twice bitten, almost cured,' says Maggie, who has been through that hoop a couple of times.
(THE AUSTRALIAN WOMEN'S WEEKLY, January 1991)

The proverb does not have a long history. In MR SPONGE'S SPORTING TOUR (1853), Robert Smith Surtees, a nineteenth-century author of humorous sporting stories, writes: *Jawleyford had been bit once, and he was not going to give Mr Sponge a second chance.* Was Surtees alluding to an adage already established in popular parlance? Or was he remembering his Shakespeare: *What, wouldst thou have a serpent sting thee twice?* (MERCHANT OF VENICE, 1596) The proverb does not appear again in literature until it is recorded in G F Northall's FOLK-PHRASES (1894).

Walsh tells a humorous French story that illustrates this expression:

A young rustic told his priest at confession that he had broken down a neighbour's hedge to get at a blackbird's nest. The priest asked if he had taken away the young birds. 'No,' said he; 'they were hardly grown enough. I will let them alone until Saturday evening.' No more was said on the subject; but when Saturday evening came the young fellow found the nest empty, and readily guessed who it was that had forestalled him. The next time he went to confession he had to tell something in which a young girl was partly concerned. 'Oh!' said his ghostly father; 'how old is she?' 'Seventeen.' 'Good-looking?' 'The prettiest girl in the village.' 'What is her name? Where does she live?' the confessor hastily inquired; and then he got for an answer the phrase which has passed into a proverb, 'A d'autres, dénicheur de merles!' which may be paraphrased, 'Try that upon somebody else, Mr Filcher of blackbirds.'

BLACK

■ **There's a black sheep in every family**

Every family has one independent member who is disapproved of for not fitting into the general mould of family life

Variant: There's a black sheep in every flock

I suppose every family has a black sheep. Tom had been a sore trial to his for twenty years.
(W Somerset Maugham, COSMOPOLITANS, 'THE ANT AND THE GRASSHOPPER', 1926)

England resembles a family, a rather stuffy Victorian family, with not many black sheep in it but with all its cupboards bursting with skeletons.
(George Orwell, ENGLAND YOUR ENGLAND, 1933)

Prince Andrew, too, cuts less of a dash than in his youth – his heart broken, some say, by the failure of his marriage to the notorious figure of 'Fergie', former Duchess of York, who has now become the Royal Family's most notorious black sheep since Wallis Simpson, Duchess of Windsor.
(DAILY MAIL, 11 December 1992)

I had a reputation for being the black sheep of the family. I've always felt different: my family love me but they always recognised I was going to be slightly off-line.
(DAILY TELEGRAPH, 1 January 1993)

Black sheep have had a bad press since the sixteenth century when they were accused of being 'perylous' beasts and quite capable of giving a nasty nip:

Till now I thought the prouerbe did but iest, Which said a blacke sheepe was a biting beast.
(Thomas Bastard, CHRESTOLEROS, 1598)

In Shropshire there was, apparently, a superstition that if a black lamb were born into a flock, bad luck would dog the shepherd. A ewe giving birth to black twins would bring certain disaster.

An economic factor also contributed to the unfortunate animal's unpopularity with shepherds; the fleece of a black sheep could not be dyed and was therefore worthless.

The term 'black sheep' was applied sometime in the eighteenth century to a person who falls foul of the accepted standards of his fellows. In his play THE MAN OF THE WORLD (1792), Thomas Macklin writes *You are a black sheep: and I'll mark you.* The proverb, found in literature from the nineteenth century onwards, was originally *There's a black sheep in every flock* (or *fold*). Its scope of application today is largely, though not exclusively, to the family, hence its more frequent contemporary form.

Usage: The 'crime' of which the black sheep stands accused can consist in, for instance, the adoption of the alternative lifestyle of New-Age travellers, or it can be a genuine matter of concern for the Courts. In any event, the non-conformity, the deviation, the rejection of standard values are all disapproved of.

■ Two blacks don't make a white

It is no justification for an action that someone else has committed it previously, or has made you suffer similarly

See also: Two wrongs don't make a right

It may be urged that the prostitution of the mind is more mischievous, and is a deeper betrayal of the divine purpose of our powers, than the prostitution of the body, the sale of which does not necessarily involve its

misuse. But whatever satisfaction the pot may have in calling the kettle blacker than itself the two blacks do not make a white.
(George Bernard Shaw, THE INTELLIGENT WOMAN'S GUIDE TO SOCIALISM AND CAPITALISM, 1928)

In his SCOTTISH PROVERBS (1721) James Kelly defines the proverb *Two blacks make no white* as *answer to them who, being blam'd, say others have done as ill or worse.* The slightly more modern form *Two blacks don't make a white* has been in common use since that time. See also *Two wrongs don't make a right* for a similar nineteenth-century expression.

BLIND

■ **If the blind lead the blind, both shall fall into the ditch**

When a person lacking in understanding or expertise attempts to guide another like himself, both will suffer serious consequences

As an 'intellectual', I was given the job of political education. Never can there have been a more signal instance of the blind leading the short-sighted.
(C Day Lewis, THE BURIED DAY, 1960)

If only . . . books were sold by men of taste, familiar with their contents, the public would buy more good literature: as things are, the blind bookseller leads the blind customer.
(J C Squire, A HORRIBLE BOOKSELLER, 1918–21)

There are numerous variants of this phrase in the ancient world: Homer (c 850 BC) has *the vile leading the vile;* Varro (c 50 BC) *the old leading the old;* and Horace introduces the blind man: *It is as if a blind man sought to show the way.* (EPISTLES, c 20 BC)

Undoubtedly the formulation we recognise today comes from similar verses in the New Testament gospels of Luke and Matthew: *They be blind leaders of the blind. And if the blind lead the blind, both shall fall into the ditch.* (MATTHEW 15:14) These verses were included in the earliest translations, such as the Anglo-Saxon Gospel of AD 995, and subsequently by Wycliffe (c 1384), Tyndale (1525), Coverdale (1535), etc. The great collections of proverbs, such as Erasmus's (1536), Heywood's (1546) and Fuller's (1732), list the saying in one form or another, and it is used by famous authors such as Cervantes and Bunyan.

One could hardly ask for a better literary pedigree. There is also an artistic heritage. The proverb has been illustrated by many famous painters: Hieronymus Bosch (c 1450–1516), Pieter Brueghel the Elder (c 1520–1569), Pieter Brueghel the Younger (1564–1638), and Jan Verbeeck (c 1569–1619).

Usage: Often the full proverb is simply alluded to in a comment such as: *It's a case of the blind leading the blind.*

■ **In the country of the blind, the one-eyed man is king**

A man of even limited ability is at a great advantage in the company of those less able

'Make a rule for yourself not to speak to anyone, and nobody's going to guess you can see. It was only being quite unprepared that landed you in that mess before. "In the country of the blind the one-eyed man is king."'

'Oh, yes – Wells said that, didn't he? – Only in the story it turned out not to be true.'

The crux of the difference lies in what you mean by the word "country" – patria in the original,' I said. 'Caecorum in patria luscus rex imperat omnis – a classical gentleman called Fullonius said it first: it's all anyone seems to know about him. But there's no organized patria, no State here – only chaos. Wells imagined a people who had adapted themselves to blindness. I don't think that is going to happen here.'

(John Wyndham, THE DAY OF THE TRIFFIDS, 1951)

In the Bible we read that when the blind lead the blind they both fall into the ditch (MATTHEW 15:14). An English proverb cited by John Ray (1678) tells us that *a man were better be half blind than have both his eyes out*. Not only can he then avoid the ditch but, when in company with others who are totally blind, he might even find himself in a position of leadership. *In the kingdom of the blind the one-eyed man is king* is a proverb quoted by Erasmus in ADAGIA (1536). It also occurs in John Palsgrave's translation (1540) of the COMEDY OF ACOLASTUS by Fullonius, and John Skelton tells us that: *an one eyed man is Well syghted when he is amonge blynde men* (WHY COME YE NOT TO COURT?, 1522). The expression is also common to other languages.

John Wyndham's science fiction novel THE DAY OF THE TRIFFIDS (1951), subsequently made into a TV serial and film, tells the story of William Masen who finds himself one of the few people in the world able to see after a meteorite shower. Because of his gift of sight, he becomes a leader in the fight against the Triffids, animate vegetable hybrids threatening to take over the world. The quotation gives Wyndham's own etymology for the saying. The H G Wells' work referred to is THE COUNTRY OF THE BLIND, short stories published in 1911. Fullonius is better known as Gulielmus Gnapheus. His five act play COMEDY OF ACOLASTUS, in Latin verse, was first published in Antwerp in 1529.

■ **There are none so blind as those who will not see**

It is pointless reasoning with a person who does not want to listen to sense

Variant: There are none so deaf as those who will not hear

I fronted up to him straight away and said: 'What drugs are you taking?' . . . The big thing is to admit it's happening to you and someone you love dearly. There are none so blind as those who don't want to see.
(NEW ZEALAND WOMAN'S WEEKLY, 14 January 1991)

With Bruno, one still wonders about the ultimate cost. His insistence he has placed into perspective the risk of further retinal problems leads one to suspect there are none so blind as those who can see.
(DAILY TELEGRAPH, 22 November 1991)

In PROVERBS (1546) John Heywood records this rhyme which expresses the age-old frustration felt towards someone who refuses to face up to facts:

Who is so deafe, or so blynde as is hee,
That wilfully will nother hear nor see?

Shortly afterwards the deaf and the blind part company permanently so that the proverb grumbles about either those who are blind to reason or deaf to it but never both together. Thomas Ingeland laments in DISOBEDIENT CHILD (c 1560) *None is so deaf as who will not hear*, and Andrew Boorde in his BREVIARY OF HEALTHE (1547) complains *Who is blynder than he yt wyl nat se.*

BLOOD

■ **Blood is thicker than water**

The family relationship is stronger than any other

'Do you mean that no one asked after me?'
'No one.'
'Really. And then they say that blood is thicker than water. They know perfectly well that I have had hay-fever. I made your mother write and tell them so. And yet they don't inquire after me.'
(Anthony Powell, FROM A VIEW TO A DEATH, 1933)

Her father's first cousin was Robert Fellowes, the husband of the Princess of Wales's sister Jane, and the Queen's Private Secretary. But Cousin Robert would prove to be an implacable obstacle to her in the

years to come. Blood may be thicker than water, but it is a lot thinner than monarchial juice. And, to a committed courtier like Robert Fellowes, there was never any question of siding with his cousin whenever there was a contest between what she wanted and what her staff dictated.
(AUSTRALIAN WOMAN'S WEEKLY, August 1992)

The expression's first written appearance was in John Ray's collection of proverbs (1670). The link between the words of the proverb and its actual meaning is not an easy one to make. Blood, it seems, is of thicker consistency, and suggests commitment. Ridout and Witting suggest that when blood and water are spilt the former leaves a stain whereas the water will evaporate. The blood of oxen, along with its hair, has been used in the preparation of mortar, to give greater consistency. In other realms, conspirators, martyrs and those betrothed have signed their allegiance to a cause or to each other – in blood, of course. Blood ties endure, then, while other relationships, such as friendships or business connections, can disappear without a trace.

Water, on the other hand, has a poor reputation. *Unstable as water* is the potent biblical phrase from Genesis 49:4, which is echoed (c 1384) by the great Bible publisher, John Wycliffe, and by Shakespeare in OTHELLO (1604). The proverbial tradition that Ray records was doubtless aware of the connotations of the words in the expression.

Although it is mostly used to refer to the immediate family, the expression has been used to cement relationships on a national level. In 1859 US Commodore Josiah Tattnall went to the assistance of the British Navy who were engaged in a skirmish with the Chinese. In his dispatch to US Navy headquarters the Commodore quoted the proverb as his reason for taking supportive action.

Not everyone, however, finds the proverb rings true. Family feuds which last to the grave are not unheard of, and sometimes family ties are felt more strongly on one side than the other. An old Jewish proverb which compares the strength of paternal and filial feeling says *One father can support ten children; ten children cannot support one father.* There are times, too, when another allegiance proves a tighter bond than blood: *If any survived they had grown rich and lost touch with their poor relations; for money is thicker than blood* (George Orwell, KEEP THE ASPIDISTRA FLYING, 1936). And some people just prefer water:

Blood, as all men know, than water's thicker;
But water's wider, thank the Lord, than blood.
(Aldous Huxley, NINTH PHILOSOPHER'S SONG, 1920)

BORROWER

■ **Neither a borrower nor a lender be**

The best way to stay on good terms with one's friends is never to offer any of them a loan nor, indeed, to ask for a loan for oneself

'Neither a borrower nor a lender be' was also dinned into us relentlessly, and a joyless old existence that would have led us all into (although I daresay the economy might be in a better state today had we heeded it).
(GOOD HOUSEKEEPING, November 1992)

The proverb in the form we know it is from Shakespeare's HAMLET (1602). Ophelia's brother, Laertes, is about to leave Denmark to study in Paris. As he bids farewell Polonius, his father, gives him a few final words of advice, amongst them these:

Neither a borrower nor a lender be;
For loan oft loses both itself and friend,
And borrowing dulls the edge of husbandry.
(Act 1, scene iii)

Borrowing in particular had been the subject of previous comment, with which Shakespeare would surely have been familiar. The Old Testament has: *The borrower is servant to the lender* (PROVERBS 22:7). Just a few years before HAMLET, Thomas Tusser had written in his FIVE HUNDRETH POINTES OF GOOD HUSBANDRIE (1573):

Who goeth a-borrowing
Goeth a-sorrowing.

As so often happens, it was Shakespeare's genius to take disparate elements and mould them into a memorable saying that enters popular wisdom.

BOTH

■ You can't have it both ways

You can't benefit from two courses of action, adopt two policies, espouse two beliefs, etc that are mutually incompatible

Variant: You can't have things both ways

See also: You can't have your cake and eat it

'Stand on your own two feet,' we say – and yet, 'Support us when we need you.' But you can't have it both ways. In other cultures – Mediterranean, Indian, African – parents move over to give the younger generation more elbow room.
(GOOD HOUSEKEEPING, September 1991)

The proverb is a common synonym for *You can't have your cake and eat it.* The earliest reference in literature comes in Shaw's FANNY'S FIRST PLAY (1911).

Usage: Informal. An idiomatic alternative phrase is *to want it both ways.*

BOYS

■ Boys will be boys

Don't be surprised when young boys behave with the mischievous and immature conduct characteristic of their age

Would old Mr Anstruther consider an outrage perpetrated on the person of Bertram Wooster a crime sufficiently black to cause him to rule Thos out of the race? Or would he just give a senile chuckle and mumble something about boys being boys?
(P G Wodehouse, VERY GOOD JEEVES!, 1930)

Then he went indoors and wrote a letter to Vin. From the time it took, and the look of his shoulder-blades, Mrs Miniver was afraid that for once in a way he was being over-stern; but when he leant back in his chair to re-read the letter she saw that it was profusely illustrated down the margin with his own particular brand of pin-man picture: so she knew it was all right. And Mrs Downce, as she brought in the tea, remarked amiably and with an air of discovery that boys would be boys. Mrs Miniver breathed more freely. The trough of low pressure was already over: it was going to be a fine week-end.
(Jan Struther, MRS MINIVER, 1939)

When a boy does terrible things, people always know what he is: he's a thug, a hooligan, a lout . . . You know where you are with a yob, for he is just a boy spelt backwards, and for every pious pinhead who dreams that virtue resides in the thwack of a cleansing birch, there is another for whom boys will always be boys. Vexing they may be, and in need of stern policing, yet the jitterbugging genes of the male juvenile are ultimately accepted as a necessary part of Mother Nature's plan.
(SUNDAY TIMES, 21 March 1993)

A Latin proverb *Pueri sunt pueri, pueri puerilia tractant* (Children are children and employ themselves with childish things) is the root of the adage, although it received scant attention over the centuries. Not until the nineteenth century did *Boys will be boys* emerge as a popular English proverb. It is interesting that boys are mentioned and not girls. Possibly this arises from mistranslation of the Latin, *pueri* being the word for both 'children' and 'boys'. Equally possible is the suggestion that, although fond Victorian papas were prepared to overlook the pranks committed by their young sons, they expected an altogether more decorous standard of behaviour from their daughters.

Usage: Remark explaining, even excusing, boisterous behaviour in boys. Often said by indulgent, complaisant parents. May also be used rather scathingly by women of their boyfriends or husbands.

BREAD

■ **Half a loaf is better than no bread**

We should be grateful for what we do get rather than complain about what we don't receive

Benton turned to Jane Keller, said, 'You have thirty thousand dollars at stake, Mrs Keller. Sometimes half a loaf is better than no bread. I have the island at stake; Sometimes a poor compromise is better than a good lawsuit. Now then, Shelby, what's your proposition?'
(Erle Stanley Gardner, THE CASE OF THE HALF-WAKENED WIFE, 1945)

In Moscow, where there is an acute housing shortage, when an unmarried woman is pregnant, it often happens that a number of men contend for the legal right to be considered the father of the prospective child, because whoever is judged to be the father acquires the right to share the woman's room, and half a room is better than no roof.
(Bertrand Russell, UNPOPULAR ESSAYS, 'AN OUTLINE OF INTELLECTUAL RUBBISH', 1950)

A proverb since at least the sixteenth century, it is recorded in John Heywood's PROVERBS (1546). The context of the proverb is that a gift should not be despised because it is smaller than was hoped for. Heywood writes:

Throw no gyft agayne at the geuers head;
For better is halfe a lofe than no bread.

Seventeenth and eighteenth century collections of proverbs by John Ray, John Clarke and Thomas Fuller record a number of other like sayings:

Better a louse (mouse) in the pot than no flesh at all
Half an egg is better than an empty shell
Better are small Fish than an empty Dish

But *Half a loaf is better than no bread* alone survives.

A French version is *Faute de grives, on mange des merles* (If there's a lack of cranes, we can eat blackbirds), a reference to eating habits in the Middle Ages and later. (See *A bird in the hand is worth two in the bush.*)

BREVITY

■ **Brevity is the soul of wit**

A witty remark is by its nature best expressed in short and pithy form

Brevity is the soul of lingerie.
(Dorothy Parker, attrib.)

Exhortations to brevity are age old and universal. In one form or another, Terence, Plautus, Pliny, Martial, Horace, Erasmus, Gracián and La Fontaine have commented on the value of concision. In England, although this proverb was not coined by Shakespeare, its contemporary form is familiar to us through his use of it in HAMLET (1602), where a worried Polonius tells Claudius and Gertrude why he thinks Hamlet is behaving so strangely:

Therefore, since brevity is the soul of wit . . .
I will be brief. Your noble son is mad.

Here wit means 'understanding, reasoning' (we still refer to *the wit and wisdom of man*); Polonius is less likely to be misunderstood if he comes directly to the point. Today wit is more likely to be understood as the art of making telling remarks in a lively and amusing way. The best wisecracks and put-downs are often one-liners. They can be very funny (Groucho Marx made a career from the humorous witticism) or acerbically critical. Theatre critics are noted in this second category for remarks such as:

'House Beautiful' is play lousy (Dorothy Parker)

It opened at 8.40 sharp and closed at 10.40 dull (Heywood Broun)
It is the sort of play that gives failures a bad name (Walter Kerr)

However, the proverb more properly refers to a weightier comment that is concisely and memorably expressed:

I can resist everything except temptation (Oscar Wilde)
God has made man in his own image – man has retaliated (Pascal)
To acknowledge you were wrong yesterday is simply to let the world know that you are wiser today than you were then (Jonathan Swift)
Many a man aims at nothing and hits it with remarkable precision (Archbishop Richard Whately)

BRICKS

■ **You can't make bricks without straw**

Nothing can be accomplished without the right materials for the job

You can only acquire really useful general ideas by first acquiring particular ideas, and putting those particular ideas together. You cannot make bricks without straw.
(Arnold Bennett, LITERARY TASTE, 'WHERE TO BEGIN', 1909)

'That', said Byng, 'was the case you put up to the Crown? It's no wonder they pulled it off. It left us no chance at all. What do you say, Heppenstall?'
'I never thought we had any chance,' Heppenstall declared.

'Can't make bricks without straw,' Quilter pointed out cheerfully.

'Can't make them without clay, at all events,' Heppenstall returned.
(F W Crofts, THE 12.30 FROM CROYDON, 1934)

They blame the media for misrepresenting them. The media cannot make bricks without straw, however, and the straws flying in the wind recently have darkened the sky.
(WEEKEND TELEGRAPH, 16 January 1993)

The proverb comes from the Bible. The children of Israel were slaves in the land of Egypt where they received brutal treatment from their Egyptian overlords. EXODUS, Chapter 5, tells how Moses went to Pharaoh to ask if the Israelites might go on a three-day pilgrimage into the desert to offer a sacrifice. Pharaoh, already concerned by the size of the Israelite population in his country, was alarmed that they had found the courage to come and ask for time off. He issued a command that the people were to be kept even busier. From then on they were no longer to be supplied with straw to make their bricks but had to find their own as well as keep up their daily quota of bricks. Not surprisingly the Israelites found this an impossible task. Allusion to the story from EXODUS has been current since at least the beginning of the seventeenth century.

BRIDGE

■ **Don't cross a bridge until you come to it**

Don't deal with anticipated problems until they become realities. Don't look for problems.

Variant: Never cross a bridge until you come to it

See also: Sufficient into the day (is the evil thereof); Tomorrow is another day

The USTA [United States Tennis Association] president next year, a man called, believe it or not, J Howard 'Bumpy' Frazer, was asked if there was a players' rebellion in the air. He said: 'That's a hard question for me to answer. I very much respect our players, and I think we have to cross that bridge a little later.'
(THE TIMES, 8 December 1992)

The earliest recorded use is in THE GOLDEN LEGEND (1851) by Longfellow, who called this 'a proverb old, and of excellent wit'. It may well be a variant of the much more ancient sixteenth century saying: *You must not leape ower the stile before you come to it* (Henry Porter, THE TWO ANGRIE WOMEN, 1599).

BRIGHT SIDE

■ **Always look on the bright side**

Take the optimistic view of every situation

See also: Every cloud has a silver lining

Teenagers rarely make the headlines because they've done something right, but Laurie Graham takes a look on the bright side and finds all the positive advantages teenagers bring.
(GOOD HOUSEKEEPING, November 1992)

We must always look for the bright side. I knew there would be some positive aspects to the Maastricht rebellion in the Parliamentary Conservative Party. It now emerges that filibustering tactics adopted by rebel Tories in the House of Commons have put an end to any further efforts by the Government to solve our economic problems, our juvenile crimewave, our inadequate fire safety arrangements at the Tower of London or anything else which crops up in the morning newspapers.
(DAILY TELEGRAPH, 13 March 1993)

One authority hazards the suggestion that the allusion may have been to the splendid and polished appearance of the decorated face of a shield contrasted with the dull hidden side. This is an imaginative but rather fanciful account,

since the proverb has only been in use since the nineteenth century, long past the days when soldiers carried shields. But there may be a shred of truth in it, for the polished is more pleasing than the tarnished and a bright day lifts the spirits more than a dull one. Perhaps it refers rather to the bright side of a black cloud, an allusion to the silver lining. (See *Every cloud has a silver lining.*)

BROKEN

■ **If it isn't broken, don't fix it**

Don't try to improve on something that is working perfectly well

Variants: If it ain't broke, don't fix it; If it isn't broken, don't mend it

See also: Let sleeping dogs lie; Leave well alone

Graeme Souness arrived at the club where he had performed so ably as player, and he was desperate to make his mark. Had he asked me for a word of advice before starting to work, I would have said: 'Graeme, old chap, if it ain't broke, don't fix it.'

But Souness did his best to improve on the Liverpool system of excellence, with the results we now see.
(THE TIMES, 8 March 1993)

NO WAY TO TREAT AUNTIE
For 70 years the BBC was a magnificent programme-making machine. It wasn't broken – so why is it now being fixed?
(GUARDIAN, 30 March 1993)

How well accepted is the wisdom of proverbs? One small piece of evidence is from Germany. A scholar there reported the results of a test carried out in 1964. Out of 24 proverbs, *Es is nicht alles Gold, was glänzt* ('Not all that glitters is gold') came top, yet only 69 per cent of respondents believed it to be an acceptable truth.

It seems to be a universal human desire to meddle with something that is working perfectly well, in order to make it work better. The consequences are usually dire. There is another natural inclination to want the latest and what the advertisers claim is the best. But, says the proverb, what is the point of the latest model of car, the newest computer, when the existing one is effectively doing the job that has to be done?

This is a very modern expression. It has widely caught on in America and the United Kingdom since its first use, according to American columnist William Safire, by Bert Lance in 1977 when he was Director of the Office of Management and Budget for President Carter.

It has been particularly popular as a source for comment on anything from government to business and to sport, occasioning some clever witticisms: *If it ain't broke, don't fix it – unless you're a consultant.* (Winton G Rossiter)

Usage: American, informal. The alternative form in particular is spoken colloquial and probably more common than its more grammatical elder brother.

BROOM

■ **A new broom sweeps clean**

A person appointed to a new position of responsibility will set out on an enthusiastic programme of reform

He'd negotiated the concession and if it hadn't been for Erkhard they might have been drilling there now. But Erkhard was the new broom.

(Hammond Innes, THE DOOMED OASIS, 1960)

BET's new-broom chief executive John Clark has ruthlessly slashed costs – head office staff alone have fallen from 300 to only 60 – and installed tough financial controls. Last year's £425m debt figure has been cut to £107m.

(DAILY MAIL, 16 June 1992)

Stevenson records a tradition which traces the origin of the proverb to the intense trading rivalry between Britain and the Netherlands in the seventeenth century. During the first Dutch war of 1652 the scornful Dutch admiral Van Tromp is said to have bound a broom to his flagship's mast. He would, he declared, sweep the British off the seas. In reply the English navy, led by Robert Blake, tied a horsewhip to their flagship. As it was, the Dutch ships were routed. There may be truth in the story but the expression, besides having equivalents in other European languages, had already been recorded by John Heywood in PROVERBS by the middle of the preceding century.

The origin is much more mundane. Brooms in the sixteenth century were bundles of green stems lashed to a long handle. (The scoparius bush takes its common name, broom, from its usefulness here.) It was not long, however, before the green stems became worn and stubbed with use and less springy as the twigs dried out. The

Italians have an expression *A new broom is good for three days* which illustrates its limited life.

This said, one wonders if the English had much use for brooms at all. Erasmus was just one of the foreign visitors who complained about the hygiene in most ordinary households. There were, of course, no carpets. Instead the floors were strewn with rushes which it was customary to renew when a visitor was expected, hence the sixteenth century proverb of welcome *Strew green rushes for the stranger.* Perhaps Erasmus would have been happier if the old floorcovering had been removed before his welcoming layer, for he writes: *The floors are made of clay and are covered with layers of rushes, constantly replenished, so that the bottom layer remains for twenty years, harbouring spittle, vomit, the urine of dogs and men, the dregs of beer, the remains of fish, and other nameless filth* (P S and H M Allen, eds, OPUS EPISTOLARUM DESIDERII ERASMI ROTERODAMI). Clearly *Cleanliness is next to godliness* was not much considered by the ordinary English citizen.

BULLET

■ **Every bullet has its billet**

Death will only come at its appointed time

Variant: If the bullet has your name on it . . .

This proverb is universally attributed to William of Orange. The problem is,

which William? Stevenson comes down on the side of William I, Stadtholder of the Netherlands (1533–84), possibly because George Gascoigne seems to allude to the saying in FRUITES OF WARRE (1575): *Sufficeth this to prove my theme withal, That every bullet hath a lighting place.* If William I did coin the phrase then it has an ironical twist, for he was assassinated with a pistol shot in 1584 at the instigation of Philip II of Spain.

Other authorities, however, Bartlett among them, attribute the proverb to William III of England (1650–1702), also Prince of Orange. Certainly references to King William in literature rather lead one to suppose that the sovereign of England is under discussion. In TRISTRAM SHANDY (1759) Laurence Sterne writes: *King William was of an opinion, an' please your honour, quoth Trim, that everything was predestined for us in this world; insomuch, that he would often say to his soldiers, that 'every ball had its billet'.* And six years later John Wesley makes this reference in his JOURNAL (6 June 1765): *He never received one wound. So true is the odd saying of King William, that 'every bullet has its billet'.*

Military commanders must perhaps of necessity have a certain fatalism about them. Horatio Nelson once responded to a warning to take care in battle with: *The bullet which hits me will have on it 'Horatio Nelson, his with speed'.* This remark may well be part of the history of the variant *If the bullet's got your name on it . . .* Napoleon is several times recorded assuring others that one predestined bullet, and that one alone, can be the cause of death. When asked by his brother, King Joseph of Spain, if he had ever been hit by a cannonball, he answered: *The bullet that is to kill me has not yet been cast.* He was right – he went on to die of natural causes after six years of exile on St Helena in 1821. Less eminent soldiers are not so invulnerable. In every collection of Famous Last Words, there is always quoted the comment of General Sedgewick, as he peered out at the enemy during the American Civil War: *They couldn't hit an elephant at this dist . . .*

The proverb is a biblical one and can be found in MATTHEW 5:15. In his Sermon on the Mount, Jesus encourages his disciples to bear witness to their faith, telling them that they are the light of the world. He goes on to explain that a lamp is of no value if it is placed under a bushel (a meal-tub big enough to contain a bushel of grain). Its proper place is on a lampstand. If his disciples are to influence those about them by word and example, they must not hide away but mix with others and act out their faith.

BUSHEL

■ **Don't hide your light under a bushel**

Don't hide your talents or merits away through modesty or shyness

One has responsibilities. The lamp mustn't be hidden under a bushel. One must let it shine, especially on people of good will.
(Aldous Huxley, POINT COUNTER POINT, 1928)

The Bishop urged Brownson not to hide his light under a bushel. As well urge a bull not to pretend to be a lamb! The rugged fiery Brownson was happy to learn that truculence had an apostolic value.
(V W Brooks, THE FLOWERING OF NEW ENGLAND, 1936)

The promise of a new love life could be rent to shreds and there are few shreds left to rend these days if you insist on hiding your light under a bushel.
(GIBRALTAR AIRWAYS IN-FLIGHT MAGAZINE, October 1991)

Business matters

It is hardly surprising that the massive growth in business and business studies in the twentieth century has re-invigorated older sayings (*Time is money* of Benjamin Franklin in ADVICE TO A YOUNG TRADESMAN, 1750; *Money talks* of O Henry in THE TALE OF A TAINTED TENNER, 1915) and spawned many memorable new ones, of which some at least have reached proverbial status. Milton Friedman, the Nobel Prize winner, said: *There's no such thing as a free lunch.* Leo Durocher has it that *Nice guys finish last,* and there's the anonymous *Buy low, sell high.* Fred Adler, a leading American venture capitalist, put money in its place: *Happiness is a positive cash flow.* There are many other witty memorable sayings from the business world that have been collected together in anthologies of business quotations. This may well encourage their common currency and assimilation into the proverb stock of the language. See *The customer is always right.*

Animals

Until the nineteenth century most of the British population lived from the land. They observed the creatures about them, both domesticated and wild, and drew lessons from their behaviour to apply to their own. From the shepherd, for instance, we learn that:

- *There is a black sheep in every flock*
- *A pet lamb makes a cross ram*
- *One foolish sheep will lead the flock*
- *Shear your sheep when elder blossoms peep*

The herdsman would know that:

- *Many a good cow hath a bad calf*
- *Milk the cow that stands still*
- *A lowing cow soon forgets her calf* (excess grief does not last long)

Observation of the pig scavenging freely in the village street would show that:

- *Pigs grow fat where lambs would starve*
- *A pretty pig makes an ugly sow*
- *Pigs might fly, but they are most unlikely birds*

Until the nineteenth century, oxen were often used for ploughing:

- *An old ox ploughs a straight furrow*
- *A man must plough with such oxen as he hath*

Cats were kept as mousers:

- *Cats in mittens catch no mice*
- *That which comes of a cat will catch mice*
- *Cats that drive the mice away are as good as they that catch them*

but other traits in their behaviour were also recognised:

- *The cat loves fish but she is loath to wet her feet*
- *The more you rub a cat on the rump, the higher she sets her tail*
- *Honest is the cat when the meat is out of reach*
- *An old cat laps as much as a young kitlin.*

Dogs were kept to guard a house:

- *A dog is a lion when he is at home*
- *Why keep a dog and bark yourself?*
- *Let sleeping dogs lie*

or to hunt:

- *The hindmost dog may catch the hare*
- *You cannot run with the hare and hunt with the hounds*

and will do anything for a meal:

- *If you wish a dog to follow you, feed him.*

All in all they lead a dog's life:

- *A dog's life, hunger and ease*

Aesop, writing in the sixth century BC, often made foxes the subject of his fables. He depicted them as sly, cunning creatures, a reputation which is reflected in European proverbs:

- *An old fox need learn no craft*
- *The fox may grow grey but never good*
- *He that will get the better of a fox must rise early* (French)
- *Foxes prey furthest from their earths*
- *A fox should not be of the jury at a goose trial*
- *An old fox is shy of a trap*

And last, but not least, the birds and the bees have something to teach us all:

- *Birds in their little nests agree*
- *It is a foolish bird that soils its own nest*
- *You cannot catch old birds with chaff*
- *Every bee's honey is sweet*
- *What is not good for the swarm is not good for the bees* (Latin)
- *Old bees yield no honey*
- *Bees that have honey in their mouths, have stings in their tails.*

Early versions of the Bible translate the correct 'lamp' as 'candle'. Sixteenth century uses of the proverb, therefore, speak of hiding a candle under a bushel. Interestingly, this continued until about the beginning of the twentieth century, when candles were no longer the main source of lighting.

Usage: 'Bushel' is a rather dated word, and it gives a somewhat antiquated flavour to the whole saying. The scope of application is now far wider than Christian witness to the world. It may refer to any hidden virtues that are undervalued

BYGONES

■ **Let bygones be bygones**

We should forget our past grievances and start over again

See also: Forgive and forget

Lately, however, prompted by curiosity or by remorse, he had asked her to spend a week or so of his declining years with him. And she had so far let bygones be bygones as to come and gratify the old man's whim.
(Max Beerbohm, ZULEIKA DOBSON, 1911)

He had made up his mind to tell her that he was reconciled with her father. In future bygones must be bygones.
(John Galsworthy, THE MAN OF PROPERTY, 1906)

What is painfully apparent is that a wrangle or dispute is liable to go from bad to worse

this week unless you are prepared to let bygones be bygones.
(RADIO TIMES, 9-15 January 1993)

This expression is based on a recurrent phrase from Homer's *Iliad* (c 850 BC): *These things will we let be, as past and done.* John Heywood echoes Homer's words imploring forgiveness in his PROVERBS (1546):

God taketh me as I am, and not as I was,
Take you me so to, and let all things past pas.

The word 'bygones', used to describe events, usually offences, that have happened in the past, was first used as a noun in the 1560s. By the time Samuel Rutherford wrote his LETTERS in 1636 it had been assimilated into a fixed proverb expressing the gist of Homer's phrase: *Pray . . . that bygones betwixt me and my Lord may be bygones.*

CAKE

■ **You can't have your cake and eat it**

You can't benefit from two incompatible plans, actions, etc. at the same moment

Variant: You can't eat your cake and have it

See also: You can't have it both ways

The conclusion [that if you live for others, you must live for others, and not as a roundabout way of getting an advantage for yourself] conflicts with his desire to eat his

cake and have it – that is, to destroy his own egoism and by so doing to gain eternal life.
(George Orwell, SHOOTING AN ELEPHANT, 'LEAR, TOLSTOY AND THE FOOL', 1950)

Its expense and its cornering of the child market tend to mean that Woolley Grange's guests are much of a muchness: well-off thirty-somethings liberal enough to want to bring their children with them to the hotel for the weekend but illiberal enough to dump them in a nursery when they get there. The first-time visitor to Woolley Grange will notice many such people lolling about contentedly, smug looks playing on their faces for having had their cake and eaten it.
(SUNDAY TIMES, 28 June 1992)

In short, BA wants to have its cake and eat it – enter the American market and gain access to passengers travelling from various American cities to international gateways and on to Europe, without significantly increasing the competition it faces at Heathrow. No wonder that United, American Airlines and Delta see this deal as terribly inequitable.
(SUNDAY TIMES, 22 November 1992)

Because teleworking allows you to work at home, it could be the ideal way of having your cake and eating it in the future. You could raise your children at home while you carried on with your thriving career.
(COMPANY, January 1993)

In all of this, I see a standard British mess – of wanting to have cakes and eat them. We want the old university system, but we won't give it either the money or the discipline that used to make it work.
(SUNDAY TIMES, 17 January 1993)

But it is more than just a mystique: the Palace is seen to be the pinnacle of a constitutional system which provides a sense of security, not just for those at the top, but for millions of ordinary people. In the end the British will have to choose, if it is not already too late, between having their Establishment and eating it.
(DAILY TELEGRAPH, 20 January 1993)

This proverb was first recorded by John Heywood in his collection of PROVERBS in the middle of the sixteenth century and has made frequent appearances in the literature of every century since. This age-old tendency to want absolutely everything and on one's own terms is not peculiarly British but crosses national frontiers: the French say *You can't have the cloth and keep the money*, and the Italians ask *Do you want to eat your cake and still have it in your pocket?*

Usage: There is an interesting variation in the form of the saying. The version *You can't eat your cake and have it* shares the same reasoning as the French and Italian proverbs; however, *You can't have your cake and eat it* is probably more frequent, though illogical.

CAP

■ **If the cap fits, wear it**

If you find the words of blame or criticism apply to you, then accept them

If indeed thou findest . . . that the cap fits thy own head, why then . . . e'en take and clap it on.

(Samuel Richardson, CLARISSA, 1748)

If the cap fits, Rector, you must wear it, and if you want to take your custom away from me for saying it, you'll be provin' to me that it fits right well.

(A G Street, THE ENDLESS FURROW, 1934)

The expression originally spoke of the fool's cap, headgear decorated with bells which was worn by fools and jesters. In Nicholas Breton's PASQUIL'S FOOLSCAP (1600) we read: *Where you finde a head fit for this Cappe, either bestowe it upon him in charity, or send him where he may haue them for his money.*

Fools were entertainers who, from medieval times, held permanent positions at court or in the households of distinguished noblemen. Shakespeare's KING LEAR (1605) gives us an insight into the role of one fool who delivers penetrating insights in a jesting fashion. The popularity of the jester dwindled in the seventeenth century and Swift's epitaph on the Earl of Suffolk's fool written in 1728 must be a tribute to the last of his kind.

Mention of the fool's cap remained in the proverb until well into the eighteenth century, fools and jesters being in living memory. Thomas Fuller records the expression in GNOMOLOGIA (1732): *If any Fool finds the Cap fit him, let him wear it.* But by the middle of that century direct reference to the fool's cap was being dropped and the proverb finds its way into Samuel Richardson's novel CLARISSA (1748) without it.

Usage: By using the phrase, the speaker points to a logical – usually unpalatable – conclusion that the listener should draw

CAT

■ A cat has nine lives

Applied to a person who has lived to a very old age, despite many setbacks

She joked about her illness and said that she was a cat with nine lives, eight of which had been lived to the full; the next attack, she said in her charming deep voice, would be the grand finale.

(Noël Coward, FUTURE INDEFINITE, 1954)

I'm like a cat with nine lives; each one lasts ten years, and I've just had my eighth. I'm going to live to be ninety, you'll see. I'm not too old to have some fun!

(J Byrom, OR BE HE DEAD)

Mischief was Captain's middle name. One time, I remember he decided to take a look at the roof of the conservatory. Portly little Captain found his way out on to the roof much to Mr Woolley's dismay. He then followed in the Captain's foot-steps, or should I say paw prints, in order to rescue his poor hound. Unfortunately Mr Woolley slipped and spent the next few days unconscious in hospital. But Captain was fine. Talk about a cat's nine lives!

(AMBRIDGE VILLAGE VOICE, LAMBING ISSUE, February 1993)

One cat took me three and a half weeks to coax from the [bombed] ruins of his home . . . I caught him . . . A week later he was sleek, gentle and loving again. One life gone, eight to go.
(B Lloyd-Jones, THE ANIMALS CAME IN ONE BY ONE, 1966)

Cats are agile creatures who, when they fall, land nimbly upon their four legs, the impact absorbed by their well-padded paws. An old proverb likened people whose fortunes always turned out favourably to a cat for this very reason: *He's like a cat; fling him which way you will he'll light on 's legs* (John Ray, ENGLISH PROVERBS, 1678). Today we would say *He always falls on his feet.* This agility has made the cat appear resilient in life-threatening situations, so that he is said to have nine lives.

The tradition, however, is not European but an ancient Indian one. It is contained in the FABLES OF PILPAY (or BIDPAI), an ancient collection of Sanskrit stories. They had widespread influence on European folklore through an eighth century Arabic translation, subsequent renderings into various Continental languages and a translation of 1570 into English. THE GREEDY AND AMBITIOUS CAT tells the story of a cat who lives on the edge of starvation with its owner, an old woman. One day she sees another cat. This one, however, is not skinny but fat and sleek. Surprised at this, the lean cat asks her new acquaintance how she comes to look so well and is told that there is plenty of food to be had at the king's house at dinner time. The lean cat resolves to accompany her sleek companion to this house of plenty the following day. Unfortunately, that very day, the servants had been ordered to rid the house of cats – many were in the habit of going there because of the rich pickings to be had. Nevertheless the lean cat entered and, spying a dish of meat, unobserved, dragged it under the dresser. Here she gorged herself on her prize until a servant noticed her and threw his knife at her, wounding her in the breast.

However, as it has been the providence of Nature to give this creature nine lives instead of one, poor Puss made a shift to crawl away, after she had for some time shammed dead: but, in her flight, observing the blood come streaming from her wound, 'Well,' said she, 'let me but escape this accident, and if ever I quit my old hold and my own mice for all the rarities in the King's kitchen, may I lose all my nine lives at once.'

The earliest known record of the proverb in English says that women share the cat's remarkable fortune, a comparison that remained current well into the eighteenth century: *A woman hath nyne lyues like a cat* (John Heywood, PROVERBS, 1546).

Other literary references just make mention of the cat's many lives. In Shakespeare's ROMEO AND JULIET (1591), Mercutio, incensed that Romeo refuses to stand up to his enemy Tybalt, himself picks a quarrel with Tybalt. When Tybalt asks him *What would thou have with me?* Mercutio replies, *Good King of Cats, nothing but one of your nine lives.*

The cat is not totally invincible, however. Even she must take heed lest care, curiosity or a murderous hand dispatch her prematurely. (See *Care killed a cat, Curiosity killed the Cat, There's more than one way to kill a cat than by choking it with cream.*

■ **A cat may look at a king**

Used to justify what others may see as an imposition or intrusion. Even the lowliest have rights

'Couldn't you give a hint to Almeric, not to keep staring at Alison? I am afraid Father will notice.'

'Oh, I think there is no harm in that, dear. A cat may look at a king; and it is only in that spirit that my poor brother looks at Alison.'
(Ivy Compton-Burnett, A HOUSE AND ITS HEAD, 1935)

Well, I will proceed to business, for in business even a cat can look at a king. I am now established in a humble way, in the basement, so to speak, of Hilliard, Lampeter and Hilliard.
(L P Hartley, EUSTACE AND HILDA, 1947)

Both French and German have variants of this proverb and each has a story behind it. The French version *Un chien regarde bien un évêque* (Even a dog may look at a bishop) is said to be a reference to a sixth century decree that forbade bishops from keeping dogs in case the animals should bite those coming to seek counsel. The German equivalent *Darf doch die Katze den Kaiser ansehen* (Even a cat may look at an Emperor) claims to stem from an incident in

which Maximilian I visited the shop of a man who made wood-cuts. During the entire visit the craftsman's cat lounged upon the table staring at the Emperor in a suspicious fashion. The fact that two European languages have equivalent proverbs with different stories to tell casts doubt upon the veracity of the tales. English boasts no anecdote to account for the origin of its particular version which was recorded by John Heywood in his collection of proverbs of 1546.

Usage: Those using the expression see it as an assertion of rights; those so addressed, from a different perspective, may interpret it as insolent. Now rather dated.

■ **Care killed a cat**

Anxiety can wear out even the most resilient people

If a cat, who is blessed with nine lives, can be worn out with care, then frail human beings, so easily given to worrying and fretting, are especially vulnerable.

The proverb is a warning and, in literature, is sometimes accompanied by an exhortation to help matters and put care aside. Shakespeare writes: *Though care killed a cat, thou hast mettle enough in thee to kill care* (MUCH ADO ABOUT NOTHING, 1599); and George Wither determines to enjoy Christmas: *Hang sorrow! Care will kill a cat, And therefore let's be merry* (CHRISTMAS, 1615). Others, however, are more realistic, or pessimistic depending on your point of view. Thomas Fuller owns: *Care will kill a Cat; yet there's no living without it* (GNOMOLOGIA, 1732). If he is right, perhaps the best remedy is to limit the scope of our anxiety for, as another proverb wisely teaches, *Sufficient unto the day is the evil thereof.*

Usage: Dated

■ **There are more ways of killing a cat than by choking it with cream**

There is more than one way of achieving one's aim

Variant: There's more than one way to skin a cat

This proverb does not make an appearance in English literature until the mid-nineteenth century when Charles Kingsley used it in WESTWARD HO (1855). A twentieth century variant of the saying suggests choking the cat with butter rather than cream. In either case, the proverb is right: this is not the only way of killing the animal. Traditionally cats and their unwanted litters were drowned; far more direct and cost-effective than the cream and butter method. Little Johnny Green in the old rhyme had obviously seen cats sent to a watery grave:

Ding, dong, bell, Pussy's in the well.
Who put her in? Little Johnny Green.
Who pulled her out? Little Tommy Stout.
What a naughty boy was that,
To try to drown poor pussy cat,
Who never did him any harm,
But killed the mice in his father's barn.

A variant, current in America, is *There's more than one way to skin a cat.* Mark Twain made use of the saying in CONNECTICUT YANKEE (1889).

■ **When the cat's away, the mice will play**

The followers of a leader will take advantage of his absence for their own ends

Variant: While the cat's away, the mice will play

President Yeltsin's statement on his sudden return from China, 'The master must return to restore order,' was delivered with the grin of a man well aware that while the cat is away the mice will play.
(THE TIMES, 21 December 1992)

Thomas Heywood, in his play A WOMAN KILL'D WITH KINDNESS (1607), calls this an 'old proverb'. It is also a proverb common to many European languages. The French, for instance, say *When the cat runs on the roofs, the mice dance on the floors;* the Spanish and Italians have *When the cat is not in the house, the mice dance;* and the Germans *Cat outside the house, repose for the mouse.*

It is impossible to say exactly when the domestic cat came to Britain or for how long it has been used as a mouser, but an article in ANIMALS (RSPCA magazine, 1979) tells how, in AD 948, the Welsh king, Howell the Good, was selling young kittens for a penny apiece, but once a kitten had caught its first mouse the price went up to twopence.

CAVEAT

■ **Caveat emptor**

Let the buyer beware

This Latin law maxim carries the rarely used English translation of *Let the buyer beware*. The full form of the maxim is *Caveat emptor, quia ignorare non debuit quod ius alineum emit* ('Let the buyer beware, for he ought not to be ignorant of the nature of the property which he is buying from another').

Formerly a buyer was totally bound by a contract with the seller. The law was amended by Chief Justice Tindal (1776–1846) who declared:

If a man purchases goods of a tradesman without in any way relying upon the skill and judgment of the vendor, the latter is not responsible for their turning out contrary to his expectation; but if the tradesman be informed, at the time the order is given, of the purpose for which the article is wanted, the buyer relying upon the seller's judgment, the latter impliedly warrants that the things furnished shall be reasonably fit and proper for the purposes for which it is required.

This was an important influence on our present day consumer law. An anecdote from Reuter, published in THE TIMES OF MALTA (4 April 1993), shows how important it is to inspect merchandise for quality:

For several days a new delivery of Syrian-made shoes took the Ukrainian city of Ivano-Frankivsk by storm, snapped up by men with an eye to fashion and elegance. Then the soles began peeling away, the colours ran and finally they simply fell apart. Itar-Tass news agency said local investigators found the stylish footwear, imported and sold off at a handsome profit by a small private company, had been made for corpses at Syrian funerals.

Usage: This saying carries the simple message 'Watch out!'

CHANGE

■ **Plus ça change, plus c'est la même chose**

Things stay essentially the same, despite superficial change and activity

Plus ça change, plus c'est la même chose. In the international community's efforts to step up pressure against Serbia, the French have yet again emerged as the odd men out.
(THE INDEPENDENT, 1 June 1992)

There is a tidal wave of crime, caused by an unreachable, subhuman underclass, which threatens the traditional, peaceful, British way of life. It is blamed, variously, on urban life, working mothers, absent fathers, family breakdown, erosion of deference, weak sentencing and soggy liberals. . . . In the 20s and 30s it was Hollywood films, in the 1890s it was music hall and 'penny dreadful' magazines, and in the 1840s the essayist Thomas Beggs felt it was 'the cheap theatres, penny gaffs and dancing saloons which are an encitement to crime . . .' Plus ça change.
(DAILY TELEGRAPH, 13 March 1993)

What future does the second language have, then, if it won't fit into the normal school day and is not viable either before or after school in Year 8 and 9? . . . One solution would be to introduce an express course for able linguists in Years 10 and 11 in the one remaining option box. Plus ça change . . . !
(TIMES EDUCATIONAL SUPPLEMENT, 26 March 1993)

This French saying was coined by Alphonse Karr, in LES GUÊPES (1849). The more governments change, the more they resemble each other. It is a sentiment that has found a home on this side of the Channel as well.

Usage: Now applicable not just to governments and their policies but much more widely. Often a weary sort of comment after the latest business whizz kid or management expert has done his worst, without fundamentally changing anything much.

CHARITY

■ Charity begins at home

Look after your own interests first

We must all be very kind to Auntie Jessie,
For she's never been a Mother or a Wife,
You mustn't throw your toys at her
Or make a vulgar noise at her,
She hasn't led a very happy life.
You must never lock her playfully in the bathroom
Or play tunes on her enamelled Spanish comb.

Though unpleasant to behold
She's a heart of purest gold
And Charity you know begins at home.
(Noël Coward, WE MUST ALL BE VERY KIND TO AUNTIE JESSIE, 1920s)

Charity will begin at home at this year's Queen Charlotte's Ball: for the first time the dresses worn will be borrowed en masse, and handed out free to the debutantes – or rather, what passes for debutantes these days. 'We would hate any deb to be prevented from going because she cannot afford the white dress,' says the executive committee's Anne Hobson, whose daughter is doing the season.
(DAILY TELEGRAPH, 19 May 1992)

One day, she stopped me in the road and bemoaned the fact that her house was worth only half its value of three years before.
'I've lost more than 200,000,' she whispered, with all the embarrassment of a woman who has gone on a two-week vacation to Monte Carlo, got completely drunk on a glass of champagne, and blown her life's savings on Number Seven at the roulette wheel.
I am sure her mood is not unique; and when the government talks about restoring confidence in the economy its message – like charity – must begin at home.
(WEST SUSSEX GAZETTE, 3 December 1992)

CHARITY BEGINS AT WORK
Most people have spent a lot of time lately thinking what to give others. Many companies are now donating time, skills and resources via employees volunteering to help their local communities . . . Teams of Halifax employees across the country organised a charity fashion show, bungee

jump, raffle, and car boot sale, as well as a gala lunch, charity greyhound race and car wash.
(DAILY EXPRESS, 28 December 1992)

Although organised charities, such as Oxfam and Save the Children, did not exist in the seventeenth century, citizens were none the less no strangers to charities, as acts of benevolence were then called. Those enjoying an income and a roof over their heads were expected to offer alms for the relief of the parish poor. Indeed, they were positively forced to by various poor laws between 1563 and 1601. This provision for the needs of the local community finds a reflection in the fuller form of the proverb current at that time, *Charity begins at home but should not end there.* It covered the interests of those around as well as one's own. However, it soon became shortened to the form we have today, with a more self-centred message that charity should begin with oneself. This thought was already well known in various expressions common since Wycliffe and Gower at the end of the fourteenth century.

It is possible that the Authorised Version of the Bible (1611) may have had some influence on the development of the proverb. There was another sense of charity, 'love', still remembered in the 1611 rendering of New Testament passages such as CORINTHIANS 13:4: *Charity suffereth long and is kind.* Since love, and 'charities' based upon it, is the basis of true piety, this may provide a link with TIMOTHY 5:4: *Let them learn first to show piety at home, and to requite their*

parents. This verse is thought by some to be the origin of the proverb.

Usage: The original positive moral exhortation now has a rather cynical, selfish sense. It is often used to justify some act of obvious self-interest.

■ Charity covers a multitude of sins

Acts of charity salve the conscience of those plagued by guilt. Acts of charity hide the flaws in a person's character

The plot is complicated, but, like Congreve's, seems a part of life, life of a world far from ours, where hearts are atrophied and polite manners and graceful bearing cover a multitude of sins.
(Allardyce Nicoll, A HISTORY OF RESTORATION DRAMA: 1600–1700, 1952)

'Pity she's so refained. I don't like women of that age who try to act the gracious lady. Bit of a prig, too.'
'Oh, I don't know. Can't really tell at this stage.'
'Ah, you always were one for a pretty face, weren't you? Covers a multitude is what I always say.'
(Kingsley Amis, LUCKY JIM, 1954)

Goodness and honesty can overcome a multitude of sins but it cannot determine success or failure on a football field. Which is why the scrutiny of Wilkinson and his team has never been stronger, nor their failings more deeply analysed.
(DAILY MAIL, 8 February 1993)

The proverb is a biblical one. PETER 4:8 reads: *And above all things have fervent charity among yourselves: for charity shall* cover the multitude of sins. Charity here, of course, is Christian love. Peter is saying that the deep love and commitment amongst a group of believers freely forgives the wrongs of others.

Charity has had another long-standing sense of good-works and financial help to worthy causes. That is far and away its predominant meaning today and is the way that the proverb has been understood over the last one hundred years.

Usage: The use of this verse as a proverb is quite recent, probably from the turn of the century, and 'charity' is understood in its modern meaning.

CHICKENS

■ **Don't count your chickens before they are hatched**

Don't be overconfident and assume success before you know the outcome of a venture

See also: First catch your hare; Don't halloo till you are out of the wood; There's many a slip 'twixt cup and lip

Make Fools believe in their fore-seeing
Of things before they are in Being;
To swallow Gudgeons ere th'are catch'd,
And count their Chickens ere th'are hatch'd.
(Samuel Butler, HUDIBRAS, 1664)

We must not reckon our chickens before they are hatched, though they are chipping the shell now.
(Walter Scott, JOURNAL, 20 May 1829)

'*We haven't said anything much about it to anybody yet, so you won't mind not talking about it just yet, will you?*'

'*I shan't say a word.*'

'*The experts, you know, the big dealers – we don't want any publicity just yet. They're all hand in glove, of course. And we don't want to count our purely putative chickens before they're hatched.*'
(William Plomer, MUSEUM PIECES, 1950)

The news from Moscow, as everyone could agree, was excellent. But dealers did not want to count all their chickens before they were hatched.
(DAILY MAIL, 22 August 1991)

Records of the proverb's use in English date back to the second half of the sixteenth century but its origins lie in the fables of Aesop written in the sixth century BC.

THE MILKMAID AND THE PAIL tells of a young girl on her way home after milking carrying her pail of milk on her head. As she walked along, she began to day-dream about what she would do with the milk. First she would make cream and, with that, butter to sell. This would bring enough to buy some eggs which would hatch into chickens. The chickens would lay still more eggs and, before long, she would have a prosperous business. When prices were high she would sell some of the birds and buy herself a beautiful dress. This would bring her to the notice of the young men in the town but she would ignore their advances with a toss of her curls. At this the milkmaid tossed her head and the pail of milk fell to the ground. Such are the disappointments of those who *count their chickens before they are hatched.*

Some writers show an exceptional fondness for using proverbs. Martin Luther (1483–1546) uses them in all his varied types of writing, from the theological through to the popular. Some lesser-known French writers of the seventeenth century also used considerable numbers of popular sayings: Adrien de Montluc (1589–1646), Gédéon Tallement des Réaux (1619–90) and Antoine Furetière (1619–88). Their contemporary, Jean de la Fontaine (1621–95), is famed for his celebrated FABLES, in which he made good use of many moral proverbial sayings. Goethe (1749–1832) showed a fondness for proverbs, and for reformulating them, which has been the subject of articles and a book-length study. Mieder (1975b) gives a thorough review of the use of proverbs in all the significant German authors.

CHILD

■ **A burnt child dreads the fire**

One does not repeat a painful lesson twice

See also: Once bitten, twice shy

The proverb is an old one. Its earliest appearances in English literature are in the PROVERBS OF HENDYNG (c 1320) and the DOUCE MANUSCRIPT (c 1350).

According to Trench (LESSONS IN PROVERBS, 1853), a similar French proverb, *A scalded dog fears cold water,* carries an even stronger message; that those who have experienced great pain or difficulty will not only draw back from the instrument of that pain in the future but will be fearful even where there is no cause.

Other languages have like proverbs:

A dog which has been beaten with a stick fears its own shadow (Italian)
Whom a serpent has bitten a lizard alarms (Southern Italy?)
One bitten by a serpent is afraid of a rope's end (Jewish)
The man who has received a beating with a firebrand runs away at the sight of a firefly (Singhalese)

And an old English proverb teaches:
Hang a Dog on a Crabtree, and he'll never love Verjuice (crab-apple liquor).

■ **Spare the rod and spoil the child**

A child who is not punished when he deserves it will become a spoilt brat

Variant: Spare the rod, spoil the child

See also: You've got to be cruel to be kind

A teacher who could be lawfully beaten by his own master was probably not inclined to spare the rod of authority over little children entrusted to his care.
(Charles and Mary Beard, THE RISE OF AMERICAN CIVILISATION, 1927)

SPARE THE ROD AND SPOIL THE SEXUAL PLEASURE
Can the painful be political? Loretta Loach talks to female sado-masochists.
(GUARDIAN, 29 April 1992)

The adage is from a verse in the Old Testament, PROVERBS 13:24, which reads: *He that spareth his rod hateth his son: but he that loveth him chasteneth him betimes.* The first part of the verse was referred to as a wise saying of Solomon's by writers throughout the Middle Ages. It was not until the seventeenth century that the verse was adapted and the modern proverb coined.

A Moroccan proverb advocates a sensitive approach to the discipline of a child. *Obey your children if you don't want them to be cursed,* it says. The proverb wisely exorts parents to take the age of the child as well as its character and temperament into consideration when considering discipline.

■ **The child is the father of the man**

The child's character gives insight into the kind of man he will grow up to be

The proverb comes from MY HEART LEAPS UP (1802), a poem by Wordsworth:

My heart leaps up when I behold
A rainbow in the sky:
So was it when my life began,
So is it now I am a man,
So be it when I shall grow old
Or let me die!
The Child is Father of the Man:
And I could wish my days to be
Bound each to each by natural piety.

The thought had been expressed by other illustrious poets before Wordsworth. These words, for instance, are Dryden's:

By education most have been misled,
So they believe, because they so were bred:
The priest continues what the nurse began,
And thus the child imposes on the man
(THE HIND AND THE PANTHER, 1687)

and these Milton's:

The childhood shows the man
As morning shows the day
(PARADISE REGAINED, 1671)

but Wordsworth's concise rendition encapsulated the thought and became proverbial.

CHILDREN

■ **Children should be seen and not heard**

Children may be present but not obtrusively noisy

See also: Speak when you are spoken to

Another common problem for women is that they have been taught to be seen and not heard. 'Women tend to sound apologetic when they speak, upping the pitch at the end of sentences almost as though asking questions,' says Phillipa.

(HELLO, 4 April 1992)

Children should be seen and not hurt.

(TEXACO CAR STICKER)

Women should be obscene, not heard.

(ANONYMOUS GRAFFITO)

This proverb is commonly thought of as being of Victorian origin but, although it may have gained renewed attention from the strict Victorian family, it is much older than that. Aristophanes' play THE CLOUDS, written in 423 BC, cites the expression and calls it an old rule. In medieval England it was not children but chattering young girls who were compelled to look decorous and remain silent: *For hyt ys an old Englysch sawe: 'A mayde schud be seen, but not herd'* (John Mirk, MIRK'S FESTIAL, c 1450).

Swift quotes this older form of the proverb in his POLITE CONVERSATION of 1738 but by 1866 the shift from maidens to children has taken place for we find E J Hardy coming to their defence and roundly declaring *'Little people should be seen and not heard' is a stupid saying* (HOW TO BE HAPPY THOUGH MARRIED). Nowadays the proverb is quoted by exasperated parents but not even heard above the din their offspring are making. Harry Graham shows the extent to which the distracted parent might go:

Father heard the children scream,
So he threw them in the stream,
Saying as he drowned the third,
'Children should be seen, not heard!'

(RUTHLESS RHYMES FOR HEARTLESS HOMES, 1899)

Usage: In these progressive days the expression has a patronising tone to it, where used directly as a form of order to unruly youngsters. More frequently, perhaps, it would be found today as an unavailing and unfulfilled longing of parents bombarded with the blare of pop culture and insolence.

CHURCH

■ **The nearer the church, the further from God**

Superficial religiosity is a long way from true religion

Variant: The nearer the church, the further from heaven

The proverb is old. Its first appearance in print dates back to the early years of the fourteenth century and makes it clear that it was a well-established saying even then:

Tharfor men seye, an weyl ys trowed,
The nere the chuchen, the fyrther fro God.
(Robert Manning of Brunne, HANDLYNG SYNNE, c 1303)

Abelard, writing 150 years earlier, identified the contemporary problems within the church:

We, who ought to live by the labour of our own hands . . . do now follow after idleness, that enemy of the soul, and seek our livelihood from the labours of other men . . . so that entangling ourselves in worldly business and striving under the sway of earthly covetousness to be richer in the cloister than we have been in the world, we have subjected ourselves to earthly lords, rather than to God . . . We take from great men of this world in the guise of alms, manors, tenants, bondsmen and bondswomen . . . and to defend these possessions we are bound to appear in outside courts before worldly judges. (See also *The cowl does not make the monk.*)

St Bernard of Clairvaux in the same period was a reforming Cistercian who did much to set matters to rights. However, after his death his strict standards were not maintained. A contemporary poem records the renewed worldliness of the Church:

*Livings and churches they buy
And many ways to cheat they try.
They buy and sell at profit
Awaiting settling day.
And well they sell their corn
And I have heard they do not scorn
To lend their money to the Jews.*

It is not surprising that Ray in 1678 should give a French origin for the phrase. In France and a good number of other countries, a parallel form of the proverb exists, in common recognition that *The religious are not necessarily the good.* Taylor (1931) points out some variants that are very typical of the Reformation: *The nearer Rome, the worse Christian* and *The nearer the Pope, the worse Christian.* These two date from Germany around 1500.

The Church cannot be unredeemably bad – at least it has shown a sense of humour. In his Christmas sermon on the

Nativity before King James I in 1622, Bishop Lancelot Andrewes applied the maxim both to himself and to the King as head of the Church: *With us the nearer, lightly the farther off: our proverb is, you know, 'the nearer the church the farther from God'.*

CLOUD

■ **Every cloud has a silver lining**

Every difficult or depressing circumstance has its hidden consolations. There is always a reason for hope in the most desperate situations

See also: Always look on the bright side; Hope springs eternal in the human breast

The lights disclosed the curate gazing at her with something in his expression that seemed to suggest that, although all this was no doubt deplorable, he had spotted the silver lining.
(P G Wodehouse, THE INIMITABLE JEEVES, 1924)

But this is Moscow where every silver lining is securely wrapped in a cloud. And this is some cloud.
(BBC RADIO 4, FROM OUR OWN CORRESPONDENT, 5 October 1991)

The silver lining to the snow cloud is that the heavy seas are likely to help the dispersal of the oil coming from the wreck.
(BBC RADIO NEWS, 11 January 1993)

If you think the HRT story sounds too good to be true, you probably won't be surprised to discover that there is a cloud with this

silver lining. One of the most controversial aspects of HRT is suggestions of a link with breast cancer. The fear of this stops many women taking it and many doctors prescribing it.
(DAILY EXPRESS, 10 February 1993)

The farside of the darkest cloud reflects the moonlight and gleams silver, a sign of hope. The proverb has its origins in John Milton's masque COMUS (1634):

Was I deceiv'd, or did a sable cloud
Turn forth her silver lining on the night?

but it was Dickens who, over two centuries later, brought the lines to popular attention with his reference to 'Milton's cloud': I turn my silver lining outward like Milton's cloud (BLEAK HOUSE, 1852). After Dickens others made mention of silver-lined clouds but W S Gilbert's reference in THE MIKADO (1885) comes close to the present day proverb: Don't let's be downhearted. There's a silver lining to every cloud.

In the grim years of the First World War people sang to encourage themselves. By now the silvery cloud was far removed from its august origins; it had become a proverb that was on the tip of the popular tongue, finding its way into one of the best-remembered wartime songs, KEEP THE HOME FIRES BURNING:

There's a silver lining
Through the dark clouds shining,
Turn the dark cloud inside out,
Till the boys come home.
(Ivor Novello and Lena Guilbert Ford, 1915)

And shortly after the Great War, looking for a silver lining remained a remedy for keeping those weary of life's troubles cheerful:

Look for the silver lining
When 'ere a cloud appears in the blue
Remember somewhere the sun is shining
And so the right thing to do
Is make it shine for you.
A heart full of joy and gladness
Can always banish sadness and strife
So always look for the silver lining
And try to find the sunny side of life.
(Jerome Kern, LOOK FOR THE SILVER LINING, 1920)

Usage: The proverb that had such grand literary beginnings has now become a rather trite cliché but, if it has suffered from overuse, it is because it answers the universal need for a ray of hope in adversity.

COAT

■ Cut your coat according to your cloth

Trim your expenditure according to the means or income you have available; adapt to your circumstances

With characteristic decision old Jolyon came at once to the point. 'I've been altering my arrangements, Jo,' he said. 'You can cut your coat a bit longer in the future – I'm settling a thousand a year on you at once. June will have fifty thousand at my death, and you the rest.'
(John Galsworthy, THE MAN OF PROPERTY, 1906)

The Expansion of England *was a grand thing while it lasted, but it has reached its natural and inevitable limit. We must cut our coat according to our cloth and adapt ourselves to changing circumstances.*
(W R Inge, LAY THOUGHTS OF A DEAN, 1926)

You are probably dreading yet another reference to the state of your finances and being told to wise up . . . However, deep down you know that it is not simply a question of cutting your coat according to your cloth – it's more the need to get others to come clean and to face up to their responsibilities.
(RADIO TIMES, 9–15 January 1993)

It all has rather more to do with emotion than economics: a sense of immense complacency and easing of the economic conscience; the most feckless among us feel better at a public display of thrift (and it usually is very public), however counter-productive it may be.

It is not so much cutting one's coat according to one's cloth, I'd suggest, as cutting up a perfectly good coat and using it for dusters.
(GOOD HOUSEKEEPING, April 1993)

In 1533 Parliament introduced legislation governing expenditure ('sumptuary laws') that laid down the clothing permitted to be worn by the different social ranks: knights, squires, yeomen, merchants, artisans and labourers earning less than 40 shillings a year. Legislation was deemed necessary to keep people in their respective social strata, since there had been considerable pressures that might break down the traditional ranks. One of these was an economic pressure. A result of the Black Death was to decimate the working population. This meant that labourers could demand (and obtain, despite laws explicitly forbidding increases) higher wages than previously, enabling them to adopt the dress, at very least, of ranks above them. The fourteenth and early fifteenth centuries became very concerned with the boundaries of social status which seemed to be changing, a theme that continued into the sixteenth century.

From this background may well have come our contemporary proverb. In John Heywood's PROVERBS of 1546 there is recorded *I shall cut my cote after my cloth* and Lyly has in 1580 *Cut thy coat according to thy cloth* in EUPHUES AND HIS ENGLAND.

The original sense of living within one's rank is now restricted to living within one's financial means or, sometimes more generally, within the constraints of circumstance. Mr Micawber was quick to point out the advantages of financial prudence:

'My other piece of advice, Copperfield,' said Mr Micawber, 'you know. Annual income twenty pounds, annual expenditure nineteen nineteen six, result happiness. Annual income twenty pounds, annual expenditure twenty pounds ought and six, result misery. The blossom is blighted, the leaf is withered, the God of day goes down upon the dreary scene, and – and in short you are forever floored. As I am!'
(Charles Dickens, DAVID COPPERFIELD, 1849)

COBBLER

■ **Let the cobbler stick to his last**

Concern yourself only with things that you know something about

Variant: The shoemaker should stick to his last

The origin of the proverb is said to be in an anecdote told about Apelles, the famous Greek painter of the fourth century BC. The story goes that Apelles was wont to display his work to public view while he hung around, undetected, listening to their comments. One day a passing cobbler criticised a shoe latchet in one of the pictures. Apelles obliged by correcting the fault. The cobbler passed by again the next day and noticed the correction. Emboldened by his success he ventured to comment upon the way the thigh was painted but Apelles, who was hiding behind the picture, called out, 'The shoemaker should not go beyond his last.'

Erasmus alludes to the expression (*Ne sutor ultra crepidam*, 'let the cobbler not go beyond his last') in his ADAGIA (1536). William Hazlitt created the word *ultracrepidarian*, based on Erasmus's rendering, to refer to a critic who is ignorant or presumptuous. He first used it in 1819 of William Gifford who, before being helped with his education, was an apprentice shoemaker. The proverb itself has been used in English literature since the sixteenth century.

COCK

■ **Every cock crows on his own dunghill**

People feel safe to brag about their bravery on their own patch

Variant: Every cock is bold on his own dunghill

If in your sympathy for Mr Rouncewell you call Dickens the champion of a manly middle-class Liberalism against Chesney Wold, you will suddenly remember Stephen Blackpool – and find yourself unable to deny that Mr Rouncewell might be a pretty insupportable cock on his own dunghill.
(G K Chesterton, VICTORIAN AGE IN LITERATURE, 1913)

Cock of the dunghill. He's got to be cock – even if it's only of the tiniest little Fabian dunghill. Poor old Mark! What an agony when he can't get to the top of his dunghill!
(Aldous Huxley, EYELESS IN GAZA, 1936)

Bartlett traces the saying *A cock has great influence on his own dunghill* to Publilius Syrus writing in the first century BC, and Seneca employed a like expression in LUDUS DE MORTE CLAUDII (AD 55): *The cock is worth most on his own dunghill.*

The unknown author of the devotional work ANCREN RIWLE (c 1220) used the saying which also appeared in fourteenth and fifteenth century writings before being included in John Heywood's 1546 collection of proverbs. Forms have varied through the centuries; the cock is *mighty, bold, proud* before crowing on his own dunghill.

Spanish, French and German cocks behave in the same way on their home middens.

Usage: An expression now fading from use

COMPANY

■ **A man is known by the company he keeps**

You can tell what a person is like by the kind of friends he associates with

Written records of the proverb in English date back to the turn of the seventeenth century: *As a man is, so is his company* (Arthur Dent, THE PLAINE MAN'S PATH-WAY TO HEAVEN, 1601). The proverb is common to many other European languages which all have close variants. This diversity is reflected in English; the saying does not settle into the familiar English form until the nineteenth century. Lord Chesterfield terms *Tell me who you live with and I will tell you who you are* a Spanish proverb and Cervantes uses *Tell me what company you keep, and I'll tell you what you are* in DON QUIXOTE (1615). Sixteenth century Italian diplomat, Stefano Guazzo, refers to the proverb twice in his CIVILE CONVERSAZIONE (1574): *Tel me with whom thou doest goe, and I shall know what thou doest,* which he refers to as 'this common proverb', and *wee are always taken for suche as those are, with whom we are conversant* he calls 'that common rule'. French, Portuguese and Dutch also share the proverb.

The wisdom is ancient. Greek playwright Euripides, writing in the fifth century BC, says *Every man is like the company he is wont to keep* (PHOENISSAE) and Aesop tells fables which make this same point. The ASS AND THE PURCHASER (c 570 BC) tells of a man who wanted to try out an ass before deciding whether or not to buy it. He took it home and led it to the stable where he kept his other asses. Straight away it sought out the laziest animal there. 'My mind is made up,' the man declared. 'It is easy to judge this ass's temperament by the companion he chooses.'

A Moroccan proverb also illustrates the point with the behaviour of an ass. *If you let your ass mix with other asses,* it says, *you will teach it to moan, to bray and to leave the straight road.* The Egyptians, proud of their great river, say that *Even the water of the Nile loses its sweetness when it mingles with that of the sea.* Hebrew reminds us that *Dry wood sets green wood alight,* while an English alternative states that *Bad company is the ruin of a good character.*

A wealth of advice, spanning the centuries, encourages actively seeking out good company and shunning bad. Earl Rivers' translation of the *Seyinges of [H]Omer* provides a summary: *Acompanye the[e] with good people and thou shalt be on[e] of them; acompanye the[e] with badde & thou shalt be on[e] of thoos* (DICTES AND SAYENGES OF THE PHILOSOPHIRS, 1477).

COMPARISONS

■ **Comparisons are odious**

Comparing (often one person with another) upsets and offends

Comparisons are odious; but I think that by the side of German English generally has the advantage in expressiveness. Thunder is a much more expressive word than Donner.
(W R Inge, MORE LAY THOUGHTS, 1931)

'Which do you think the prettiest girl in the room?'

He looked at her quizzically, laughing heu, heu, heu behind his silly little moustache.

'Aha! Comparisons are odious, my sweet.'
(Rosamand Lehmann, INVITATION TO THE WALTZ, 1932)

'I think he's the silliest man who's ever been here.'

'Comparisons are odious.'

'There just isn't anything nice about him. He's got a silly voice and a silly face, silly eyes and silly nose.'
(Evelyn Waugh, A HANDFUL OF DUST, 1934)

This is an old and much-used proverb that is common to many European countries. Its use in French can be traced back at least as far as the thirteenth century. The earliest known English records, however, are in John Lydgate's DEBATE BETWEEN THE HORS, SHEPE AND GHOOS (c 1430): *Odyous of olde been comparisonis,* and then in John Fortescue's DE LAUDIBUS LEGUM ANGLIAE (1471), where the author uses the proverb in his comparison of English common and civil law.

Later Shakespeare uses the saying to humorous effect in MUCH ADO ABOUT NOTHING (1599) where Dogberry declares *Comparisons are odorous* (Act 3, scene v).

Francis Hawkins, writing in the seventeenth century, has this to say about comparing one with another: *Take heed that thou make no comparisons, and if any body happen to be praised for some brave act, or virtue, praise not another for the same virtue in his presence, for every comparison is odious* (YOUTH'S BEHAVIOUR, 1663). Sydney Smith (1771–1845) needed no such warnings. He was the very essence of tact and gallantry. On one occasion he met two attractive ladies of his acquaintance, Mrs Tighe and Mrs Cuff. 'Ah, ladies, there you are,' he greeted them. 'The *cuff* that everyone would wear and the *tie* that no one would loose.'

COOKS

■ **Too many cooks spoil the broth**

When too many people are involved in a project the result will be confusion

TOO MANY COOKS SLICING THE SALAMI
As a research and development officer, I am of necessity a compulsive journal scanner and I have recently noticed an increasing trend in coauthorship of professional papers with the number of authors sometimes even exceeding the number of words in the title.
(TIMES HIGHER EDUCATIONAL SUPPLEMENT, 26 February 1993)

George Gascoigne tells us that *there is the proverb, the more cooks the worse pottage* (LIFE OF CAREW, 1575). Large sixteenth century households, comprising of the family, their retinue and guests, had many cooks and scullion boys, each with his own particular job to do. Any cook who insisted on interfering with another's dish would neglect his own and perhaps be guilty of over-spicing his colleague's. Even in more modest establishments food is easily spoilt if everyone who passes through adds a little more of this and that. A Dutch proverb concurs: *Too many cooks make the porridge too salt.*

The proverb in its modern form was current by the seventeenth century. It was used by Sir Balthazar Gerbier in PRINCIPLES OF BUILDING written in 1662.

Usage: The proverb is not, of course, restricted to the kitchen. It can be used of any situation where more than the appropriate number for the particular task get involved and make a contribution that cancels out the efforts of others.

COUNTRIES

■ So many countries, so many customs

Every land has its own culture and its own way of life

That there are marked differences in the way different nationalities conduct their daily affairs is obvious on a world scale but is equally true within the bounds of a single continent. In his PROVINCIAL GLOSSARY, Francis Grose (1731–91) speculated on what would happen if a number of European nations colonised an island: *In settling an island, the first building erected by a Spaniard will be a church; by a Frenchman, a fort; by a Dutchman, a warehouse; and by an Englishman, an alehouse.* Once established the colonialists would doubtless set about making life more comfortable. This drinking rhyme, of unknown origin, underlines still more differences in national taste and character:

A Frenchman drinks his native wine,
A German drinks his beer;
An Englishman his 'alf and 'alf,
Because it brings good cheer.
The Scotchman drinks his whiskey straight
Because it brings on dizziness;
An American has no choice at all –
He drinks the whole damn business.

Where there are men, there are customs is just one of a number of Latin and Greek sayings which express this idea of the cultural diversity of mankind. There are very early references to this in English texts. Amongst some Anglo-Saxon gnomic verses from the turn of the twelfth century we find: *An equal number both of countries and customs* and in the PROVERBS OF HENDYNG (c 1320): *So many countries, so many customs.* Chaucer's rendition in TROILUS AND CRISEYDE (c 1374) is: *In sondry londes, sondry ben usages.*

The proverb is known in several other European languages, as is a similar saying *Different times, different manners*, meaning that people's way of life and code of conduct change as the years go by. This proverb is found in a hymn from the fifth century BC by the great Greek poet Pindar.

CRADLE

■ **The hand that rocks the cradle rules the world**

A mother's influence is greatest of all

Actress Rebecca de Mornay, 30, portrays a psychotic nanny who destroys a family in The Hand That Rocks The Cradle . . .
(Film title, TODAY, 12 May 1992)

My theory is that it's in the genes all right . . . but it's not got a lot to do with guilt. It's because women just can't be bothered with all the excuse making. They have too many other things to think about and do . . . than to rush around seeking out a suitable door and then piling up the blame at it. The hand that rocks the cradle stops the buck; and it's not an entirely ignoble thing to do.
(GOOD HOUSEKEEPING, July 1992)

CLUBS AND SCHOOLS VIE TO BE HAND THAT ROCKS CRADLE
. . . there remain shortcomings as a potentially damaging power struggle for the minds and bodies of young talent is played out. In one corner are the professional clubs, who believe they are best qualified to give youth its head; in the other the English

Schools FA, seeing themselves as guardians and providers of football for boys (and girls, too, these days), not boys for football.
(DAILY TELEGRAPH, 15 March 1993)

The proverb was coined by William Ross Wallace in a poem THE HAND THAT RULES THE WORLD, published in John o'London's TREASURE TROVE (1881):

They say that man is mighty,
He governs land and sea,
He wields a mighty sceptre
O'er lesser powers that be;
But a mightier power and stronger
Man from his throne has hurled,
For the hand that rocks the cradle
Is the hand that rules the world.

The recognition of the mother's influence being paramount in a child's early years finds expression in several European cultures, perhaps most memorably in the Spanish *What is sucked in with the mother's milk runs out with the shroud.*

Walsh gives two anecdotes that illustrate this proverb in reverse. The first goes back to Themistocles, who claimed his son was the most powerful person in Greece: *For the Athenians govern Greece, I the Athenians, my wife me, and my son my wife.*

The second is from the PERCY ANECDOTES by Reuben and Sholto Percy (1823):

A nobleman accosted a lame school-master and asked him his name. 'I am R T,' was the answer, 'and the master of this parish.' 'Why, how so?' 'I am the master of the children of the parish, the children are masters of the mothers, the mothers are the rulers of the fathers, and consequently I am the master of the whole parish.'

It is hardly surprising that humorists have found such potent themes as the exercise of power and the relationship between man and woman as perfect targets for their wit. American short story writer O Henry begins with a play on words in his title THE HAND THAT RILES THE WORLD (in GENTLE GRAFTER, 1907) and proceeds to poke fun at his typically folksy characters.

Usage: The hand that rocks the cradle in this abbreviated form is often used as a simple synonym of 'mother'

CROWD

■ **Two's company, three's a crowd**

The presence of a third person prevents intimacy

Variant: Two's company, three is none

One's too few, three's too many is a proverb quoted by John Ray in ENGLISH PROVERBS (1678) which has the same meaning as the saying recorded in the nineteenth century by William Carew Hazlitt: *Two is company, three is none* (ENGLISH PROVERBS, 1869). More than one source has pointed out that the proverb was particularly suited to courting couples both then and now. *Two's company, three's a chaperon,* writes Philip Moeller (MADAME SAND, 1917). Discretion is a Lancashire virtue. A correspondent of NOTES AND QUERIES (1871) describes how the saying would

be used in that county as an excuse to avoid playing gooseberry. *'When a lover meets his intended with her companion,'* he says, *'the latter will say, "Two are company, but three are none", and pass on another road.'*

Usage: The popular variant *Two's company, three's a crowd* is modern.

CRUEL

■ **You've got to be cruel to be kind**

It may be necessary to do something unpleasant in the short term, for long term benefit

See also: Spare the rod and spoil the child

Parents were last night warned they are driving their children to obesity, idleness and an early grave . . .
   Leaflets urging parents: 'Be cruel to be kind' and telling them to make their children walk are now being circulated in some areas. (DAILY EXPRESS, 20 April 1992)

The current contexts in which *You've got to be cruel to be kind* are used are fairly ordinary – a parent insisting a child takes some unpleasant medicine, for example. It was not always so.
   Catherine de Medici was born in Florence and came from one of the most influential families in Italy. She married Henry II of France. She would be conversant with the Italian proverb *Sometimes clemency is cruelty and cruelty is clemency.* She also knew the words of Bishop Corneille Muis in his SERMON

(c 1550): *Against rebels it is cruelty to be humane, and humanity to be cruel.* On the eve of St Bartholomew's Day, 24 August 1572, she quoted this saying to her son, Charles IX, to spur him on to begin the purge of the French Huguenots. His scruples allayed, the carnage started in Paris and the provinces, with a death toll that probably reached 50,000.

The linguistic history of the expression is much less dramatic. Sophocles was the first to make the association of cruelty and clemency (c 409 BC). In English, Shakespeare introduced the thought in a precursor of our contemporary expression: *I must be cruel, only to be kind* (HAMLET, 1602)

CUP

■ **There's many a slip 'twixt cup and lip**

Beware of being over-confident, for many things can go wrong between the starting and finishing of a project

Variants: There's many a slip between cup and lip; There's many a slip 'twixt the cup and the lip

See also: Don't count your chickens before they are hatched

Charles had little fear that the old man would have changed his mind. All the same he had seen nothing in writing on the subject, and he could not help being worried by dark thoughts of slips between cups and lips. (F W Crofts, THE 12.30 FROM CROYDON, 1934)

When it became known that Ouse Valley Sludge's Saturday Sport programme had got the exclusive rights for screening synchronised swimming and volley ball, plus the World Marbles Championships at Tinsley Green, their success in gaining the franchise seemed secure. But of course there's many a slip . . .
(MID SUSSEX TIMES, 30 August 1991)

From the sixteenth to the eighteenth centuries the proverb was *Many things fall* (or *happen*) *between the cup and the lip.* Then, sometime during the first quarter of the nineteenth century, the rhyme we are familiar with today, together with a more rhythmical turn of phrase, gave *There's many a slip 'tween the cup and the lip.* 'Twixt' was a slightly later addition, possibly the inspiration of R H Barham in *The Ingoldsby Legends* (1840).

The proverb is of ancient origin. Cato cites an early form in DE AEDILIBUS VITIO CREATIS (c 175 BC): *I have often heard that many things may come between the mouth and the morsel.* When Erasmus included *Manye thynges fall betwene the cuppe and the mouth* in his ADAGIA (1523), he attached it to the following story. Ancaeus, helmsman of the Argo, had a fertile vineyard which was cultivated by slaves whom Ancaeus worked to the limits of their endurance. One day one of the slaves came to Ancaeus and prophesied that he would die before he got the chance to taste its wine. All went well with the vineyard. An abundant harvest was gathered and pressed to make fine wine. Ancaeus, goblet in hand, mocked the slave for his hasty prophecy. But he replied, 'Many things happen between the cup and the lip.' As Ancaeus was about to drink, a messenger ran up shouting that the Calydonian boar was wreaking havoc in the vineyard. Ancaeus threw down his goblet and rushed to the vineyard intending to kill the boar but, instead, the enraged animal turned on him and savaged him to death.

Stevenson, however, proposes an alternative origin to this. Homer's ODYSSEY recounts the adventures of Odysseus as he travels home after a long absence at the Trojan war. A number of suitors have gathered around his beautiful wife, Penelope, and Odysseus is determined to destroy these. The suitors are assembled in the great hall to attempt a challenge, devised by Penelope, with her hand in marriage as prize. None of them succeeds but Odysseus, disguised as a beggar, successfully performs the challenge. He then turns his bow upon Antonious, the leader of the suitors, whom he shoots in the throat just as he is about to drink, causing his goblet to fall to the ground.

Usage: The proverb employs the Middle English form *'twixt*, which is a shortening of *betwixt*. This is now used only in very few fixed expressions such as this proverb and in *betwixt and between*. The interesting thing is that no record has yet been found of the proverb including *'twixt* that predates 1840.

CURE

■ **Prevention is better than cure**

Stopping illness before it starts is better than having to treat it later

Variant: An ounce of prevention is worth a pound of cure

Margot has some advice for other families who find themselves in the same situation: 'Get help fast. Break down doors if you have to but get help. And be aware of the risk all young people are at - prevention is 100 times better than cure.'
(NEW ZEALAND WOMAN'S WEEKLY, 14 January 1991)

As if in answer to Chris Mawson's plea for more younger men . . . enter new heart-throb Dr Richard Locke, to the surgery vacated by GP Dr Matthew Thorogood. The new doctor comes from a north country group practice and believes that prevention is better than cure.
(AMBRIDGE VILLAGE VOICE, CHRISTMAS ISSUE, Winter 1992)

How much better and more useful it is to meet the trouble in time, rather than to seek a remedy after the damage has been done, says Henry de Bracton (DE LEGIBUS ET CONSUETUDINIBUS ANGLIAE, c 1240), expressing the thought behind the future proverb. Erasmus narrows it down to medicine in his ADAGIA (1500): *It is better to doctor at the beginning than at the end.* The proverb itself started to appear in written form in the seventeenth century. Thomas Adams quotes an early form in WORKS (1630):

Prevention is so much better than healing. Almost a century later the saying is much more recognisable: *Prevention is much preferable to cure* (Thomas Fuller, GNOMOLOGIA, 1732). And Dickens uses it in MARTIN CHUZZLEWIT (1844) in its modern form.

Modern practitioners seek to follow the wisdom behind this proverb, in preventative medicine and dentistry. Illness is distressing and treatment often unpleasant or painful. How much better to take steps to avoid being ill at all. Our forebears had the added incentive of avoiding all sorts of grim and excruciating cures. Some were rooted in superstition and folk medicine: in Elizabethan times tumours were treated by rubbing them with a dead man's hand and those suffering from the ague were recommended to swallow a good-sized live spider in treacle. Others were not unlike present day practice but pity the Georgian dental patient who,

David Teniers (1610–90) painted DUTCH PROVERBS in oils in 1646-7. It is currently housed at Belvoir Castle, on the borders of Leicestershire and Nottinghamshire. What is particularly interesting about it is that it illustrates some forty-five Dutch proverbs. There is another claimant for the most proverbs in one picture. A French print of 1570 illustrates some seventy-one expressions.

without the aid of anaesthetic, sat while his aching teeth were seared with a red-hot rod to kill the nerve before being filled with molten lead. Extraction by the blacksmith might be preferred.

Usage: The proverb need not only be applied to preventative medicine but nowadays can also refer to taking steps to prevent future difficulty in any sphere.

CURIOSITY

■ **Curiosity killed the cat**

Beware of poking your nose into the affairs of others; it may get you into trouble

'Light, Kurak.'
   Kurt hooded the torch glass and flashed twice across the lough, twice again in the direction of the castle ruins.
   'That for Jason?' I asked.
   'Possibly.'
   'We burying the sleepers in the castle ruins?'
   Kurt waggled a finger. 'Curiosity killed the cat, Lovejoy.'
(Jonathan Gash, THE SLEEPERS OF ERIN, 1983)

Disappointingly this proverb has no intriguing story behind it, but a quaint rhyming version of unknown origin explains why the cat died:

Curiosity killed the cat,
Information made her fat.'

A variant is *Curiosity killed a monkey.* Both animals, it seems, had a reputation for being too curious for their own good. Monkeys are quite obviously mischievous and curious but an incident reported by the British media where a cat leapt into a washing machine and was then treated to a long cycle of washing and spinning, suggests that cats are too. Unlike the unfortunate animal in the proverb, the cat who made the news headlines lived to tell the tale.

References in literature date from the beginning of the twentieth century. Some suggest an American origin.

CURSES

■ **Curses, like chickens, come home to roost**

Speaking badly of someone will rebound ultimately to one's own detriment

Curses are like young chickens,
And still come home to roost!
(Lytton)

By this time some of the merriest are past their first youth. I do not understand what then happens; but I rather think curses come home to roost, and a younger generation still shows a like indifference to whatever are the consequences of fashion.
(Frank Swinnerton, THE GEORGIAN LITERARY SCENE, 1935)

'I prefer my country to the salvation of my soul,' said Machiavelli. This is making patriotism a rival religion indeed. But may not the soul of a nation be lost? And does not sacro egoismo come home to roost?
(W R Inge, A RUSTIC MORALIST, 'SUBSTITUTES FOR RELIGION', 1937)

The problem with the Government's finances arose because public spending was allowed to soar, not as economic recovery set in during 1991 or 1992, but simply on the rash assumption that it was bound to do so. The chickens have come home to roost.
(DAILY MAIL, 17 March 1993)

English literature has several vivid similes to illustrate the notion that curses rebound and harm the very person who uttered them. The unknown author of ARDEN OF FEVERSHAM (1592) says:

Curses are like arrowes shot upright,
Which falling down light on the shuter's head.

There are echoes of this in Sir Walter Scott's OLD MORTALITY (1816): *I have heard a good man say, that a curse was like a stone flung up to the heavens, and maist like to return on the head that sent it.*

Chaucer comes close to the modern proverb in his CANTERBURY TALES: *And ofte tyme swich cursinge wrongfully retorneth agayn to him that curseth, as a brid that retorneth agayn to his owene nest* (THE PARSON'S TALE, c 1386), but the earliest known record of the present day saying comes in Robert Southey's CURSE OF KEHAMA (1809). Scholars of the period claimed it to be of Arabic or Turkish origin.

CUSTOMER

■ **The customer is always right**

Always defer to the client

Variant: The customer always knows best

'I was only trying to do what you said, love.'
She spun round on her way to the door.
'What I said?'
'The tourist is always right.'
(Jonathan Gash, THE GONDOLA SCAM, 1984)

'It might sound very simple,' says Stuart Slade, 'but really the whole Tesco turn-around has been based on Sir Ian's insistence that "The customer is always right".'
(GOOD HOUSEKEEPING, November 1992)

THE CUSTOMER ISN'T ALWAYS RIGHT
The emancipation of country-house-hotel cooking, which was steaming ahead in the boom years, has turned into a crisis of confidence. Business is now so hard to come by that even the battle-hardened survivors are tempted to play down their culinary talents and pander to the lowest common denominator.
(WEEKEND TELEGRAPH, 7 November 1992)

One of the most popular business expressions is *The customer is always right* – see also **Business Matters** (page 33). Archer Taylor, a leading student of proverbs, traces it back to 1921 and suggests that it is probably British and not American in origin. Other sources indicate that it may have been coined by H Gordon Selfridge. He was born in the USA in 1857 but later became a British citizen. He established Selfridge's department store on Oxford Street, one of the largest in Europe. The motto for all his shops was *The customer is always right*.

These days, in order to get the customer service message through to company staff, American firms surround their employees with motivational plaques:

It takes months to find a customer, seconds to lose one.

Rule 1 *If we don't take care of our customers, somebody else will.*

A customer is the most important visitor on our premises. He is not dependent on us – we are dependent on him. He is not an outsider in our business – he is a part of it. We are not doing him a favor by serving him . . . he is doing us a favor by giving us the opportunity to do so.

We shall strive for excellence in all endeavors. We shall set our goals to achieve total customer satisfaction and to deliver defect-free premium value products on time, with service second to none.

There can be no doubt that the customer is king on both sides of the Atlantic and is recognised as such. Henry Ford lets us into the secret why the customer is, and always will be, right – in successful enterprises at any rate: *It's not the employer who pays the salaries, it's the client.*

DAY

■ **Sufficient unto the day (is the evil thereof)**

Be concerned with today rather than worry about tomorrow

See also: Don't cross a bridge until you come to it; Tomorrow is another day

He never looks happy – not really happy. I don't want to make him worse, but of course I shall have to, when Jon comes back. Oh! well, sufficient unto the night.
(John Galsworthy, To Let, 1921)

Only this life with Clifford, this endless spinning of webs of yarn, of the minutiae of consciousness, these stories Sir Malcolm said there was nothing in, and they wouldn't last. Why should there be anything in them, why should they last? Sufficient unto the day is the evil thereof. Sufficient unto the moment is the appearance of reality.
(D H Lawrence, Lady Chatterley's Lover, 1928)

This is a biblical proverb. In his Sermon on the Mount, Jesus preaches on anxiety. He tells his listeners not to worry but to trust God for their needs, for he who feeds the birds of the air and clothes the lilies of the field knows what these are before they ask. Rather than fretting about and storing up belongings, they are to live a life which pleases God and so they will find that their needs are faithfully met. In concluding Jesus says: *Take, therefore, no thought for the morrow; for the morrow shall take thought for the things of itself. Sufficient unto the day is the evil thereof* (MATTHEW 6:34).

The proverb is now used in the sense of living one day at a time and refusing to give way to anxieties about tomorrow – sound advice, for *tomorrow is another day* when today's problems might well appear in a better light. As the little jingle says: *Today is the tomorrow you worried about yesterday, and all is well.*

Usage: Somewhat dated. Regularly reduced to the first phrase only.

DESPERATE

■ **Desperate diseases call for desperate remedies**

An almost insurmountable difficulty calls for bold and extreme measures to overcome it

Variant: Desperate diseases demand / require desperate remedies

It would be said that desperate ills have desperate remedies, and there would be a strong temptation to suppress the fanatic. But to arrest a man who is not breaking the law, would be an act of glaring tyranny.
(J B Bury, A History of Freedom of Thought, 1914)

Two tears trickled down Donna Caterina's cheeks. Machiavelli patted her hand in kindness. 'Desperate situations demand desperate remedies.'
(W Somerset Maugham, Then and Now, 1946)

For extreme illnesses extreme treatments are most fitting (APHORISMS, c 400 BC) was a maxim of the great Greek physician Hippocrates. (See *Art is long, life is short.*) One extreme measure might be to stand by and let a disease take its course without interfering at all. Hippocrates goes on to explain that sometimes the courage to do this is just what is needed.

Richard Taverner expressed the proverb as *Strong disease requyreth a strong medicine* (PROVERBS, 1539); in EUPHUES (1579), John Lyly writes: *A desperate disease is to be committed to a desperate doctor;* and, in Shakespeare's HAMLET (1602), Claudius reminds us that:

Diseases desperate grown
By desperate appliance are relieved,
Or not at all (Act 4, scene iii).

In which case, there is everything to gain and nothing to lose.

Proverbs can be used to 'prove' anything. In 1939 Helene Heger published a thesis in Vienna attempting to demonstrate that proverbs supported Hitler's view of the superiority of the Aryan race. She might have learnt from two volumes published in the same city in 1881–2, in which the writer warns against taking anti-semitic proverbs from various languages as indicators of national character.

Usage: The area of application of the saying goes beyond the medical to any sort of severe problem that needs drastic action

DEVIL

- **Better the devil you know than the devil you don't know**

It is better to remain with the problems one already has than to change one's circumstances and face a set of unknown, and possibly worse, difficulties. It is better to stick to a person whose faults are known to you than move on to someone whose faults you have yet to discover

Neither the Koreans nor the Chinese love overmuch the Japanese . . . The Chinese seem to prefer the old Russian devil they know, to the new devil they don't.
(B Burleigh, EMPIRE OF THE EAST, 1905)

A survey revealing that one man in four would be prepared to commit murder for a million pounds comes as no great surprise. In fact my own findings suggest a much higher percentage . . . Employees wanted to rid the world of their bosses, although one loyal secretary kissed goodbye to her million by declaring 'better the devil you know.'
(MID SUSSEX TIMES, 9 August 1991)

The thought is an ancient one. Plautus in TRINUMMUS (c 194 BC) says: *Keep what you have, the known evil is best.* Aesop, writing in the sixth century BC, had already put the idea into the form of a fable which he wrote to encourage the

Athenians who, having enjoyed a democracy, had come under the power of a tyrant who had arisen from amongst them. The Athenians bewailed their servitude, though it was not severe, and Aesop cautioned them against voicing their discontent with this story: The marsh frogs wanted a king and asked Jupiter for one. Amused, the god threw a stout piece of wood into their pool. The log made such a splash that it frightened the frogs into submission. As time passed, however, the log just lay there in the mud and the frogs became used to its presence and eventually began to abuse it with insults. Then they started to call out for another king saying the one they had was no good. This time Jupiter sent them a water snake. The snake cut swiftly through the water and started to devour the frogs one by one. The frogs, in panic, sent a message to Jupiter asking for help. The reply came 'Since you were unwilling to put up with the good you had, you must put up with this evil.' *Likewise*, said Aesop to the Athenians, *you must bear the evil that you have, lest a greater one befall you.*

Pettie echoes the ancients when he writes: *You had rather keep those whom you know, though with some faults, than take those whom you know not, perchance with more faults* (PETITE PALLACE, 1576). And Shakespeare writes of the same reluctance to abandon one's present difficulties in order to face unknown evils in HAMLET (1602): *The dread of something after death . . . makes us rather bear those ills we have, Than fly to others that we know not of.*

In the light of these more general statements, the proverb we know today was developing with two different forms. One used 'devil', one 'evil'. The variation is readily understandable because of the similarities in pronunciation, spelling and meaning. Over time, *Better the evil you know than the evil you don't know* became less used in favour of the venerable *Better the devil you know than the devil you don't know.* Trollope in BARCHESTER TOWERS (1857) refers to it as an old saying.

■ **Every man for himself, and the devil take the hindmost**

Everyone should concentrate on taking care of himself and his own interests

Summerfield set an example of nagging and irritating insistence, and he urged all his employees to the same policy. The result was a bear-garden, a den of prize-fighters, liars, cut-throats and thieves in which every man was for himself openly and avowedly and the devil take the hindmost.
(Theodore Dreiser, THE GENIUS, 1915)

So with a good conscience men took what they could get, and the devil took the hindmost.
(W R Inge, A RUSTIC MORALIST, 'SUBSTITUTES FOR RELIGION', 1937)

The devil take the hindmost was the original proverb in its entirety, *Every man for himself* being a later addition, probably nineteenth century.

Opinions differ as to the origin of this proverb. In his ADAGIA (1536), Erasmus records a phrase of Horace: *The itch take the hindmost* (DE ARS POETICA, c 20 BC).

The devil to pay

The devil is usually represented with horns, a tail and cloven hooves. This is because, in Jewish writings, the rabbis referred to him as a goat, a symbol of uncleanliness (hence the word *scapegoat*). Originally the devil was an angel in the service of God. He rebelled and, being cast from Heaven, continued his insubordination by plotting to keep men from fellowship with God. Medieval churchgoers were constantly reminded of this by vivid murals painted on church walls or detailed carvings over the door which depicted the judgement of departed souls; those at the right hand of God were accompanied by angels into eternal bliss, those at the left hand were propelled by demons into the flames of hell as prizes of the devil. The north side of the building was traditionally the devil's side, for it was here that he and his demons hovered to trap those who were not vigilant. Some churches had a small door built into the north wall which was opened during baptismal or communion services in order to let him out.

Sometimes the devil would manifest himself to a terrified congregation. At the parish church in Bungay, for instance, he appeared among the Tudor worshippers as a black dog, choking two of them and viciously tearing the back of another with his talons. The striking of church spires by lightning was also recognised as satanic work. *Talk of the devil and he will appear* was sincerely meant.

People lived with an ever-present awareness of the hovering powers of evil, which conspired to blight their lives or trick them into committing evil deeds. This belief persisted until as late as the second half of the seventeenth century. Although from then on, in a dawning age of science and reason, a more tolerant attitude led to a less fervent and credulous religious climate, it is small wonder that the devil features prominently in proverbial literature.

Some of this takes a warning tone, highlighting the consequences of flirting with evil:

- *He should have a long spoon that sups with the devil*
- *The devil finds work for idle hands.*

The proverb *The Devil dances in an empty pocket* refers to the destitute's temptation to turn to crime. Coins were minted with a cross on one side so that the devil could not enter the pocket they were kept in.

Other sayings recognise the power or presence of evil:

- *Needs must when the devil drives*
- *Better the devil you know.*

And still others exhort us to fight the temptation to ignore God's promptings in our lives:

- *The devil sick would be a monk*
- *Speak the truth and shame the devil*

The phrase *Don't hold a candle to the devil* alludes to the Catholic and High Church custom of lighting a candle as an offering to a saint, and means 'don't support or approve of something you know to be wrong'. But anyone tempted to turn his back on his conscience can be assured of one thing, *The devil looks after his own.*

This was an allusion to a children's chasing game in which the itch, or scabies, was wished upon the child who came in last. The robust seventeenth century English wished worse than scabies upon the unfortunate individual who was unable to look after himself and lagged behind. The devil himself would take the hindmost. English essayist G W E Russell agrees with this origin. In SOCIAL SILHOUETTES (1906) he writes: *He starts in life with a plan of absolute and calculated selfishness . . . His motto is Extremum occupet scabies – the devil take the hindmost.*

Brewer, however, proposes an alternative theory. He says that *The Devil take the hindmost* was a phrase from late medieval magic. It seems that there was a school of magical arts in Toledo, Spain. Part way through their studies those students who had progressed had to run through an underground corridor. The last to do so was captured by the devil and became his imp.

Usage: The entire proverb is occasionally used but either of the two phrases may be used separately, as was originally the case. *The devil take the hindmost* has one interesting restricted use in sport. In one kind of cycle racing, for instance, at the end of each lap the last person must drop out, until only the winner is left.

■ **Give the devil his due**

Even unpleasant characters deserve their share of praise when it is deserved

See also: The devil's not as black as he's painted

To give the devil its due, ours is the best Age men ever lived in; we are all more comfortable and virtuous than we ever were. (John Galsworthy, CASTLES IN SPAIN, 1927)

The Prince of Darkness has a right to a courteous hearing and a fair trial, and those who will not give him his due are wont to find that, in the long run, he turns the tables by taking his due and something over. (R H Tawney, RELIGION AND THE RISE OF CAPITALISM, 1926)

■ **He should have a long spoon that sups with the devil**

If you keep bad company you will need to be on your guard

His recent speech on foreign policy in Milwaukee, though making Carteresque nods to global democracy and human rights, also made it plain that a defence of American interests sometimes made it necessary to sup with the devil (big devil-supping question, so far unanswered: how tough would Clinton-the-president be with China?). (THE ECONOMIST, 10 October 1992)

Sharing a meal with someone usually means you are already on quite good terms with them or that you want to get to know them better. If you agree to partake of the devil's hospitality, you are on dangerous ground and need to beware. The reference to a *long spoon* is obscure; probably it emphasises the distance it is necessary to keep from the potent contamination of the devil. The proverb was current in the fourteenth century, Chaucer using it in his CANTERBURY TALES:

'Therfor bihoveth him a ful long spoon
That shal ete with a feend,' thus herde I seye.
(THE SQUIRE'S TALE, c 1386)

And Shakespeare referred to it in THE
TEMPEST (1610) where Stephano says of
Caliban: *This is a devil, and no monster; I*
will leave him; I have no long spoon.

Usage: Rather dated

■ **Needs must when the devil drives**

Used when a person is forced to take a
course of action he would rather have
avoided

The medieval mind was steeped in
superstition and very alert to the unseen
forces of evil which lurked, ever present,
awaiting any opportunity to make
mischief or cause a man to stumble. (See
The devil to pay, page 66.) The proverb,
originally *He needs must go that the devil*
drives, is a vivid picture of a man who,
though his will and better judgement
warn him otherwise, has fallen prey to
diabolical circumstances and is being
forced along a disastrous route.

An early written record of the
proverb dates back to the first half of the
fifteenth century:

Hit ys oft seyde by hem that yet lyues,
He must nedys go that the deuell dryues.
(John Lydgate, THE ASSEMBLY OF GODS,
c 1420)

This original form of the expression was
trimmed down and slightly altered in
the seventeenth century, and recorded
by John Lacey: *Needs must go when the*
devil drives (THE OLD TROOP, 1672). It was
streamlined still further in the

nineteenth century to the familiar
modern form *Needs must when the devil*
drives. But usage in the second half of
the twentieth century is more
economical still and many people,
oblivious to the malicious intervention
of the devil in their affairs, will only say
Needs must.

Usage: The fuller form *Needs must when*
the devil drives is now somewhat dated

■ **Pull devil, pull baker**

A tug-of-war of divided allegiances

To be torn between divided allegiances is the
painful fate of almost every human being.
Pull devil, pull baker; pull flesh, pull spirit;
pull love, pull duty; pull reason and pull
hallowed prejudice.
(Aldous Huxley, THOSE BARREN LEAVES,
1925)

In his capacity of organist he was for ever
pressing for more processions, more
voluptuous music, more elaborate chanting
of the liturgy, so that it was a continuous
pull devil, pull baker between him and the
rector.
(George Orwell, THE CLERGYMAN'S
DAUGHTER, 1935)

The devil has always had a bad press.
The interesting thing about this proverb
is that the humble baker's reputation is
equated with the devil's. Whichever
character you 'pull', there is nothing to
choose between them.

Medieval bakers were unpopular
figures accused of accumulating wealth
at the expense of their customers, to
whom they sold underweight loaves.

The punishment for this was a spell in the pillory, as a common proverb shows: *And so late met, that I feare we parte not yeet, Quoth the Baker to the pylorie* (John Heywood, PROVERBS, 1546). The baker's reputation did not improve in later years. They were often charged with keeping the price of bread high, hence the proverb *Three dear years will raise a baker's daughter to a portion;* the customer would indirectly finance the girl's dowry. *Tis not the smallness of the bread,* comments Ray, *but the knavery of the baker* (ENGLISH PROVERBS, 1678).

The proverb *Pull devil, pull baker* has its origins in a traditional puppet play of the sixteenth century which satirised the baker's dishonesty. The tale remained popular through the centuries for, in the nineteenth century, it was the subject of a magic lantern show. A correspondent with NOTES AND QUERIES (1856) gives details of the scenes:

Slide 1 – sets the scene with the baker's oven

Slide 2 – the baker is detected in making short weight loaves

Slide 3 – the devil enters and seizes the baker's bread and his hoard of ill-gotten wealth

Slide 4 – the baker runs after his money, grabs hold of the devil's tail and it's pull devil pull baker until the baker is pulled off the scene

Slide 5 – the devil appears with the baker's basket strapped to his back. Inside is the baker himself who is swiftly carried into hell where the flames are hotter than in his own oven.

Usage: Rather dated

■ Speak the truth and shame the devil

Be honest and resist any temptation to avoid problems by lying

Variant: Tell the truth and shame the devil

I don't like the whole change that's come over you in the last year. I'm sorry if that hurts your feelings, but I've got to – tell the truth and shame the devil.
(Thornton Wilder, OUR TOWN, 1938)

Tell the truth and shame the devil, the nuns at my convent were very fond of telling us; I learnt quite quickly that the only person shamed by the truth was me – Yes, it was me passing the rude drawing round the classroom, no, I wasn't at hockey, I was hiding in the lavatory, and actually my father did most of my maths homework – and the devil got off very lightly indeed.
(GOOD HOUSEKEEPING, November 1992)

Hugh Latimer, Bishop of Worcester, writing in the mid-sixteenth century calls this proverb *a common saying amongst us.* For the Tudors, as for their ancestors, the devil was an ever present, and sometimes even visible, figure (see **The devil to pay,** page 66). The tug against the conscience, the inner voice prompting lies rather than the truth, were all signs that the devil was about his work leading souls to hell. Hugh Latimer himself must have shamed the devil on many occasions for he had a reputation for plain and honest speaking. His determination to hold on to the truth cost him his life when in 1555 he was burnt at the stake for refusing to renounce his Protestant faith.

In 1708 Samuel Butler used the expression in the title of a publication: *Speak Truth, and Shame the Devil in a Dialogue Between his Cloven-footed Highness, of Sulphurious Memory, and an Occasional Conformist.* In this satirical verse dialogue, the Occasional Conformist makes all the arguments that one might expect from the devil (on how easy it is to buy men's allegiance, for example), such that the latter finishes the piece with these ironic lines:

Thour't such a Master-piece in Evil,
That I'll be Man, and you be Devil;
Since one that can expound so well,
Deserves the Government of Hell.

Usage: Now dated

■ **Talk of the devil and he will appear**

Said when a person who was being talked about makes an unexpected appearance

Variant: Speak of the devil and he will appear

'What's the matter, Hasselbacher?'
'Oh, it's you Mr Wormold. I was just thinking of you. Talk of the devil,' he said, making a joke of it, but Wormold could have sworn that the devil had scared him.
(Graham Greene, OUR MAN IN HAVANA, 1958)

The devil has nothing at all to do with the origin of this proverb. An ancient fable tells of a wolf who appeared without fail whenever he was mentioned. The ancients would remark upon *the wolf in the fable* whenever a person they were discussing appeared unexpectedly. This practice goes back at least to Plautus in 200 BC. Erasmus quoted the proverb *Lupus in fabula* (The wolf in the fable) in ADAGIA (1536) but, although other European languages use proverbs about the wolf in this same context, it was hardly alluded to in English, where it was replaced by the devil. That the devil should figure in the proverb is not surprising, given the prominence of him and his works in the culture of the time. (See **The devil to pay**, page 66.)

Usage: Usually reduced to *Talk of the devil* and used humorously.

■ **The devil can quote scripture for his own purpose**

A high-sounding rationale can be a cover for base motives

Variants: The devil can cite scripture for his purpose; The devil can cite scripture for his own purposes

A sort of creeping comes over my skin when I hear the devil quote scripture.
(Walter Scott, KENILWORTH, 1821)

Does any one doubt the old saw, that the Devil (being a layman) quotes Scripture for his own ends?
(Charles Dickens, MARTIN CHUZZLEWIT, 1844)

The proverb is from Shakespeare's MERCHANT OF VENICE (1596). After Shylock's speech on the multiplying of Jacob's herds, Antonio says:

The devil can cite Scripture for his purpose.
An evil soul, producing holy witness,
Is like a villain with a smiling cheek,

A goodly apple, rotten at the heart:
Oh, what a goodly outside falsehood hath!
(Act 1, scene iii)

The same theme is reiterated later in the play:

In religion,
What damned error, but some sober brow
Will bless it and approve it with a text,
Hiding the grossness with fair ornament?
(Act 3, scene ii)

Some authors deliberately coin new proverbs. Edgar Watson Howe (1853–1937) is one such. In fact many are simply variations of existing sayings. None the less, Howe, a journalist and publisher of the Kansas newspaper THE GLOBE, is credited with at least *Better safe than sorry.*

Thomas Chandler Haliburton (who wrote also under the pseudonym Sam Slick) offered these sayings, amongst many others:

• *The road to a woman's heart is through her child*
• *Youth is the time for improvement*
• *The bigger the house the bigger the fool be that's in it*
• *A man that has too many irons in the fire is plaguy apt to get some of them burnt*
• *Wherever natur' does least, man does most*

See also *Appearances are deceptive* and *Handsome is as handsome does.*

---

and it had appeared in RICHARD III (probable first performance 1594):

But then I sigh; and, with a piece of Scripture,
Tell them that God bids us do good for evil:
And thus I clothe my naked villainy
With old odd ends, stolen out of holy writ;
And seem a saint, when most I play the devil.
(Act 1, scene iii)

Shakespeare's inspiration may have come from the Bible itself. When Christ goes into the wilderness at the start of his ministry, Satan comes to tempt him using words of scripture. Or the notion may have come from Christopher Marlowe, whose play THE JEW OF MALTA (c 1592) contains the line: *What, bring you scripture to confirm your wrongs.* It is believed by some scholars that Marlowe may have helped in the writing of some of Shakespeare's earlier plays, among them RICHARD III which is cited above.

Usage: Narrowly, the proverb refers to quoting scripture hypocritically to justify one's own ends. More widely, the saying can be applied to any fine, moral defence where the real motive is self-serving. Modern usage prefers 'quote scripture' rather than Shakespeare's 'cite scripture'. Now rather dated.

■ **The devil finds work for idle hands**

If you are unoccupied you are likely to be bored and get into mischief

Variant: The devil finds work for idle hands to do

Have something to do so that the devil will always find you occupied, advised the wise St Jerome (EPISTLES, c AD 400). Later, in TALE OF MELIBEUS (c 1386), Chaucer quoted the good saint and his sage counsel. The proverbial form of the idea recorded by James Kelly in SCOTTISH PROVERBS (1721) and Thomas Fuller in GNOMOLOGIA (1732) was *If the devil find a man idle, he'll set him to work.* However, in 1720 Isaac Watts wrote a poem 'AGAINST IDLENESS' (DIVINE AND MORAL SONGS FOR CHILDREN) and put the wisdom into a poetic form to which our present day proverb bears a closer resemblance:

In works of labour or of skill
I would be busy too;
For Satan finds some mischief still
For idle hands to do.

The work of Satan in the life of an idle person is recognised in other cultures too. Danish calls laziness *the devil's pillow* and a Moroccan proverb says that *The head of an idle man is Satan's workshop.*

■ **The devil sick would be a monk**

Said of someone who, in times of illness or difficulty, prays and makes fervent promises which are forgotten the moment pain passes

Variant: The devil was sick

A prisoner's penitence is a thing the quality of which it is very difficult to judge until you see it . . . tried outside. The devil was sick.
(D C Murray, JOSEPH'S COAT, 1881)

The observation that men are prone to a piety under duress that is forgotten the

moment the burden lifts was certainly not a new one. Pliny the Younger remarks that *we are never so virtuous as when we are ill* (LETTERS, c AD 100), and the Jewish MIDRASH (c 550) reminds us *in the hour of distress, a vow; in the hour of release, forgetfulness.*

During the medieval period there was a vogue for making up Latin rhymes based on ideas already in circulation. This proverb, an early coining from one such rhyme, is common to very many European languages:

Aegrotavit Daemon, monachus tunc esse volebat;
Daemon convaluit, daemon ut ante fuit
(The Devil was sick, then he would be a Monk;
The Devil recovered, and was a Devil as before)

The vogue for Latin rhymes started to wane during the fifteenth century but the proverb survived translation into English. By the seventeenth century it had been polished to:

The Devil was sick, the Devil a monk would be;
The Devil was well, the Devil a monk was he.

An alternative form found in medieval literature concerned wolf and lamb:

When the wolf was sick, he wished to be a lamb;
but after he got better, he was the same as before.

The thought was also encapsulated in the English proverb *The chamber of sickness is the chapel of devotion,* known since at least the seventeenth century.

In his poem DIPSYCHUS (1869), A H Clough put forward a similar argument for the basis of belief in God:

'There is no God,' the wicked saith,
'And truly it's a blessing,
For what He might have done with us
It's better only guessing.' . . .

Some others, also, to themselves
Who scarce so much as doubt it,
Think there is none, when they are well
And do not think about it. . . .

But almost every one, when age,
Disease, or sorrows strike him,
Inclines to think there is a God,
Or something very like him.

And just to prove that disaster-induced piety is not exclusive to the Christian church, H H Hart records this apposite Chinese proverb: *When times are easy we do not burn incense, but when trouble comes we embrace the feet of Buddah* (SEVEN HUNDRED CHINESE PROVERBS, 1937).

Usage: Dated

■ **The devil's not as black as he's painted**

Said to those who are speaking worse of an unsavoury character than he truly deserves

See also: Give the devil his due

Variant: The devil's not so black as he's painted

'He's not so black as he's painted,' said his wife.

'Really we all owe him a great debt of gratitude,' said the Doctor's wife.
(David Garnett, A SHOT IN THE DARK, 1958)

Still, I was happy, doing what comes naturally. Don't misunderstand. Forgery's not as bad as it's painted. Not even factory-sized.

I mean, generations of collectors have enjoyed their 'Canaletto' paintings sublimely unaware that the young William Henry Hunt actually painted many of them as copies in Doctor Monro's so-called academy . . .
(Jonathan Gash, THE GONDOLA SCAM, 1984)

This proverb, also found in other European languages, has been current since at least the sixteenth century. In A MARGUERITE OF AMERICA (1596) Thomas Lodge writes: *Divels are not so blacke as they be painted, . . . nor women so wayward as they seeme.*

Give the devil his due, another diabolic proverb contemporary to this, also pleads justice for the wayward.

■ **Why should the devil have all the best tunes?**

Secular music is more exciting and appealing than religious music. Christianity can properly import the secular and turn it to its own ends

The Devil is said to have the best tunes, though Palestrina, Vivaldi, Bach and Handel would doubtless disagree. So would the Commission of the Archbishops of Canterbury and York, though their tastes are – dare one say – more catholic.
(DAILY MAIL, 8 May 1992)

Like his brother, John, Charles Wesley was an itinerant evangelist and hymn writer. He wrote over 5500 hymns, many of them still sung today. *Love divine, all loves excelling* and *Hark the herald angels sing* are amongst the most well known. Sometimes Wesley would popularise his hymns by setting them to the music of well-known songs of the day, including drinking songs containing a host of profanities but having undeniably catchy tunes. When questioned about bringing music from the tavern before God, Wesley's reply was *Why should the devil have all the good tunes?*

The great Spanish mystic St John of the Cross would doubtless have concurred with Charles Wesley. His poetry of love for God was often transmuted from secular verses he borrowed from others into an intense religious lyricism.

In an alternative derivation, another fervent evangelist, the Reverend Rowland Hill (1744–1833), similarly refused to accept that the devil should have all the best tunes, according to his biographer E W Broome.

Usage: Relatively infrequent

DIRT

■ **Fling enough dirt and some will stick**

Attack an opponent repeatedly and some of the accusations will be believed

See also: Give a dog a bad name and hang him

He who slings mud, usually loses ground. (Adlai Stevenson [attrib], 1954)

These days scarcely a month passes without reports of some attempt or other to embarrass a leading national or world figure. This is no new thing, however. A Latin saying, quoted by Francis Bacon in De Dignitate et Augmentis Scientiarum (1623), urged *Calumniate boldly, something will always stick*. The same expression was also quoted by some of Bacon's contemporaries, always with reference to Medius, a renowned sycophant at the court of Alexander the Great, and who, according to Plutarch, heartily endorsed this sort of behaviour.

Thomas Hall echoed the dubious advice with this robust turn of phrase: *Lye lustily, some filth will stick* (Funebria Florae, 1660) while in Hudibras Redivivus (1706) Edward Ward explains that 'scurrility' is an approved method of besmirching a person's reputation:

Scurrility's a useful trick,
Approv'd by the most politic;
Fling dirt enough, and some will stick.

American usage substituted 'mud' for 'dirt' and lead to the coining of *mud-slinging* (the act of spreading malicious gossip about another), a term frequently used in a political context. We have learnt our lesson well; the proverb is still current, as is the practice.

■ **You've got to eat a peck of dirt before you die**

Accepting imperfect food hygiene will be inevitable in the course of a lifetime

The peck in the proverb is a measurement for dry produce, although the word could also be loosely applied to mean 'a great deal', 'a heap'. No one can avoid eating a little dirt unnoticed day by day. Over a lifetime these minuscule quantities must add up to a significant amount – as much as a peck, according to the proverb.

The earliest record of the saying comes in John Clark's PAROEMIOLOGIA (1639): *You must eat a peck of ashes ere you die.* Almost a century later Thomas Fuller includes it in GNOMOLOGIA (1732): *Every Man must eat a Peck of Dirt before he dies.*

An anecdote tells how Lord Chesterfield was dining at an inn one day and complained to the waiter that the plates were rather dirty. 'Everyone must eat a peck of dirt before he dies,' came the reply. 'That may be true,' replied the earl, 'but no one is obliged to eat it all at one meal.'

Usage: Used as an excuse for dirty plates or food

DIRTY

■ **Don't wash your dirty linen in public**

Keep your affairs private; don't discuss private feuds or scandals in public

The tide of opinion turned violently against the Queen and her advisers; high society was disgusted by all this washing of dirty linen in Buckingham Palace; the public at large was indignant at the ill-treatment of Lady Flora.
(Lytton Strachey, QUEEN VICTORIA, 1921)

James had maintained that the Meeting should be an open gathering attended by any guests who happened to be present at the Court and who wished to see the brotherhood in action. Michael had declared that he had no taste, even in so would-be charitable an atmosphere, for washing dirty linen in public.
(Iris Murdoch, THE BELL, 1958)

This proverb has a French origin. Bartlett says that the French proverb, *Il faut laver son linge sale en famille* (One should wash one's dirty linen at home), has been current since about 1720. Voltaire used it memorably in a riposte to the Encyclopaedists and about some poems King Frederick II had sent him for his comments. Not surprisingly, the latter case was a main cause in Voltaire losing favour at the Prussian Court. Napoleon Bonaparte made notable use of the saying in an address he made to the French Assembly in 1815 when he returned to Paris after his short exile on Elba and temporarily restored the Empire:

What is the throne? – a bit of wood gilded and covered with velvet. I am the state – I alone am here the representative of the people. Even if I had done wrong you should not have reproached me in public – people wash their dirty linen at home. France has more need of me than I of France.

Napoleon was doubtless responsible for drawing English attention to the proverb which became current during the nineteenth century.

Usage: Informal

DISCRETION

■ Discretion is the better part of valour

It is better to avoid taking unnecessary risks

Well done, Eustace! You have shown the discretion which is the better part of valour. You could not make a scene before ladies, that is taboo; and had you attacked Sir Richard, you would now be lying senseless on the greensward, quite unable to undertake the journey that lies before you tomorrow.

(L P Hartley, EUSTACE AND HILDA, 1947)

Sometimes, however, my 'Mickey' didn't want to 'whoa' at all, and sometimes he would stop abruptly of his own volition to munch a bit of grass, to smell the air or sometimes apparently just for a bit of a think. However, we gradually got to understand each other, mainly by my not giving him any commands at all, capitulation for me being the better part of valour.

(Pauline Collins, LETTER TO LOUISE, 1992)

The proverb in the form we know it today is traditionally considered to be a misquotation of a line from Shakespeare's KING HENRY THE FOURTH, PART ONE, Act 5, scene iv (1597). The original line, *The better part of valour is discretion*, is spoken by Falstaff who has just escaped almost certain death in a fight by pretending to be fatally wounded.

Although we may owe our present day familiarity with the proverb to Shakespeare, the idea is not, however,

his alone. William Caxton in his translation of JASON (c 1477) wrote: *Than as wyse and discrete he withdrewe him sayng that more is worth a good retrayte than a folisshe abydinge.* The proper balance between wisdom and bravery is also weighed in the classical authors Plutarch, Archilocus, Tertullian and Menander. Shakespeare, it seems, was using the character of Falstaff to embody a base human instinct for self-preservation rather than as an example of prudent courage.

The literary critic Jorgensen makes a rather different case. One part of his interesting argument is that *discretion* at that period clearly means 'strategy', as in Sidney's ARCADIA of 1584: *. . . by playne force there was small apparaunce of helping Clitophon: but some device was to be taken in hand, wherein no lesse discretion then valour was to be used.* To contemporary soldiers *valour* and *discretion* were standard parts of military vocabulary, meaning together the 'sensible deployment of human courage'. Moreover, Jorgensen points out, the sense of *discretion* as 'a species of lower prudence' is not listed in the OED until 1720, more than a hundred years after Shakespeare. The playwright, then, may have been portraying Falstaff not so much as self-preserving soldier but as a posturing military professional, taking a heroic pose as a master of the newest strategic approach to war.

If all this is indeed the case, it seems that later centuries have not only re-ordered Shakespeare's original words but also attributed to them a meaning he may not have intended. (For an example of a proverb whose meaning currently appears to be in transition, see *Changing with the times.*)

Usage: Mostly used in a semi-jocular fashion. Beloved of TV scriptwriters of husband-and-wife comedies.

DO

■ **Do as you would be done by**

Treat others in the same way you would want them to treat you

Variant: Do unto others as you would have them do unto you

Do other men, for they would do you.
(Charles Dickens, MARTIN CHUZZLEWIT, 1843)

Only one little cloud darkened the glorious horizon: he appeared to have little interest in Judaism, except in so far as the traditions reminded him of a happy childhood.
'But darling, there's been a war. I've seen suffering you would never have dreamed of. How can there be a God?'
'Don't talk like that. You can't really mean it.'
'Oh, but I do! "Do unto others as you'd have them do unto you", that's the only Judaism I want.'
(Michele Guinness, CHILD OF THE COVENANT, 1985)

British Airways issued a new code of conduct to its 50,000 employees yesterday . . . BA chief executive Sir Colin Marshall listed *the new code under titles like Fairness, Honesty, Integrity and Fair Competition. He ruled out dirty tricks and wrote: 'Treat others as you would like to be treated.'*
(SUN, 23 January 1993)

The proverb stems from the Golden Rule: that of treating others in the same way as one would like to be treated by them. The principle is an ancient one. Confucius (c 500 BC) taught it as a lifelong rule of conduct, it is a Hindu precept and is fundamental to Judaism and Christianity where, along with the command to love God with all one's being, it encapsulates the Judeo-Christian message. The Golden Rule is probably most familiar to us through biblical teaching. MATTHEW 7:12 says: *Therefore all things whatsoever ye would that men should do to you, do ye even so to them: for this is the law and the prophets.*

The proverb itself appears in a sixteenth century play by an unknown author. In the eighteenth century it was proclaimed by Lord Chesterfield as *the surest method that I know of pleasing* (LETTERS, 16 October 1747) and, more seriously, as *the plain, sure, and undisputed rule of morality and justice* (LETTERS, 27 September 1748).

It is certainly the kind of lofty moral saying that is open to re-interpretation: *Do unto the other feller the way he'd like to do unto you an' do it fust* (Edward N Westcott, DAVID HARUM, 1898)

Usage: It has a rather elevated, moralising tone and could hardly be used as advice in direct address

DOG

■ **A man's best friend is his dog**

Human affection may wane but a dog remains completely loyal

You may have been led to believe that your best friend was hairy with a wet nose. In fact it's black and shiny and answers to the name of CVP-G700. . . Being a Sony it's as faithful as a hound to the original.
(Advertisement for Sony camcorders, SUNDAY TIMES, 22 November 1992)

All over Turkey there are proud new dog owners. Pouting models at Istanbul airport have poodles. Gruff, bearded intellectuals have great shaggy animals. And Dalmatians are in oversupply. This is an extraordinary change of heart, a cultural watershed for a people who have happily lived for centuries, if not millennia, with man's best friend locked firmly out of the house, charged with keeping the wolf from the sheepshed door.
(INDEPENDENT, 20 March 1993)

The faithfulness of man's companion, the dog, has been recognised for centuries, often to the detriment of the human half of the partnership: *Histories are more full of examples of the fidelity of dogs than of men.* (Alexander Pope, LETTERS, 1737)

Wordsworth, in his aptly named poem FIDELITY of 1805, told the story of a dog remaining at his dead master's side in the hills of Cumberland:

The dog, which still was hovering nigh,
Repeating the same timid cry,
This dog had been through three months'
space

A dweller in that savage place.
Yes, proof was plain that, since the day
When this ill-fated traveller died,
The dog had watched about the spot,
Or by his master's side.

Lord Byron certainly knew the close relationship of a dog. His own, Boatswain, died in 1808 and is buried at Newstead Abbey. Part of the epitaph, generally attributed to Byron but probably written by his best (human) friend, John Cam Hobhouse, reads:

Near this spot are deposited the remains of one who possessed Beauty without Vanity, Strength without Insolence, Courage without Ferocity, and all the Virtues of Man, without his Vices. This Praise, which would be unmeaning Flattery, if inscribed over human ashes, is but a just tribute to the Memory of Boatswain, a Dog . . .
The poor dog, in life the firmest friend,
The first to welcome, foremost to defend,
Whose honest heart is still his master's own,
Who labours, fights, lives, breathes for him alone.

Canine fidelity is equally legendary across the Atlantic. Stevenson quotes a speech given by Senator George G Vest in 1876. A farmer had shot his neighbour's dog for molesting livestock. The neighbour decided to prosecute. The case dragged on unresolved until Senator Vest was called in to act as counsel for the prosecution. Being unfamiliar with the case and evidence, his impromptu address was necessarily given on purely general lines but it so moved the jury that it ruled in favour of his client:

The best friend a man has in the world may turn against him and become his enemy. His son or daughter . . . may prove ungrateful. Those who are nearest and dearest to him . . . may become traitors to their faith . . . The one absolutely unselfish friend that man can have in this selfish world, the one that never deserts him, the one that never proves ungrateful or treacherous, is his dog.

All these expressions of loyalty have built up a universal picture of a dog's qualities, but it is difficult to pinpoint where the precise form of today's phrase was first used.

■ **Dog does not eat dog**

One ought not to attack or take advantage of another from one's own circle

See also: There is honour among thieves

Dog does not eat dog; and it is hard to be robbed by an Englishman, after being robbed a dozen times by the French.
(Charles Kingsley, HEREWARD THE WAKE, 1865)

Dog won't eat dog, but men will eat each other up like cannibals.
(C H Spurgeon, JOHN PLOUGHMAN, 1869)

Except where I felt it to be absolutely essential, however, I have avoided any discussion of criticism and critics: dog should not eat dog.
(J B Priestley, LITERATURE AND WESTERN MAN, 'INTRODUCTION' , 1960)

The proverb arises from the observation that, in nature, animals do not kill others of their own kind. Juvenal made this point in SATIRES (c AD 120): *Wild beasts do not injure beasts spotted like themselves.*

Shakespeare remarked that bears are not naturally aggressive towards one another and Herbert makes the same point about wolves. Many animals will fight, of course, over territory and for a mate, though rarely to the death. In extreme circumstances, even dog might eat dog. Thomas Fuller in his GNOMOLOGIA of 1732 cites two contemporary proverbs to this effect:

Dogs are hard drove, when they eat dogs.
It is an hard Winter, when Dogs eat Dogs.

Usage: Contemporary usage is often a comment on a situation. There is usually implied a comparison of what animals don't do with what man does do. Where a colleague turns viciously on another, a typical remark might be *It's a case of dog eating dog.*

■ **Every dog has his day**

Fortune smiles on everyone once in a lifetime

Every catch-phrase has its day, and this week, after the demise of Lis Howell at GMTV, the F-factor has finally bitten the dust.
(SUNDAY TIMES, 28 February 1993)

Every dog has his day, and yesterday it was the turn of an alsatian called Gunther.
The ageing pet was left a £65 million fortune by his eccentric owner, a German countess.
(DAILY EXPRESS, 1 May 1993)

In his ADAGIA (1536), Erasmus quotes from Plutarch's MORALIA: TERRESTRIAL COMPARISONS (c AD 95): *Even a dog gets his revenge.* Erasmus connects the proverb to the story of Euripides. Tradition has it that, whilst a guest at the Macedonian court, the Greek dramatist was savaged to death by a pack of dogs loosed upon him by two rival poets, Arrhidaeus and Crateuas. The original sense of the Latin and early uses in English suggested that any man, however humble, would have one day in his life to avenge past wrongs. The meaning nowadays is rather that a person will have at least one day of success or happiness in a lifetime.

Usage: It is possible to use the proverb to someone encouragingly; alternatively it can be used in surprise at the achievement of a no-hoper. In this case it is patronising and superior.

■ **Give a dog a bad name and hang him**

Ruining someone's reputation is irreversible

Variant: As well hang a dog as give him a bad name

See also: Fling enough dirt and some will stick

The Liberal impulse is almost always to give a dog a bad name and hang him: that is, to denounce the menaced proprietors as enemies of mankind, and ruin them in a transport of virtuous indignation.
(George Bernard Shaw, THE INTELLIGENT WOMAN'S GUIDE TO SOCIALISM, 1928)

Dogs have not always been looked upon as loyal friends and lovable pets. Until a serum treatment was introduced in 1899, dog bites were often fatal. Stray dogs can be dangerous carriers of disease, particularly of rabies. Notable outbreaks of rabies occurred in France in the thirteenth century, in Spain in the sixteenth century, in Germany in the seventeenth century and in France, Germany, Italy and England during the first half of the eighteenth century. An old European proverb says *He that would hang his dog gives out first that he is mad,* hanging being an accepted way of ridding oneself of a troublesome or rabid animal. The proverb meant that anyone who is planning to do something unpleasant thinks up some plausible reason for doing so first.

Give a dog a bad name and hang him is first recorded in the early eighteenth century, perhaps as a direct result of the rabies outbreak then. Certainly it reflects the same background as the earlier proverb but the meaning is slightly different; if someone's reputation is sullied he is as good as hanged for he will never regain his former standing.

Usage: Often used today without the second part of the phrase

■ **Let sleeping dogs lie**

Don't invite trouble by stirring up a potentially tricky situation

See also: Let well alone

It is euyll wakyng of a sleepyng dog.
(John Heywood, PROVERBS, 1546)

'I was wondering if I should see him.' Charles shook his head. 'Don't you. He'll go and tell the uncle and the uncle's back will be put up still further . Result: no mortgage. Let sleeping dogs lie.'
(F W Crofts, THE 12.30 FROM CROYDON, 1934)

The allusion is to disturbing a snoozing watchdog.

Chaucer provides us with the earliest English use of this proverb in TROILUS AND CRISEYDE (c 1374). When the go-between Pandarus steals into Cressida's chamber at night to prepare her for a visit by Troilus, Cressida is alarmed and wants to call in some servants. Pandarus dissuades her, saying that it is never wise to wake a sleeping dog or to give people grounds for conjecture. The saying was not unique to English, however, but was also found in other European languages. Medieval French has a use that predates Chaucer by a hundred years.

This is not the motto for an active interventionist!

■ Love me, love my dog

If you love me, you must take me as I am and be willing to put up with all my weaknesses and foibles

By the time Diana met Tony, the man who was to become her husband, she was already totally committed to her web-footed friends . . . not that Tony knew then exactly how Diana's little hobby was going to take over her life. 'He didn't stay in much doubt for long,' says Diana. 'I am afraid there was never any question about who came first. It was the ducks or nothing. In fact, marriage to me was a case of love me love my ducks.'

(GOOD HOUSEKEEPING, June 1993)

'Qui me amat, amat et canem meum' (Who loves me loves my dog too) were words penned by St Bernard of Clairvaux in the middle of the twelfth century. Writing at a time when dogs were not pampered pets but often disease-ridden menaces, he was illustrating the nature of true friendship: the acceptance of the whole person, faults and failings included.

In spite of his sympathetic reference to dogs, the large breed known as St Bernard was not named after St Bernard of Clairvaux but after another saint altogether, St Bernard of Menthon (923–1009).

■ Take the hair of the dog that bit you

A remedy for a hangover which advises the sufferer to swallow another alcoholic drink the next morning

He poured out a large bumper of brandy, exhorting me to swallow 'a hair of the dog that had bit me.'
(Walter Scott, ROB ROY, 1817)

There is no cure for a hangover – official. Some swear by milk mixed with lemon, others rely on chicken soup, bran flakes or even raw egg . . . The Consumer Association surveyed members to find out what remedies worked for them. For the strong of stomach, a fried breakfast was the answer. But forget the 'hair of the dog' – a drink the morning after. It is said to be no solution.
(DAILY MAIL, 3 December 1992)

Serum to control rabies is a relatively recent discovery (see *Give a dog a bad name and hang him*). An ancient remedy recommended that, whenever someone suffered a dog-bite, a hair from the offending animal should be bound to the wound to help it to heal and to offer protection against disease. A recipe book of 1670 repeats the centuries old advice: *Take a hair from the dog that bit you, dry it, put it into the wound, and it will heal it, be it never so sore.* The cure was still deemed good in the second half of the eighteenth century. Robert Jones recommends it in THE TREATMENT OF CANINE MADNESS (1760): *The hair of the dog that gave the wound is advised as an application to the part injured.* Procuring the important hair must have been a tricky business at times.

By the sixteenth century the remedy for dog-bites was also being recommended for hangovers. John Heywood quotes the advice in PROVERBS (1546). Samuel Pepys found it efficacious. His diary entry for 3 April 1661 reads:

Up among my workmen, my head akeing all day from last night's debauch . . . At noon dined with Sir W. Batten and Pen, who would have me drink two good draughts of sack to-day, to cure me of my last night's disease, which I thought strange, but I think find it true.

A contemporary of Pepys, William Lilly, famous for his astrological predictions and yearly almanacs, was of a more sober temperament. As the following song shows, his advice and prophecies were derided then, much as his successor, Old Moore, is today:

If any so wise is that sack he despises,
Let him drink his small beer and be sober,
And while we drink and sing,
As if it were spring,
He shall droop like the trees in October.
But be sure, over night, if this dog you do bite,
You take it henceforth for a warning,
Soon as out of your bed, to settle your head,
With a hair of his tail in the morning.

Then be not so silly
To follow old Lilly,

There's nothing but sack that can tune us,
Let his Ne assuescas be put in his cap-case,
Sing Bibito Vinum Jejunus.

■ **Why keep a dog and bark yourself?**

Why pay someone to work then do the task yourself?

There is no point in going to the expense of buying and feeding a guard dog if you are always on the look out for intruders yourself. The proverb was included in John Ray's collection of ENGLISH PROVERBS (1670): *What? Keep a dog and bark myself? That is, must I keep servants, and do my work myself?* But an earlier literary appearance was in Brian Melbancke's PHILOTIMUS (1583).

Usage: Can be condescending: scorning menial tasks that others are paid to perform

■ **You can't teach an old dog new tricks**

An older person cannot pick up successfully new ideas, practices or skills

Teaching an old sheepdog new tricks. Gwen and her champion handler Julie Deptford shepherd their flock into London's Hyde Park yesterday after arriving in traditional city fashion for the Festival of Food and Farming.
(Picture caption, FINANCIAL TIMES, 13 November 1991)

Proving that no dog is ever too old to learn new tricks is Norman Lindop, former director of Hatfield Polytechnic. Not content with returning to his old institution to take a part-time MSc in astrophysics, Sir Norman, 72, has spent the past few weeks

working hard towards acquiring another demanding retirement job – as a Labour candidate in yesterday's county council elections.
(TIMES HIGHER EDUCATIONAL SUPPLEMENT, 7 May 1993)

Old dogs, and old people too for that matter, are not incapable of learning, they've probably just lost the enthusiasm to do so. The expression is an excuse for those of a certain age and older who have tried a little and failed, or who can't be bothered to try at all. An old sixteenth century proverb tells us that *It's hard to make an olde dogge stoop.* The proverb *It's hard to teach an old dog tricks* is from the beginning of the seventeenth century.

EASIER

■ **Easier said than done**

It's easier to talk about doing something than to perform the task

Variant: Sooner said than done.

They say it is most restful of all to make the mind a complete blank, but as I know that is easier said than done.
(Elizabeth Bowen, THE HEAT OF THE DAY, 1949)

'Beware of Greeks bearing gifts,' runs the old proverb. But as with so many proverbs, it is a case of easier said than done. When their gifts reach such colossal proportions, it seems an act of folly to show them the door.
(EVENING STANDARD, 20 October 1992)

Plautus and Livy are amongst the ancients who used the expression. Early English records date back to the fifteenth century. Heywood quotes *Sooner said than done* (PROVERBS, 1546) but *Easier said than done* prevailed from the eighteenth century onwards.

EASY

■ **Easy come, easy go**

Anything that is come by without effort is casually lost. Money that is easily come by is easily spent.

See also: A fool and his money are soon parted

The proverb teaches that money which has been gained through little effort is rapidly frittered away. Money earned through hard work is spent carefully as its value is appreciated.

The saying is a variant of an earlier proverb. *Lightly come, lightly go* was known to Chaucer and was still current in the nineteenth century. Its meaning is well expressed in Arbuthnot's JOHN BULL (1712): *A thriftless wretch, spending the goods and gear that his forefathers won with the sweat of their brows; light come, light go.* A sixteenth century variant of this form was *Lightly gained, quickly lost,* and yet another *Quickly gained, quickly lost,* which also survived to the nineteenth century. But that century also coined its own variant. *Easy come, easy go,* wrote Samuel Warren, *is . . . characteristic of rapidly acquired commercial fortunes* (DIARY OF A LATE PHYSICIAN, c 1832).

Usage: Applied to money itself, or to the things that money can buy. The emphasis is not so much on the means of acquisition but on its ease.

EAT

■ **We must eat to live and not live to eat**

We should eat to keep alive, not live to indulge our greed

Variant: Live not to eat but eat to live

See also: The eye is bigger than the belly

The story goes that King Archelaus invited Socrates to leave Athens and live a more luxurious existence at his court instead. Socrates declined the offer, replying that, as meal was cheap in Athens and water free of charge, his needs were already being met. Diogenes Laertius and Athenaeus both attribute the words *Other men live to eat, while I eat to live* to Socrates. Plutarch, however, credits the philosopher with *Bad men live that they may eat and drink, whereas good men eat and drink that they may live* (MORALIA, c AD 95)

According to Rabelais, sixteenth century monks were characterised by gluttony; the proverb was well applied to them. Other writers use the proverb and manage to sound a touch smug: *Let us therefore rejoyce, that we are not in the number of those, which live onelie to eate and whose hunger is bigger than their panches* (Stefano Guazzo, CIVILE

CONVERSATION, 1574). Still others give it very short shrift. There is more to life than mere existence, as Robert Burton points out: *Eat and live, as the proverb is, . . . that only repairs man which is well concocted, not that which is devoured* (THE ANATOMY OF MELANCHOLY, 1621). American philosopher Ralph Waldo Emerson concurs: *Let the stoics say what they please, we do not eat for the good of living, but because the meat is savory and the appetite is keen* (ESSAYS: NATURE, 1844). Fielding even manages to preach this message illicitly. In his comedy, L'AVARE (1668) Molière uses the proverb correctly but Fielding, in his translation of the play, omits the all-important *not,* thus rendering it as 'We must eat to live *and* live to eat.'

Those subscribing to this view may take comfort from scripture's endorsement. In ECCLESIASTES 8:15 we find: *I commended mirth, because a man hath no better thing under the sun than to eat, and to drink, and to be merry.* Owen Meredith's LUCILE of 1860 (cited by Walsh) puts everything in proper proportion:

We may live without poetry, music, and art;
We may live without conscience, and live without heart;
We may live without friends; we may live without books;
But civilized man cannot live without cooks.
He may live without books, – what is knowledge but grieving?
He may live without hope, – what is hope but deceiving?
He may live without love, – what is passion but pining?

But where is the man that can live without dining?

Usage: Though doubtless sound sense, the proverb has a rather ascetic, puritanical ring to it

EGGS

■ **Don't put all your eggs in one basket**

Don't entrust all your hopes or resources to one single venture

It was odd how, with all this ingrained care for moderation and secure investment, Soames never put his emotional eggs into one basket. First Irene – now Fleur.
(John Galsworthy, To Let, 1921)

With most slow-moving sea-animals, it is the food question which restricts size. It is usually more advantageous to the race to have a number of medium-sized animals utilizing the food available in a given area than to put all the biological eggs into the single basket of one big individual.
(J Huxley, Man in the Modern World, 'The Size of Living Things', 1947)

Dr Elizabeth Tylden, a psychiatrist who has been counselling people leaving cult religions for the past 20 years, said that members would have gone through the ultimate bereavement.

'You are talking about people who have put their friendship networks, jobs, financial security and all their interests in one basket – and lost the lot,' she said.
(The Times, 21 April 1993)

This is a business proverb dating from at least the turn of the seventeenth century. Eggs are fragile and easily broken. It would be unwise of any poultry keeper to put all his eggs into the same basket when taking them to market in case an accident occurred and all his income were lost. It would be better to spread the risk over several containers. Several hundred years later, farmers still know a good thing when they see one, under the Common Agricultural Policy of the European Community:

Spread your eggs between several baskets, taking care to keep the amount saved at, or below, the maximum compensation level.
(Good Housekeeping, November 1991)

The proverb was used by Cervantes in Don Quixote de la Mancha. The novel, published in 1605, was immediately successful both in Spain and further afield. Possibly it is by this route that the proverb came into the language, English already having an equivalent expression from an old Greek proverb, *Don't venture all your goods in one bottom (ship),* for which it became an alternative.

■ **You can't make an omelette without breaking eggs**

Nothing can be achieved without sacrifices or losses along the way

She would be very upset, she would cry, perhaps. In war soldiers themselves sometimes cried, and their relations cried quite often. You can't make an omelette without breaking eggs. It was better to have

A matter of form

A feature of proverbs is that many of them exhibit characteristic forms or fit into set patterns. This partly explains why we so readily interpret them as proverbs. You might like to work out the patterns from the following sets of examples, and add more of your own.

- *Better safe than sorry*
- *Better late than never*

- *Never say die*
- *Never put off till tomorrow what you can do today*
- *Never look a gift horse in the mouth*
- *Never judge by appearances*

- *Money talks*
- *Time flies*

- *He who hesitates is lost*
- *He who laughs last laughs best*

- *Time is money*
- *Seeing is believing*
- *Virtue is its own reward*
- *Honesty is the best policy*

- *Enough is enough*
- *Boys will be boys*

- *Nothing ventured, nothing gained*
- *Out of sight, out of mind*

- *An ounce of prevention is worth a pound of cure*
- *One man's meat is another man's poison*

- *Practice makes perfect*
- *Familiarity breeds contempt*

- *You can't make a silk purse out of a sow's ear*
- *You can't get blood from a stone*

- *Like it or lump it*
- *Do or die*

- *Live and let live*
- *Live and learn*

- *Man proposes but God disposes*
- *Jack of all trades is master of none*
- *The spirit is willing but the flesh is weak*

The sound of the proverb to the ear is very important in making it memorable, as some of the examples above show. Consider the common features of these further sets:

- *Spare the rod and spoil the child*
- *In for a penny, in for a pound*
- *Where there's a will there's a way*
- *Waste not, want not*

- *Little strokes fell great oaks*
- *A friend in need is a friend in deed*
- *Every bullet has its billet*
- *Haste makes waste*

a good cry than to marry a man who was keeping another woman with your money.
(L P Hartley, THE HIRELING, 1957)

This is a translation of an old French saying which has been credited to both Robespierre and Napoleon. It reached respectability on being accepted into the 1878 edition of the DICTIONNAIRE DE L'ACADEMIE. Examples of its use in English literature date from the mid-nineteenth century.

Usage: Often used today by a businessman, politician or military leader on announcing a decision that will call for sacrifice of jobs or lives – always someone else's.

ELEPHANT

■ **An elephant never forgets**

Said of someone with a prodigious memory, usually for slights and wrongs

It was not the memory of the elephant but that of the camel that was renowned amongst the Greeks long ago. A Greek proverb ran *Camels never forget an injury.* Proverbial reference to the elephant's memory is relatively recent. In REGINALD: REGINALD ON BESETTING SINS (1910), the camel is usurped by the elephant: *Women and elephants never forget an injury.* The author, Saki, was no stranger to elephants having been born in Burma and lived there, and would have appreciated the intelligence of the animal. The working elephant memorises a large number of

commands given by its mahout and recognises many other animals and people, thus remembering both kindnesses and injuries. Since its life-span is 50 or 60 years these memories are long-lived.

Usage: Usually said of a person who does not forget injuries, but an 'elephantine memory' could just be a good one

ENDS

■ **All's well that ends well**

When the outcome is happy, it makes up for any difficulty or unpleasantness that went before

I had got rid of the farmer, . . . dog, . . . bull, . . . and the bees – all's well that ends well.
(Captain Marryat, MR MIDSHIPMAN EASY, 1836)

All's well that ends with a good meal.
(Arnold Lobel, FABLES, 1980)

All's well that ends well, as the saying goes. Strenuous but productive aspects allow you to end a long-running altercation this month.
(HOUSE BEAUTIFUL, February 1993)

This proverb, common to many European languages, immediately brings Shakespeare to mind since it is the title of one of his plays. Shakespeare, however, did not coin the expression – it was already at least three hundred years old, being recorded in PROVERBS OF HENDING (c 1300) – he merely borrowed it. The comedy (1601) tells of the young Helena and the rejection, difficulty and subterfuge she has to undergo before Bertram, her husband, willingly owns her as his wife. The ending is a happy one, making amends for all the hurt and deceit and demonstrating the truth of the proverb that *all's well that ends well*.

ENOUGH

■ Enough is enough

It is unnecessary or even harmful to do more. There is a limit to everything

See also: Enough is as good as a feast

Fun is fun, but enough's enough.
(Ogden Nash, FOR THE MOST IMPROBABLE SHE, 1938)

A good publisher never lets an editor forget that without the ads there is no revenue; and a good editor never stops complaining about this, nor making the necessary compromises. It is not fair. But then neither is the fact that, in this country, black models and 'real women' on covers are not thought to sell magazines. Steinem knew this, decided to confront it and then committed potential commercial suicide by naming the meddling advertisers in the relaunch issue's exposé 'Sex, lies and advertising'. Enough was enough, she and the new editor, Morgan, had decided.
(SUNDAY TIMES, 22 November 1992)

The film brought back disturbing memories of school in Bradford, where she endured racial taunts daily. She became so emotional she had to scream out: 'Enough is enough!'
(SUNDAY MIRROR, 14 February 1993)

The best censorship in a free society is self-censorship. The best hope for the cinema is if leading practitioners such as Sir Anthony Hopkins do indeed say enough is enough. But how often have we heard that before? Who would bet on there being no Silence of the Lambs II?
(THE TIMES, 3 March 1993)

Iam satis est, meaning 'now there is enough' is a phrase not uncommonly found in the writings of Roman poets and playwrights. This plea for moderation passed from Latin literature into various European languages. Italian has the rhyming *Assai basta, e troppo guasta* (Enough is enough, and too much spoils). French and Dutch concur with this sentiment. French has *Mieux vaut assez que trop* and Dutch *Genoeg is meer dan overvloed*, both phrases meaning that enough is better than too much. English is more economical; John Heywood includes *Enough is enough* in his PROVERBS (1546) and that has been the common form ever since. In English speech, it seems, enough really is enough – the rest is common-sense.

Usage: Often uttered as a warning to stop, when reasonable limits are in danger of being breached. May refer to words or actions.

■ Enough is as good as a feast

Moderation is ultimately more satisfying than excess

See also: Enough is enough

At nineteen he had commenced one of those careers attractive and inexplicable to ordinary mortals for whom a single bankruptcy is good as a feast.

(John Galsworthy, IN CHANCERY, 1920)

Beauty is that which satisfies the aesthetic instinct. But who wants to be satisfied? It is only to the dullard that enough is as good as a feast. Let's face it: beauty is a bit of a bore.

(W Somerset Maugham, CAKES AND ALE, 1930)

Euripides in SUPPLIANTS (c 421 BC) tells us that there is no virtue in gluttony and that *enough is as a feast.* The proverb was known in England in the fifteenth century for John Lydgate uses it in THE ASSEMBLY OF GODS (c 1420). In PROVERBS (1546) John Heywood quotes the expression in its familiar form.

When Euripides inspired the proverb he was discussing gluttony. Although happy to accept the call for moderation in many areas, when it comes to food we tend to justify our desire to indulge. A modern variant of the proverb reflects this tendency: *Enough is as good as a feast; too much is as good as a banquet.* Penny Vincenzi would endorse the modern dictum:

Enough is as good as a feast, my great aunt Daisy was wont to say to me, as I reached an ever-chubbier hand towards the chocolate biscuits. I can remember to this day the sense of outrage this induced (greater even than the removal of the biscuits); I was only about 4 years old at the time, but able to distinguish fact from fiction and I knew perfectly well even then that enough was nothing like as good as a feast. What was 'enough' chocolate biscuits anyway? By

adult standards, it seemed to be two at most, possibly only one; and enough for what, I wanted to know? Enough to tantalise, to remind me of the taste, the texture, to give the sensation of intense pleasure, but enough? Enough! Enough chocolate biscuits (in much the same way as enough champagne, raspberry Pavlova and cheese and onion crisps) is enough to stop you wanting any more for a bit; maybe even quite a bit. That could arguably be as good as a feast, but not some neat, nannyish portion that teeters around the tastebuds and then becomes a memory.

(GOOD HOUSEKEEPING, November 1992)

Usage: Nowadays the proverb is not restricted to food but can be applied to any area where excess is a danger and moderation should be called for.

EVILS

■ Of two evils choose the lesser

When faced with unappetising alternatives, choose the less damaging one

Variant: Choose the lesser of two evils

The saying has its origins in Greek philosophy. It was already proverbial in Aristotle's day: *We must choose the lesser of two evils, as the saying is* (NICOMACHEAN ETHICS, c 335 BC). The proverb is found in French texts from the thirteenth century. Its earliest recorded use in English is in Chaucer's TROILUS AND CRISEYDE (c 1374): *Of harmes two, the lesse is for to chese.*

According to Plutarch a Spartan with a sense of humour used the proverb as a quip upon his marriage to a short wife. The joke was successful for it is found repeated in a seventeenth century book of CONCEITS, CLINCHES, ETC (1639): *One persuaded his friend to marry a little woman, because of evils the least was to be chosen.*

But, of two evils, which is the lesser? Indecisiveness was ever a human failing. An American story, quoted by Walsh, tells of a traveller who stopped to ask the way. He was given the choice of two roads, one long and one short, and told that it didn't matter which he chose, since either way he was bound to regret his decision and wish he had taken the other.

Usage: The saying need not exclusively refer to high ethical dilemmas. It can be used more lightly of two strategies in sport, or even of walking to town versus waiting for an infrequent bus.

EXCEPTION

■ **The exception proves the rule**

Anomalies put to the test the validity of the generalisation

Variant: Exceptions prove the rule

The exception proves the rule . . . has often been greatly abused . . . The exception in most cases merely proves the rule to be a bad one.

(Julius and Augustus Hare, GUESSES AT TRUTH, 1827)

There is no general rule without some exception, as the old proverb has it. North said so in his translation of PLUTARCH'S LIVES 'Alexander and Caesar' (1579), as did Heywood, Shelton and Burton some years later, perhaps after Cicero in PRO BALBO. There is no question, then, that exceptions exist, but what is their significance? As our contemporary proverb puts it, can they be said to *prove the rule?*

The meaning of the word 'prove' has undergone a change since the proverb was first recorded in the seventeenth century. Today we understand 'prove' to mean 'demonstrate' but an older sense of the word was 'test' (see also *The proof of the pudding is in the eating*). It is known to us today in this sense from the 1611 Authorised Version of the Bible. 1 THESSALONIANS 5:21, for instance, has: *Prove all things; hold fast that which is good.* The proverb does not therefore mean that an exception shows the rule to be correct but that an exception tries out the wisdom of the rule. It may be true – or not.

Usage: Few use the proverb in its original sense nowadays. Usually said as a comment after something unexpected has occurred.

EXPERIENCE

■ **Experience is the teacher of fools**

Everyone learns from the lessons of life

The fool in the proverb is everyone for, as Oscar Wilde pointed out, *Experience is the name everyone gives to his mistakes* (LADY WINDERMERE'S FAN, 1891).

The proverb comes from Livy's HISTORY OF ROME (c 10 BC). When the saying was used in England in the sixteenth century, experience was described as the *mistress* of fools, probably a reference to the Elizabethan Dame schools charged with the teaching of young children.

In his well-known book on education, THE SCHOLEMASTER (1570), Roger Ascham, tutor to Lady Jane Grey and the young Princess Elizabeth, considered that *It is costly wisdom that is bought by experience.* His life proved the truth of his words. In spite of his elevated position, he died a poor man owing to his addiction to gambling, a pastime he condemned. His theme was taken up by others, however. Thomas Fuller acknowledged that *Experience is good, if not bought too dear* (GNOMOLOGIA, 1732) and Benjamin Franklin brought both Livy's and Ascham's maxims together when he wrote that *Experience keeps a dear school, yet Fools will learn in no other* (POOR RICHARD'S ALMANACK, 1743). But take heart. A cheaper education is available and Publilius Syrus points the way: *Happy is he who gains wisdom from another's mishap* (SENTENTIAE, c 43 BC).

EYE

■ **An eye for an eye, and a tooth for a tooth**

See also: Revenge is sweet

Whatever evil has been meted out should be returned in equal measure to its perpetrator

'Well that's [fresuicilleye's] a mouthful. You can't make anything out of that.'
'Can't I though? Why, it's clear as clear. Fre is short for Fred and Suici for Suicide and Eye; that's what I always say – an eye for an eye and a tooth for a tooth.'
(Graham Greene, BRIGHTON ROCK, 1938)

From the continued existence of the old theory, 'an eye for an eye' condemned to death over nineteen hundred years ago, but still dying very hard in this Christian country.
(John Galsworthy, THE SPIRIT OF PUNISHMENT, 1910)

It was with his own children in mind that Tony set out to demystify the Bible in the TV shows Blood And Honey and now The Good Book Guide. 'I realised they were unfamiliar with those stories. How can you understand the British judicial system or concepts like an eye for an eye without the Bible?'
(DAILY MAIL, 1 February 1993)

The more aggressive assert that 10-year-olds nowadays are as mature as 15-year-olds used to be. There's too much do-gooding round here, said one mother who wouldn't give her name. 'It ought to be an eye for an

eye,' she added. 'Let whoever done this awful thing pay the proper price for the crime.'
(TODAY, 23 February 1993)

An eye for an eye and a tooth for a tooth is a helpful motto for those bent on revenge and seeking justification for pursuing it. The words are from the Bible and are listed amongst the penalties for slaying and injuring which God gave to Moses along with the rest of the Law. LEVITICUS 24:20 reads: Breach for breach, eye for eye, tooth for tooth: as he hath caused blemish in a man, so shall it be done to him again.

Nevertheless, this law was never intended to give licence for revenge but to exact justice. Neither did it permit taking matters into one's own hands since every case was subject to public judgement.

Jesus saw the question in a different light. In the Sermon on the Mount he urges his listeners to fight evil with good: Ye have heard that it hath been said, An eye for an eye, and a tooth for a tooth; But I say unto you that ye resist not evil, but whosoever shall smite thee on thy right cheek, turn to him the other also. And if any man will sue thee at the law, and take away thy coat, let him have thy cloak also. And whosoever shall compel thee to go a mile, go with him two (MATTHEW 5:38–41). The intention is not to show weakness but to prove that one is free from the spirit of hate and revenge by offering more than was first demanded.

■ **The eye is bigger than the belly**

The visual appeal of food makes us eat when we have no appetite

See also: We must eat to live and not live to eat

The proverb is from the sixteenth century. John Lyly makes reference to it in EUPHUES AND HIS ENGLAND (1580): Thou art like the Epicure, whose bellye is sooner filled than his eye.

For the Tudors the main meal of the day was taken at noon and, in reasonably prosperous households, might last for up to two hours whilst the family and their guests ploughed their way through copious amounts of food. Foreigners writing home were wont to express their amazement at how much their English counterparts could consume. The RELIQUIAE ANTIQUAE (c 1540) reported that Englysshemen ar callyd the grettyste fedours in the worlde. But with a large variety of colourful dishes on offer at each meal it is small wonder that diners tried to make room for a little of everything and found their eyes were bigger than their appetites.

Abundance at the English dining table continued into the following centuries, leading Thomas Fuller to pronounce in one of his sermons: Gluttony is the sin of England; . . . our ancientest carte is for the sin of gluttony (JOSEPH'S PARTI-COLOURED COAT, 1640). And with good reason. In his diary Samuel Pepys records the menu he offered a few friends for a special dinner in 1663:

A fricassee of rabbit and chickens, a leg of mutton boiled, three carps in a dish, a great dish of a side of lamb, a dish of roasted pigeons, a dish of four lobsters, three tarts, a lamprey pie, a most rare pie, a dish of anchovies, good wine of several sorts, and all things mighty noble, and to my great content.

With such enticement to gluttony, pity, then, the poor character in Dean Swift's POLITE CONVERSATION (1738) who is forced to admit defeat over a mere mouthful: *I thought I could have eaten this wing of a chicken; but my eye's bigger than my belly.* (For conspicuous consumption at medieval feasts, see *A bird in the hand is worth two in the bush.*)

Usage: Somewhat dated

■ What the eye doesn't see, the heart doesn't grieve over

Being unaware of something unpleasant stops us from being concerned about it

Variant: What the eye don't see, the heart don't grieve over

See also: Ignorance is bliss

This proverb, recorded by John Heywood in 1546 as *That the eie seeth not, the hert rewth not* was called a 'common saying' by George Pettie in 1576. The proverb teaches quite logically that we can only be troubled by things that we know about. It is the sight of the caterpillar on the lettuce that puts us off our salad; had we unknowingly eaten it we could not have given it a thought. In his TRAVELS IN FRANCE AND ITALY (1766), Tobias Smollett recounts the tale of a young man whose heart was very much grieved upon witnessing his beloved's table manners:

I know no custom more beastly than that of using water-glasses, in which polite company spirt, and squirt, and spue the filthy scourings of their gums, under the eyes of each other. I knew a lover cured of his passion, by seeing this nasty cascade discharged from the mouth of his mistress.

Turning a blind eye makes the path of true love run smooth!

Usage: Quite often used to excuse deliberately keeping quiet about something

■ You should never touch your eye but with your elbow

The best health for eyes is preserved by not touching them

This sensible proverb, spoken to discourage people from touching their eyes, has been in circulation in Europe since at least the middle of the seventeenth century. Various forms warn against touching or rubbing the eye except with the elbow. George Herbert, along with the Portuguese, prescribes that *Diseases of the eye are to be cured with the elbow* (JACULA PRUDENTUM, 1640). In England the advice was extended to include the ear, and nineteenth century nursemaids would encourage good manners from their young charges by forbidding them to pick their teeth at the table until they could first do it with their elbow.

This is a proverb which begs for revival and its scope could be extended still further to include the nose.

Usage: The original health warning against contagious diseases and cross-infections may now in its variant forms be an exhortation to good manners. Rather dated

FAMILIARITY

■ **Familiarity breeds contempt**

When one becomes used to someone or something, one's respect degenerates into disregard

See also: A prophet is not without honour save in his own country

Perhaps if I had heard Tennyson talking every day, I shouldn't read Tennyson. Familiarity does breed contempt.
(Trollope, HE KNEW HE WAS RIGHT, 1869)

'I confess I do not care about my grandfather or Marcia; of the two I prefer my grandfather, but that is saying very little. Philip alone has been very nice to me, indeed more than kind.'
'More! What does Marcia say to that?'
'Oh! there is nothing between them; I am sure of that. They either hate each other, or else familiarity has bred contempt between them; as they avoid each other all they can, and never speak unless compelled.'
(M Hungerford, MOLLY BAWN, 1878)

One would have thought that once an object was recognised as beautiful it would contain enough of intrinsic worth to retain its beauty indefinitely. We know it doesn't. We get tired of it. Familiarity breeds not contempt perhaps, but indifference; and indifference is the death of the aesthetic emotion.
(W Somerset Maugham, A WRITER'S NOTEBOOK, '1941', 1949)

Victor, aged 27, joined the Chippendales six years ago having graduated from a Californian university in business and finance. *Familiarity has not bred contempt for the adoration of strange women: he still insists that the photograph sessions after the show – and the calendar signings beforehand – are 'really kinda fun. It's an opportunity to get personable with the ladies.'*
(WEEKEND TELEGRAPH, 9 May 1992)

Aesop's THE FOX AND THE LION (c 570 BC) tells of how a fox, upon meeting a lion for the first time, nearly died of fright and ran away. The next time he saw the lion the fox was still a worried but stood his ground. At their third meeting, however, the fox felt no nervousness at all and dared to approach the powerful beast. Familiarity took the edge off his fear until eventually he felt none.

From here it is only a short step to contempt. Another fable, THE CAMEL, expresses the same idea:

When the first men first set eyes
On a camel, they were staggered by its size
And ran away in fear.
In time, seeing the beast seemed fairly mild,
They plucked up courage to go near.
Finally, when they came to realise
That it was docile and their fears were idle,
They used it with contempt, gave it a bridle
And put it in the charge of a child.
(John Vernon Lord and James Michie (trs.), AESOP'S FABLES, 1989)

Publilius Syrus concurred. In SENTENTIAE (c 43 BC), he writes: *Too much familiarity breeds contempt*, a statement which was much echoed thereafter by Plutarch in particular, Martial and other ancient writers. The earliest recorded use of the expression in English is in Alanus de Insulis's SATIRES (c 1160). It has been taken up widely ever since.

FATHER

■ Like father, like son

A son is likely to have the same character and behaviour as his father

When Thomas Mann peeped at the diary of his 13-year-old son Klaus, he found it 'disturbing'. It showed 'coldness, ingratitude and lack of affection'. Like father, like son? Thomas Mann's diaries reveal a man who was not only cold and ungrateful but also a cynical opportunist, disagreeable and at times downright detestable.
(GUARDIAN, 21 January 1993)

Stevenson suggests a fable by Aesop (sixth century BC) as the origin for the proverb. A mother crab scolded her son for walking sideways, whereupon the youngster replied that he would be pleased to walk straight if she would show him how to do it.

The proverb was known in England in the fourteenth century. The Latin proverb Qualis pater, talis filius is quoted by Langland in PIERS PLOWMAN (1362), and in LEGEND OF GOOD WOMEN (c 1385) Chaucer writes: As doth the fox Renard, [so doth] the foxes sone.

A complementary proverb exists for mothers and daughters, but there is a suggested biblical origin for this. EZEKIEL 16:44 reads: Behold, every one that useth proverbs shall use this proverb against thee, saying, As is the mother, so is her daughter.

FEATHERS

■ Fine feathers make fine birds

Expensive clothes give the wearer an appearance of respectability and breeding

See also: Appearances are deceptive

We all know that fine feathers make fine birds, but a house doesn't have to look like a palace in order to sell.
(FOUNDATIONS: LEEDS MAGAZINE, Spring/ Summer 1991)

Some birds are more pleasing to look at than others. The familiar simile as proud as a peacock arises from the observation that the male bird's bearing, together with the magnificent display of his plumage, gives him a haughty look. Plucked before being cooked for a medieval banquet, however, the cock bird would look as unremarkable as his dowdy hen. The Italian diplomat, Stefano Guazzo, recognised that the meanest personalities can hide behind expensive apparel. In CIVILE CONVERSATION (1574) he writes: It may rightly be sayde of these costly clad carkases, that the feathers are more worth than the byrde.

In the spirit of Guazzo's cynicism the earliest uses of the proverb were often tongue-in-cheek. In THE SCOURGE OF FOLLY (1611), John Davies of Hereford writes:

The faire Feathers still make the faire Fowles.
But some haue faire feathers that looke but like Owles.

But if John Ray is to be believed, the saying was not necessarily always intended to be uncomplimentary: *Fair feathers make fair fowles. Fair clothes, ornaments and dresses set off persons . . . God makes and apparel shapes* (ENGLISH PROVERBS, 1670).

By the time Bunyan wrote PILGRIM'S PROGRESS (1678) the proverb was shifting to a more recognisable form: *They be fine feathers that make a fine bird,* and thirty-six years later Bernard Mandeville in THE FABLE OF THE BEES (1714) uses the exact form we know today.

Usage: Always used ironically or sarcastically

FESTINA LENTE

■ **Festina lente**

The best way to make good progress is to proceed with caution

Variant: Make haste slowly

See also: More haste, less speed

The tortoise was sent to me when I became a clergyman by someone who knew the importance of making haste slowly.
(TELEGRAPH MAGAZINE, 6 February 1993)

This proverb is often quoted in Latin although its origins are Greek. It was popularised by the Emperor Caesar Augustus, who quoted it frequently in that language. It was also made much of by Erasmus, who considered its message so worthy of attention that he would have had it inscribed everywhere to bring it into public view.

A contemporary version of the maxim was propounded by Lee Iacocca, former president of General Motors, who warned that *Action should not be confused with haste.*

Usage: One of the few instances where the Latin form is still in fairly common currency, alongside the English translation

---

FEVER

■ **Feed a cold and starve a fever**

The best medicine for a cold is to eat well, for a fever to fast

Variant: Stuff a cold and starve a fever

I've always been told that you should feed a cold and starve a fever. Is there any medical basis for this?
(DAILY MAIL, November 1992)

This medical proverb seems to have originated sometime in the nineteenth century, when some gave it an alternative form and meaning. Originally the wording was *Stuff a cold and starve a fever.* A correspondent with NOTES AND QUERIES points out that the saying is elliptical and says the advice should be . . . *[if you] stuff a cold, [you will have to] starve a fever.* This, of course, changes the wisdom of the proverb for it suggests that anyone foolish enough to eat heartily while suffering from a cold will soon bring a fever upon himself. Other nineteenth and early twentieth century writers agree, however, that this is indeed the import of the proverb.

Modern medical advice is at odds with this view and supports the contemporary sense of the saying: a good intake of healthy food is recommended for a cold, with no suggestion that a fever will result. Those who have a fever do not usually feel like eating anyway but need plenty to drink when the fever eventually 'breaks'.

FINGERS

■ **Fingers were made before forks**

An explanation or excuse for not using cutlery for eating

It is said that John the Good, Duke of Burgundy, in the fourteenth century, was the proud possessor of two forks but, if he was, the novelty did not catch on. Diners continued to use their knives (carried permanently tucked into their belts and used for all sorts of purposes) or fingers to dig into the variety of communal dishes placed upon the table. In the previous century Fra Bonvicino, who had obviously been treated to stomach-churning spectacles at the monastic dinner table, had issued a few guidelines for those about to dip into the pot with their companions:

Let thy fingers be clean.
Thou must not put thy fingers into thine ears,
Or thy hands on thy head.
The man who is eating must not be cleaning
By scraping with his finger at any foul part.

(See also Smollett's account of Continental table manners in *What the eye doesn't see, the heart doesn't grieve over*, page 94.) It was Venetian polite society at the beginning of the sixteenth century that hit upon the idea of using forks. THE FRANK MUIR BOOK (1976) quotes Thomas Coryat, on his travels through Italy in the early seventeenth century, who could not quite believe his eyes when he saw them being used:

I observed a custom in all those Italian cities and towns through which I passed that is not used in any other country that I saw in my travels, neither do I think that any other nation in Christendom doth use it, but only in Italy. The Italian and also most strangers that are commorant in Italy do always at their meals use a little fork when they cut their meat. For while with their knife which they hold in one hand, they cut the meat out of the dish, they fasten their fork which they hold in their other hand upon the same dish, so that whatsoever he be that sitting in the company of any others at meal, should unadvisedly touch the dish of meat with his fingers from which all at the table do cut, he will give occasion of offence unto the company, as having transgressed the laws of good manners, in so much that for his error he shall be at the least brow-beaten, if not reprehended in words.

(CORYATS CRUDITIES, 1611)

It was nearly two hundred years before such niceties were wholeheartedly embraced by the English, however. And when society diners in the late seventeenth century eventually adopted the custom, there were inevitably those who would inadvertently slip back into the old ways or even just prefer them. Then, to cover their embarrassment on being noticed, they would retort, *Fingers were made before forks*.

The proverb was easily coined, being modelled on an earlier one known since at least the second half of the sixteenth century. Swift uses them both together in POLITE CONVERSATION (1738), the new with the old: *They say fingers were made before forks, and hands before knives*.

Usage: Part of the folk wisdom of children rather than in active use amongst adults in any literal sense. Sometimes metaphorically used in support of a less sophisticated approach.

FISH

■ All is fish that comes to the net

It is best to take advantage of anything that comes your way. Also, a comment made on evidence of a lack of discrimination

See also: All is grist that comes to the mill

She's had Emmott and Coleman dancing attendance on her as a matter of course. I don't know that she cares for one more than the other. There are a couple of young Air Force chaps too. I fancy all's fish that comes to her net at present.
(Agatha Christie, MURDER IN MESOPOTAMIA, 1936)

A fisherman may be hoping for a particular kind of catch but, if he is sensible, he will make use of whatever fills his net to make his livelihood. Uses in literature date from the first half of the sixteenth century.

Usage: One sense approvingly suggests taking advantage of whatever opportunities present themselves; another sense negatively implies a lack of scrupulousness and discrimination in choosing between the chances that come our way

■ Don't cry stinking fish

Don't speak about yourself or your efforts in a detrimental way

I replied that I was a young gentleman of large fortune (this was not true; but what is the use of crying bad fish?)
(William Thackeray, BARRY LYNDON, 1844)

You're very disillusioned, Garston. I've noticed it before. I think it's a bad thing not to have faith in your work, y'know. It's no use crying stinking fish, is it?
(Nigel Balchin, MINE OWN EXECUTIONER, 1945)

The proverb, which dates back to the seventeenth century, alludes to street vendors who would advertise their wares by shouting out about them, sometimes in song or rhyme.

This street cry from the Stuart period, contemporary with the proverb, belongs to an apple vendor:

Here are fine golden pippins,
Who'll buy them, who'll buy?
Nobody in London sells better than I,
Who'll buy them, who'll buy?

And this song to a seller of brooms:

Here's one for the lady,
Here's a small one for the baby;
Come buy my pretty lady,
Come buy o' me a broom.

Robert Herrick's love poem, CHERRIE-RIPE (1648), opens with the call of someone with cherries to sell:

Cherrie-Ripe, Ripe, Ripe, I cry,
Full and faire ones; come and buy.

These cries emphasise the excellence of the wares on offer. There would be little point, then, in a fish vendor crying out 'Come and buy my fish, rotten fish, stinking fish,' if he wanted to sell what was in his barrow. The proverb encourages us, therefore, to present ourselves and what we have to offer in a good light.

Usage: Somewhat dated

FOOL

■ **A fool and his money are soon parted**

A foolish person gives little consideration as to how he spends his money and soon finds himself without any at all

See also: Easy come, easy go

A fool and his money are soon married.
(Carolyn Wells)

I have another friend, a great gourmet who treats Fortnums as a supermarket, and has a freezer stuffed with smoked salmon, and a larder hung with grouse and pheasants, but show her a sell-by date on a packet of ham or a tub of cream and she feels compelled to go far beyond it, seeing it as an elaborate plot by the manufacturers to see foolish women and their money parted a lot sooner than necessary.
(GOOD HOUSEKEEPING, April 1993)

Hilaire Belloc described the sad case of Peter Goole, a young man who had all the hallmarks of the fool in the proverb:

It seems he wholly lacked a sense
Of limiting the day's expense,
And money ran between his hands
Like water through the Ocean Sands.
Such conduct could not but affect
His parent's fortune, which was wrecked
Like many and many another one
By folly in a spendthrift son:
By that most tragical mischance,
An Only Child's Extravagance.
('PETER GOOLE', MORE CAUTIONARY TALES, 1930)

Fools are often helped to dispose of their income by sharp fellows who recognise spendthrift tendencies in others. Walsh hazards a story which may have been the origin of the proverb. It is equally possible that the anecdote is merely an instance of the saying being used or even that it is a pure fabrication. Here, at any rate, is the story.

George Buchanan, renowned historian and wit and one-time tutor to James VI of Scotland, once made a wager with a courtier. Buchanan bet that if they both produced a piece of vulgar verse his would be the coarser. The courtier lost and Buchanan scooped up his winnings remarking, 'A fool and his money are soon parted.'

The proverb appears in literature as a maxim in Thomas Tusser's FIVE HUND-RETH POINTES OF GOOD HUSBANDRIE (1573):

A foole and his monie be soone at debate
Which after with sorrow repents him too
late.

Although Tusser farmed in Suffolk, it may be that he was familiar with the above anecdote since his book was produced during the period Buchanan spent as tutor at the Scottish court.

■ **Fools rush in where angels fear to tread**

Unwise people thoughtlessly and rashly tackle situations that even the wisest think twice about

A kind of mixture of fools and angels – they rush in and fear to tread at the same time
(William O'Henry, THE MOMENT OF VICTORY, 1909)

At length a plump woman (who was, in fact, no other than Mrs Ruddle's friend) remarked, with that feminine impulsiveness which rushes in where the lords of creation fear to tread.
(Dorothy L Sayers, BUSMAN'S HONEYMOON, 1937)

The proverb comes from Alexander Pope's AN ESSAY ON CRITICISM (1711). Pope is discussing critics who, he says, have the audacity to voice opinions where even more enlightened readers would hesitate to criticise:

No place so sacred from such fops is barr'd,
Nor is Paul's church more safe than Paul's
churchyard:
Nay, fly to altars; there they'll talk you dead;
For fools rush in where angels fear to tread.

■ **You may fool all of the people some of the time, some of the people all of the time, but not all of the people all of the time**
It is possible to deceive people to different degrees, but not totally

Variant: You may please all of the people . . .

Nancy: *You make it sound so simple.*
Sid: *That's because it is. When you've got a single-supplier market and a big enough advertising budget, you really can fool all of the people . . .*
(MACUSER, 19 February 1993)

You can't fool all the people all the time, and certainly not if they live in St Albans or Pitlochry. These are people who would have been elbowing their way to the front of the crowd to shout: 'Look – the Emperor's got no clothes on!'
(SUNDAY TIMES, 28 February 1993)

This saying is attributed to Abraham Lincoln by two different sources citing two separate occasions. William P Kellog asserts that Lincoln used the saying in a speech given at Bloomington, Illinois on

29 May 1856, while Alexander K McClure, in his book LINCOLN'S YARNS AND STORIES (1904), claims that Lincoln was in discussion with a caller at the White House and said: *If you once forfeit the confidence of your fellow citizens, you can never regain their respect and esteem. It is true that you may fool all the people some of the time; you can even fool some of the people all the time; but you can't fool all of the people all the time.*

Lincoln's words were, however, anticipated in thought and formula, as correspondents with NOTES AND QUERIES have pointed out. One of his illustrious predecessors as President of the United States expressed a similar idea: *You may be too cunning for one, but not for all* (Benjamin Franklin, POOR RICHARD'S ALMANACK, 1750), while the form has echoes in La Rochefoucauld's *One may be more clever than another, but not more clever than all the others* (MAXIMES, 1665). And just a few years before Lincoln's Bloomington speech, English essayist John Sterling (1806–1844) wrote: *There is no lie that many men will not believe; there is no man who does not believe many lies; but there is no man who believes only lies* (ESSAYS AND TALES: THOUGHTS).

Perhaps ultimate credit should be given to Pliny the Younger who, around AD 10, said: *Individuals may deceive and be deceived; but no one ever deceived everybody, nor has everybody ever deceived any one* (PANEGYRICS: TRAJAN).

Usage: Regularly reduced to the allusive *You can't fool all the people all the time . . .*

FORGIVE

■ Forgive and forget

Do not bear a grudge but rather put out of mind all past wrongs

See also: Let bygones be bygones

She told herself then that she could never forgive or forget the insult to which she had been subjected.
(D Garnett, A MAN IN THE ZOO, 1924)

But there's something the people of Gildsey and the Leem (and not just them but people everywhere) wanted to do more than forgive; and that was forget.
(Graham Swift, WATERLAND, 1983)

SCORPIO (George Barford, Peggy Archer, Alf Grundy, Brian Aldridge, Kylie Richards): Still thinking about that wrong someone did to you all those years ago? Forget it Scorpio; revenge is not the answer. It will only make you bitter, so make this the year you forgave and forgot.
(AMBRIDGE VILLAGE VOICE, LAMBING ISSUE, Spring 1992)

I forgive and forget appears in Philo's DE IOSEPHO which was written in about AD 40. Whether or not Philo's charitable sentiments were the inspiration behind the proverb is not known but the phrase certainly put in an early appearance in English literature. The unknown author of the devotional manuscript ANCREN RIWLE (c 1200) used it in his work and a century and a half later William Langland applied the expression to the grace of Christ:

So wil Cryst of his curteisye,
and men crye hym mercy,
bothe forgiue and forgete.
(PIERS PLOWMAN, 1377)

As so often happens, Shakespeare had an influence in fixing the phrase in the language. In ALL'S WELL THAT ENDS WELL (1601) there is the present day order: *I have forgiven and forgotten all.* In KING LEAR (1605) we have the variant: *Pray you now, forget and forgive.* Usage today has settled for the logical *forgive and forget,* in that forgiving must reasonably precede forgetting. However, as W E Norris points out: *We may forgive and we may forget, but we can never forget that we have forgiven.*

Usage: A laudable exhortation which – perhaps because it is easier said than done – might be resented by the person to whom it is addressed

■ **To err is human, to forgive divine**

It is human nature to make mistakes and find it hard to forgive others; true forgiveness is a godly quality

See also: Even Homer sometimes nods

What is a history teacher? He's someone who teaches mistakes. While others say, Here's how you do it, he says, And here's what goes wrong. While others tell you, This is the way, this is the path, he says, And here are a few bungles, botches, blunders and fiascos . . . It doesn't work out; it's human to err (so what do we need, a God to watch over us and forgive us our sins?)
(Graham Swift, WATERLAND, 1983)

To err is human, to forgive divine is a worthy maxim, Grebby, anywhere but at Perkins Ltd.
(Cartoon caption, TELEGRAPH MAGAZINE, 24 January 1993)

The frailty of human nature has been recognised and lamented for centuries. *Being human I erred* confessed Menander (PHANIUM, c 300 BC). *It is human to err* pronounced a more matter-of-fact Seneca (NATURALES QUAESTIONES, c AD 62). This Latin proverb, itself drawing on a Greek tradition, was quoted extensively by ancient writers and so, not surprisingly, slipped easily into the writings of most Romance languages.

St Augustine gave a Christian cast to the proverb in encouraging his readers to fight against the flesh: *It is human to err; it is devilish to remain wilfully in error* (SERMONS, c AD 400), possibly taking his inspiration from the secular Cicero: *Any man may err, but nobody but a fool persists in error* (PHILIPPICS, 43 BC).

But it was Alexander Pope who, with remarkable insight into human nature and a genius for condensing great truth into a few telling words, gave the proverb yet another dimension and coined the wording we know today: *To err is human, to forgive divine* (AN ESSAY ON CRITICISM, 1711). There is a contrast between the tendency in man to sin and the characteristic in God to forgive. When man does forgive, it is in imitation of his maker. In a more secular age, it is perhaps not surprising that the second phrase is frequently omitted today!

Usage: Where the proverb is reduced to just the first part, the emphasis is particularly that, because we are all human and prone to mistakes, we should therefore be as forgiving as possible to others

FRIEND

■ **A friend in need is a friend indeed**

A friend who will support you when you are in need of help is a true friend

Variant: A friend in need is a friend in deed

The petitioners for compensation had begun to regard the Poultry and Damage Fund as a regular friend in need, and complaints from poultry farmers were far too frequent.
(Siegfried Sassoon, MEMOIRS OF A FOX-HUNTING MAN, 1928)

A friend in need is a friend to be avoided.
(Lord Samuel)

Men have pondered upon the nature of true friendship since ancient times and, unsurprisingly, have concluded that the test of a relationship comes in time of difficulty. Aesop tells of two friends who were travelling together when they saw a bear. One of them quickly climbed a nearby tree, the other, seeing no chance of escape, lay down on the ground pretending to be dead. The bear began to nuzzle him, and he held his breath, for no bear will touch a corpse.

At last the bear gave up and went away and the man's companion came down from the safety of his tree. 'What was it that the bear was whispering in your ear?' he asked. 'The wise bear advised me not to travel in future with friends who abandon one in times of trouble,' came the reply. Bartlett traces the proverb back to the playwright Plautus who, in EPIDICUS (200 BC), writes: *Nothing is there more friendly to a man than a friend in need.*

References to companions proving themselves in time of need are found in English literature from the twelfth century onwards, though the saying is variously expressed. In William Caxton's fifteenth century translation of FABLES OF ESOPE (1484), for instance, we find: *The very and trewe frend is fond in the extreme nede* and also *A trewe frend is oftyme better at nede than a Royalme.* Just over half a century later John Heywood extends the thought, meditating upon the fickleness of friendships which he had assumed strong:

A freende is neuer knowen tyll a man haue neede.
Before I had neede, my most present foes
Semed my most freends, but thus the world goes
(PROVERBS, 1546)

He was proving the truth of a French proverb which says *Prosperity gives friends, adversity proves them,* which itself goes back to Publilius Syrus.

During the sixteenth century writers working in rhyme found the words 'need' and 'indeed' a convenient coupling when expressing the proverb.

By 1678 they were linked permanently, the proverb appearing in John Ray's collection of ENGLISH PROVERBS in its present day form.

Usage: The two variants in the form of the proverb sound alike to the ear and reflect an interesting ambiguity of sense. *Indeed* acts as an adverb, intensifying what has gone before. *In deed* means that a friend is the one that actually does something practical to help out, rather than just making encouraging noises.

FRUIT

■ **Forbidden fruit is the sweetest**

If we are forbidden to do or have something, the object of our desire becomes all the more alluring

Variants: Stolen fruit is always the sweetest; Stolen apples/cherries are always the sweetest

See also: The grass is always greener on the other side of the fence

His father successfully prevented Galileo from even knowing that there was such a subject as mathematics until at the age of nineteen, he happened, as an eavesdropper, to overhear a lecture on geometry. He seized with avidity upon the subject, which had for him all the charm of forbidden fruit.
(Bertrand Russell, RELIGION AND SCIENCE, 1935)

Does your child spend more than 30 minutes a day playing computer games? . . . Here's what to do:

1. *Limit the time your child's allowed to play.*
2. *Don't let your child take games to school.*
3. *Talk to teachers.*
4. *Encourage your child to invite friends round and invent interesting games.*
5. *Vet any games you buy.*
6. *Use computer games as a reward rather than punishment.*
7. *Don't ban games: forbidden fruit is sweeter.*
(DAILY EXPRESS, 29 April 1993)

There are two areas of variation in the form of this proverb: *forbidden* or *stolen* fruit? Stolen *apples* or stolen *fruit*?

The distinction between *stolen* or *forbidden* fruit is not sharply made. An Arabic proverb has it that *Everything forbidden is sweet* and there are innumerable references in English literature through the ages to the same effect. Bohn's HANDBOOK OF PROVERBS (1855), for example, records *Forbidden fruit is sweet*. Similarly, there are plentiful instances of the attraction of the stolen. One of the oldest references to this idea is in the Old Testament book of PROVERBS 9:17: *Stolen waters are sweet and bread eaten in secret is pleasant.*

Two millennia later, Thomas Randolph phrased it beautifully in SONG OF FAIRIES (c 1635):

Stolen sweets are sweeter;
Stolen kisses much completer;
Stolen looks are nice in chapels;
Stolen, stolen be your apples.

As to the issue of stolen *apples* (as in this verse) or stolen *fruit*, there is a long tradition back to Plutarch in c AD 100 that refers to the allure of stolen apples. There is also the influence of the popular confusion that Eve plucked the forbidden apple in the Garden of Eden. In fact the book of Genesis talks only of forbidden fruit.

Surprisingly with such a venerable history, the combined efforts of all the great students of English proverbs have not yet come up with a recorded example in anything like its present form that predates one in Mrs Gaskell's NORTH AND SOUTH of 1855. The Spanish analogue on the other hand, which draws on exactly the same traditions, has had a recognised shape since its first rendering in Garcilaso de la Vega's THIRD ECLOGUE of 1536.

GOD

■ **God helps those who help themselves**

Self-help stimulates divine assistance

Things improve gradually, but remember that 'God helps those who help themselves'. A medical check-up would not go amiss – some of you are suffering from eye strain or stress.
(DAILY MIRROR, 21 January 1992)

He was a burglar stout and strong,
Who held, 'It surely can't be wrong,
To open trunks and rifle shelves,
For God helps those who help themselves.'
But when before the court he came,
And boldly rose to plead the same,
The judge replied, 'That's very true;
You've helped yourself, now God help you!'
(SCOTTISH EPIGRAM)

Ancient literature holds many references which tell us that we can only expect help from God if we are prepared to play our part, too. One of Aesop's fables (c 570 BC), HERCULES AND THE WAGGONER, carries this message. A waggoner was driving along a muddy track when his cart skidded into a ditch. Instead of doing something about it, the waggoner called upon the mighty Hercules for help. The god appeared and told the waggoner to put his shoulder behind the wheel and goad his oxen on. Hercules then scolded the man, forbidding him to call upon him ever again unless he had first made an effort himself.

English and other European languages have coined a number of quaint proverbs to express the idea of self-help: the French, for instance, say *God never builds us bridges, but he gives us hands;* and the Spanish *While waiting for water from heaven, don't stop irrigating.*

Similarly many European languages have the proverb *God helps those who help themselves.* In English before the eighteenth century, the thought was variously expressed: John Baret tells us that *God doth help those in their affaires, which are industrious* (AN ALVEARIE, 1580); and George Herbert in his JACULA PRUDENTUM (1640) has *Help thyself, and God will help thee.* Then in his POOR RICHARD'S ALMANACK of 1736, Benjamin Franklin coins or records the present day form of the proverb.

■ **God made man, man made money**

Humanity shapes and extends God's creation

The following rhyme, claimed to be the origin of the proverb by the LONSDALE MAGAZINE of 1820, was written by John Oldland at the beginning of the eighteenth century. It was inspired by the lawyer who sued him for debt:

God mead man,
And man mead money,
God mead bees,
And bees mead honey,
But the Devil mead lawyers an' 'tornies,
And pleac'd 'em at U'ston and Doten i' Forness.

There is, however, at least one other variant of the rhyme. This offering was written on the flyleaf of an old Bible belonging to a miner:

God made bees, and bees made honey,
God made man, and man made money,
Pride made the devil and the devil made sin;
So God made a cole-pit to put the devil in.

It is impossible to say which came first or, indeed, if either was the origin of the saying.

■ **God made the country, and man made the town**

The beauty of the countryside is preferable to urban sprawl

The proverb is a line from Cowper's poem THE TASK (1785) but he in turn found inspiration in DE RE RUSTICA (c 35 BC), a work by the Roman scholar Varro: Divine nature gave the fields, human art built the cities.

Early appearances in English literature give a biblical slant to the saying. Bacon writes: God Almighty first planted a garden (OF GARDENS, 1625), while Abraham Cowley in his essay THE GARDEN (1656) writes: God the first garden made, and the first city Cain. Cowley was possibly inspired not only by Varro and Bacon but by Rabelais who, in PANTAGRUEL (1532), wrote: I found in Holy Scripture that Cain was the first builder of cities. But Cowper's rendering is simpler and, therefore, more quoteable and this is the version that has become proverbial.

It is not surprising that the saying should find ready acceptance. There is a long tradition of the beauties of rural bucolic life and of the noble savage who lived there. The Greeks revered the Arcadians, the Romans the Scythians. Rousseau had an enormous influence on eighteenth and nineteenth century Romantic writing. Chateaubriand, for instance, celebrated the pastoral life of the Red Indian in his ATALA (1801) and LES NATCHEZ (1826).

■ **God tempers the wind to the shorn lamb**

God is especially tender in his protection of the weak. God softens the trials that his defenceless children have to endure.

Although we cannot turn away the wind, we can soften it; we can temper it, if I may say so, to the shorn lambs.
(Charles Dickens, THE OLD CURIOSITY SHOP, 1841)

An accumulation of wisdom

The last of Erasmus's editions of his great ADAGIA (see **Erasmus's Adagia**, page 8) was published in 1536, some ten years before the first collection of English proverbs: John Heywood's A DIALOGUE CONTEINING THE NUMBER IN EFFECT OF ALL THE PROVERBES IN THE ENGLISHE TONGUE (1546). He subsequently produced three collections of epigrams at five-year intervals from 1550 to 1560.

From Heywood, a king's entertainer, to Fergusson, a king's minister. The latter was Moderator of the General Assembly of the Church of Scotland and at the court of the king. He died in 1598 but his SCOTTISH PROVERBS was not published until 1641. This was the beginning of quite a British clerical tradition (although it could be argued that this began with Erasmus who had been an Augustinian monk and, while in England, had received the benefice of Aldington in Kent from Archbishop Warham). Thomas Draxe was an English clergyman who published in 1612 his BIBLIOTHECA SCHOLASTICA INSTRUCTISSIMA OR, A TREASURIE OF ANCIENT ADAGIES, AND SENTENTIOUS PROUERBES. Next in line was Pastor John Clarke and his PAROEMIOLOGIA ANGLO-LATINA of 1639. George Herbert was another churchman who interested himself in proverbs. His OUTLANDISH PROVERBS was published in 1640, some seven years after his death. It is best known in its 1651 edition, extended by a later editor as JACULA PRUDENTUM. Perhaps that same editor was responsible for the inspired new title – it means 'javelins of the wise'.

The next collections of especial note are those of James Howell (1659) and John Ray (1670). The former is strong on proverbs from other cultures and languages, resulting from the author's wide study and travel; the latter is well organised, with many new entries and learned notes.

The succeeding centuries brought reprints of these old works or 'new' collections that were the same old ones, but with additions. Landmarks are:

James Kelly (1721) COMPLETE COLLECTION OF SCOTTISH PROVERBS

Thomas Fuller (1732) GNOMOLOGIA: ADAGIES AND PROVERBS

William Carew Hazlitt (1869) ENGLISH PROVERBS AND PROVERBIAL PHRASES

Vincent Stuckey Lean (1902–4) COLLECTANEA

George Latimer Apperson (1929) ENGLISH PROVERBS AND PROVERBIAL PHRASES

In more recent years there have been several editions of THE OXFORD DICTIONARY OF ENGLISH PROVERBS since its first publication in 1935.

In the United States of America there have been a number of works of real importance. Benjamin Franklin's POOR RICHARD'S ALMANACK flourished from 1733 to 1758. In the twentieth century undoubtedly the major work is Burton Stevenson's BOOK OF PROVERBS, MAXIMS AND FAMILIAR PHRASES of 1949. Its 3000 pages are a master work of scholarship. Parœmiology – the study of proverbs – is fortunate to have had the benefit of the prodigious energies and intellect of so many writers through the centuries. Nor are these endeavours at an end. Projects under way include a scholarly proverb collection by the American Dialect Society.

Books come out so quickly and in such numbers that there is, at best, time only to review them (in the technical sense of that verb). And reviewers, however conscientious, do not always have time to be critics. Standards fluctuate and vary. Reviewers sometimes temper the wind to the shorn (not slaughtered) lamb.

(K W Gransden, 'THOUGHTS ON CONTEMPORARY FICTION' in A REVIEW OF ENGLISH LITERATURE, VOL 1 No 2, 1960)

Aristocrats still exist; but they are shorn beings, for whom the wind is not tempered – powerless, out of place, and slightly ridiculous.

(Lytton Strachey, BIOGRAPHICAL ESSAYS, 'LADY MARY WORTLEY MONTAGU', 1949)

Those who do not think the proverb biblical often attribute it to Laurence Sterne. In his SENTIMENTAL JOURNEY THROUGH FRANCE AND ITALY: MARIA (1768), Sterne meets up with Maria, a character from TRISTRAM SHANDY, an earlier work. Maria is a little mad. Since their last meeting she has roamed all over Lombardy, penniless and with no shoes on her feet. Asked how she had borne it and how she had fared Maria can only reply, *God tempers the wind to the shorn lamb.*

The saying is, in fact, Sterne's poetic rendering of an old French proverb *Dieu mesure le froid à la brebis tondue* (recorded by Henri Estienne in 1594), which he properly puts into the mouth of a French character. A literal translation of a variant recorded by Labou in 1610 can be found in Herbert's JACULA PRUDENTUM (1640): *To a close shorn sheep, God gives wind by measure.* Although correctly only sheep and not lambs are shorn, it is easy to see why Sterne's version came into popular speech.

Usage: For all its poetic qualities, the proverb is not frequent today

■ **Man proposes but God disposes**

People may make plans but without control over the outcome

The ancients acknowledged the power of the gods to order puny man's plans:

Man intends one thing, Fate another.
(Publilius Syrus, SENTENTIAE, c 43 BC)

By many forms of artifice the gods Defeat our plans, for they are stronger far.
(Euripides, FRAGMENTS, c 440 BC)

But, 'Man proposes, God disposes' – how everlasting true is that old saying of the good Thomas à Kempis!
(DAILY NEWS, 20 December 1898)

Such a view is easily assimilated into Christian thinking with an all-powerful, all-knowing, loving God taking the place of the jealous and capricious ancient deities. Thomas à Kempis, in his DE IMITATIONE CHRISTI (c 1420) finds the source of the proverb in two biblical texts. PROVERBS 16:9 reads: *A man's heart deviseth his way: but the Lord directeth his steps;* and JEREMIAH 10:23 has: *O Lord, I know that the way of man is not in himself: it is not in man that walketh to direct his steps.* Other authors have pointed to several passages of Scripture (PROVERBS 16:33, JAMES 4:15) on the same theme.

William Langland, however, thinks the origin lies with Plato, as this passage from PIERS PLOWMAN (1377) indicates:

Homo proponit, *quod a poete, and Plato he hyght,*
And Deus disponit, *quod he, let God done his wille.*

Nothing in Plato's work, however, matches the wording of the proverb – the nearest being a reference to an ancient proverb *Human affairs are not what a man wishes, but what he can bring about*. The biblical source, then, is the more likely.

Langland's words serve to indicate just how long the proverb has been in circulation in England. It has an equally long history throughout Europe, being found from Sweden to Italy. Quite different cultures also acknowledge it. The following are from collections of Chinese proverbs:

Man may plan, but Heaven executes

Men, without divine assistance,
Cannot move an inch of distance.

Man says, so! so!
Heaven says, no, no.

■ **Whom the gods love dies young**

Words of comfort on a person's early death

Variant: God takes soonest those whom he loves best

I was meant to die young and the gods do not love me.
(Robert Louis Stevenson, LETTERS, 1894)

It has never been satisfactorily determined whether the saying about the darlings of the gods dying young means young in years or young in heart.
(E V Lucas, ADVISORY BEN., 1923)

The Greek historian Herodotus includes in his HISTORY (c 445 BC) this incident told by the wise Athenian statesman Solon. A woman was anxious to go to the temple for the festival of Here but the oxen who drew her cart could not be found, so her two young sons, Cleobis and Biton, took the yoke on their own backs and pulled her there themselves. Touched by their thoughtfulness, the mother beseeched Here to bestow upon her sons the greatest of all blessings. When the two young men lay down to rest they never awoke. The Greek poet Menander coined the phrase *Whom the gods love dies young* from this story 125 years later. The proverb which celebrates the virtue and blissful reward of Cleobis and Biton spread throughout the ancient world.

In the centuries which passed before the benefits of present day medical understanding, early death was common and the proverb was a solace for grief. In 1553 Thomas Wilson published his ARTE OF RHETORIQUE in which he remodelled Menander's adage: *Whom God loueth best, those he taketh soonest*. Wilson's wording came to be used on many tombstones in all parts of the country. One such stone from Rainham churchyard in Kent, dated 1626, reads:

Here slepes my babe in silance, heauen's his rest,
For God takes soonest those he loueth best.

Another from Morwenstow in Cornwall runs:

Those whom God loves die young!
They see no evil days;
No falsehood taints their tongue,
No wickedness their ways.

Baptized, and so made sure
To win their blest abode,
What shall we pray for more?
They die and are with God.

The following delight comes from near Hartford, Connecticut:

Here lies two babies so dead as nits;
De Lord he kilt them with his ague fits.
When dey was too good to live mit me,
He took dem up to live mit He,
So he did.
(HARPER'S MAGAZINE, August 1856)

But the proverb seems to brush aside those who live to a good old age yet whose life is a rich source of blessing to those it touches. Are they less worthy than those plucked in their youth? Elbert Hubbard pondered the same question and found a true answer: *Whom the gods love die young, no matter how long they live* (EPIGRAMS. 'THE PHILISTINE', Vol xxiv, 1907).

■ You can't serve God and Mammon

You cannot seek to live a wholeheartedly godly life if you are trying to amass worldly riches

See also: No man can serve two masters; The love of money is the root of all evil

It was indeed a cause for rejoicing that in disposing of their personal enemies they had done an important service to the Church. They proved thus that it was in point of fact possible to serve God and Mammon.
(W Somerset Maugham, THEN AND NOW, 1946)

The boss's son is made to start, almost ostentatiously, at the bottom and is taught above everything else – since it serves Mammon and Demos equally well – to mingle.
(L Kronenberger, COMPANY MANNERS, 'THE DECLINE OF SENSIBILITY', 1954)

In his Sermon on the Mount, Jesus makes the point that it is impossible for someone to serve two masters, *for either he will hate the one, and love the other; or else he will hold to the one, and despise the other* (MATTHEW 6:24). Jesus, of course, had two particular masters in mind when he spoke. *Ye cannot,* he said, *serve God and mammon.*

The word 'mammon' is a transliteration of the Aramaic 'màmônâ', which means riches or gain. Jesus is saying that service to God cannot be wholehearted if a person is consumed with the idea of accumulating wealth; the two purposes conflict. Medieval writers make Mammon, imbued with the spirit of covetousness, as the chief of one of the nine orders of devils. Wynkyn de Worde speaks of *a deuyll named Mammona* (ORDYNARYE OF CHRISTEN MEN, 1502). In PARADISE LOST (1667)

Milton also personified Mammon as one of the main fallen angels:

Mammon led them on,
Mammon, the least erected Spirit that fell
From heav'n'; for even in heaven his looks and thoughts
Were always downward bent, admiring more
The riches of heaven's pavement, trodden gold,
Than aught divine and holy else enjoyed.

In the centuries which followed other writers have followed suit. The main personification today is Mammon, the god of Money and Money-making, with the religious overtones less prominent than in earlier centuries. It is particularly used in business, with a growing realisation that the raw pursuit of money is to the prejudice of other worthwhile moral and ethical values.

Godliness

■ **Cleanliness is next to godliness**

Keeping clean is of spiritual as well as practical value

Mrs Joe . . . had an exquisite art of making her cleanliness more uncomfortable and unacceptable than dirt itself. Cleanliness is next to Godliness, and some people do the same by their religion.
(Charles Dickens, GREAT EXPECTATIONS, 1861)

They say Cleanliness is next to Godliness, Mable. I say it's next to impossible.
(Edward Streeter, DERE MABLE, 1918)

Much importance was given to personal cleanliness in Middle Eastern countries. Herodotus, the Greek historian writing in the fifth century BC, informs us that it was the practice of Egyptian priests to bathe four times a day. He writes that the Egyptians *set cleanliness above seemliness.* The Jewish Talmud, a foundation upon which Jewish law rests, insists that every Jewish community should maintain a public bathhouse. The pursuit of cleanliness and hygiene became very much a cult of purity – incidentally ensuring a high standard of health. The Talmud explicitly links the physical to the spiritual:

'Cleanliness is next to godliness, ' it is said. Carefulness leads to cleanliness, cleanliness to purity, purity to humility, humility to saintliness, saintliness to fear of sin, fear of sin to holiness, and holiness to immortality.

And no excuses can be made for lapses in purity, for a Talmudic precept states: *Poverty comes from God, but not dirt.*

It is impossible to say exactly how or when the proverb arose from these beginnings but the notion that cleanliness and spirituality are linked was current in Christian thinking long before the early seventeenth century, as Francis Bacon tells us: *Cleanliness of body was ever deemed to proceed from a due reverence to God* (OF THE ADVANCEMENT OF LEARNING, 1605). According to Thomas Fuller, Sir Edward Coke concurred with this doctrine, so that he was very particular about his own personal cleanliness: . . . *and the jewel of his mind was put into a fair case, a beautiful body, with a comely countenance; a case which he did wipe and keep clean, delighting in good cloaths, well worne, and being wont to say, that the outward neatness of our bodies might be a monitor of purity to our souls* (THE WORTHIES OF ENGLAND, 1655).

In similar vein, the proverb itself was used by the great evangelical John Wesley to reinforce his message. Discussing the view that I PETER 3:3–4 teaches that one should not pay much attention to one's outward appearance but should concentrate on one's spiritual state, he comments:

Slovenliness is no part of religion; neither this, nor any text of Scripture, condemns neatness of apparel. Certainly this is a duty, not a sin; 'cleanliness is indeed next to godliness' (SERMONS: ON DRESS, c 1780).

In Victorian England keeping one's home clean was regarded as a moral duty which had to be performed before the Lord's Day. Cleanliness became so closely associated with purity that people assumed those who were known to live in sin would necessarily have filthy houses. In the diary written in the 1870s while he was vicar of Bredwardine, Francis Kilvert expresses his astonishment at the cleanliness of one such household.

But not everyone found absolute wisdom in the proverb. Mary Baker Eddy, founder of the Christian Scientist sect, did not like to take its injunction to extremes. In SCIENCE AND HEALTH (1875) she tried to loosen the bond between cleanliness and godliness, perhaps fearing that, on the one hand, people might imagine themselves spiritual simply by virtue of having a daily wash-down and, on the other, that they might do themselves irreparable harm by exposing their bodies to too much water: *Cleanliness is next to godliness; but washing should be only for the purpose of keeping the body clean, and this can be effected without scrubbing the whole surface daily. Water is not the natural habitat of humanity.* In these days of the daily, sometimes twice daily, bath or shower one wonders if Mrs Eddy's concern for our bodily welfare will be proved right.

Usage: The sanctimonious overtones probably result from its overuse in previous generations to keep in check children's natural tendency to get dirty! It is dated in all applications today. May be used for humorous effect.

Gold

■ **All that glitters is not gold**

Nothing should be judged by its external appearance. Superficial attractiveness does not necessarily denote solid worth

Variant: All is not gold that glitters

See also: Never judge by appearances; Appearances are deceptive

Black sheep dwell in every fold,
All that glitters is not gold;
Storks turn out to be but logs;
Bulls are but inflated frogs.
(Sir William Gilbert, HMS PINAFORE, 1878)

A story with a moral appended is like the bill of a mosquito. It bores you, and then injects a stinging drop to irritate your conscience. Therefore let us have the moral first and be done with it. All is not gold that glitters, but it is a wise child that keeps the stopper in his bottle of testing acid.
(O Henry, 'THE GOLD THAT GLITTERED', STRICTLY BUSINESS, 1910)

The early alchemists believed that any metal that could be made to look like gold, for instance, was thereby transformed into gold. For them all was gold that glittered.
(J Sullivan, THE LIMITATIONS OF SCIENCE, 1933)

I mean that all is not the gold that glitters. I mean that, though this lady is rich and beautiful and beloved, there is all the same something that is not right. And I know something else.
(Agatha Christie, DEATH ON THE NILE, 1937)

Many proverbs do not remain unique to any one language. This one is no exception. Real Eurospeak. It makes it difficult, even for experts, to be sure of the ultimate origin. Samuel Singer affirms a French origin, but Archer Taylor (1958, 1959) in two learned articles takes this very expression to show that it is extremely hard to establish the earliest written record and subsequent history of many phrases. We can, however, go back many centuries with some certainty.

Non teneas aurum totum quod splendet ut aurum,
Nec pulchrum pomum quodlibet esse bonum.
(Do not hold to be gold everything that shines like gold,
Nor every fine apple to be good.)

These words, recorded in the Winchester College Hall-book of 1401–2, are lines from the PARABOLAE of Alanus de Insulis, a French monk and poet writing in the twelfth century. The idea that outward appearance can be misleading was already an old one, having been thoroughly explored by the ancients: several of Aesop's fables are on the theme, including THE LEOPARD AND THE FOX (c 570 BC), which tells us that we should *look to the mind, and not to the outward appearance;* Diogenes of Sinope discovers *In an ivory scabbard a sword of lead* (c 400 BC); Livius Andronicus explains that *In noble trappings march ignoble men* (VIRGA, c 235 BC) and Petronius remarks that *He sees the copper under the silver* (SATYRICON, c AD 60).

Chaucer took inspiration from Alanus de Insulis for his Canterbury Tales. In THE CANON'S YEOMAN'S TALE (c 1386). He writes:

But al thing which that shyneth as the gold
Nis nat gold, as that I have herd it told;
Ne every appel that is fair at ye
Ne is nat good, what-so men clappe or crey.

It was not until David Garrick used the proverb in the Prologue to Goldsmith's play SHE STOOPS TO CONQUER in 1773 that the word 'glitters' entered the expression. Before then gold had 'shone', 'shown a goldish hue', 'shown bright', 'glowed', 'glistened' and 'glistered' but Garrick's version *All is not gold that glitters* fixed 'glitter' in the proverb, with the word order remaining flexible, as it still is today.

An Italian variant of this international proverb is particularly appealing: *Every glow-worm is not a fire.*

GOOD

■ **One good turn deserves another**

Kindness should be reciprocal; if someone does you a particular favour take the opportunity to repay it

See also: You scratch my back and I'll scratch yours

A Latin manuscript written around the turn of the fifteenth century is our earliest record of the proverb which is later cited in the same form by John Heywood: *One good tourne askth an other* (PROVERBS, 1546). Bishop Joseph Hall found that one good turn 'requires' another (CONTEMPLATIONS, 1622) but, by the first half of the seventeenth century, the proverb had settled into the present day form.

In English this notion of mutual help was expressed in other forms, too. From the sixteenth to the nineteenth centuries *giff-gaff*, meaning 'give and take', was used. It appeared in the proverbs *Giff-*

gaff was a good fellow and *Giff-gaff makes good friends. Giffe gaffe is one good turn for another,* says John Ray (ENGLISH PROVERBS, 1670).

Ka me, ka thee was another favourite of the same period, though this could refer not only to reciprocal help but also to flattery or even injury; paying back kind for kind as in *You scratch my back and I'll scratch yours.* 'If you'll be so kind to ka me one good turn, I'll be so courteous to kob you another,' write Dekker and Ford in THE WITCH OF EDMONTON (c 1623). But John Skelton refers to a man in a more suspicious frame of mind: *Yea, sayde the hostler, ka me, ka thee; yf she dooe hurte me, I wyll displease her* (WORKS, c 1568).

GOOSE

■ **What is sauce for the goose is sauce for the gander**

What is good enough for one person is good enough for another in similar circumstances

'Does that apply only to men?'
If you insist I'll admit that what is sauce for the gander is sauce for the goose. The only thing to be said against it is that with a man a passing connection of that sort has no emotional significance, while with a woman it has.
(W Somerset Maugham, THE RAZOR'S EDGE, 1944)

The transferring of more and more power over policy, regulation and service quality from local authorities to Westminster is a disease of governments long in office. John

Major's government . . . is gripped by this disease. Each year a group of London-based civil servants, ministers and computers must work out the spending needs of over 400 local authorities with a population of almost 50 million. They are a good deal less answerable for their decisions than locally elected leaders. These are precisely the grounds on which ministers have repeatedly opposed the transfer of powers from London to Brussels. Local authority capping is part of the same argument. Sauce for the goose . . .
(THE TIMES, 8 May 1992)

Not many chairmen are prepared to go as far as arriving on a bicycle or in a mini in order to convince staff that times are hard and wage rises out of the question. But plenty will leave the Rolls Royce at home and commute in a Jaguar four-litre or 3.2.

But the sauce for the head goose applies equally to senior and middle management ganders, and in the interest of the environment and company image everyone should be prepared to drive a smaller vehicle.
(DAILY TELEGRAPH, 27 May 1992)

The sixteenth century had a proverb *As well as for the coowe calf as for the bull.* The proverb of goose and gander is a variant first recorded by Ray in ENGLISH PROVERBS (1670). Ray calls it a 'woman's proverb' because it makes a plea for equality and fairness in the treatment of male and female alike. The recommended sauce is the same whether one is serving a goose or a gander for dinner. Perhaps the sauce our seventeenth century forebears had in mind was a gooseberry one. One

authority claims that gooseberries are so called because, centuries ago, their fruit went into a sauce that was enjoyed with roast goose. THE OXFORD DICTIONARY OF ENGLISH ETYMOLOGY allows that a derivation from 'goose' and 'berry' is a possibility, although it prefers an old French origin. Whatever the origin of the word, gooseberry sauce is still served with geese and ganders today, its sharp acidity cutting through the greasier taste of the meat.

Usage: The early context was of the relationship between men and women. This very quickly broadened to apply to an apparent imbalance in any sphere

GRASS

■ **The grass is always greener on the other side of the fence**

Said of people who are permanently dissatisfied, believing that others benefit from greater advantages than they do

Variant: The grass is always greener on the other side of the hill

See also: Forbidden fruit is the sweetest

I could go on to tell you more, especially about the appalling lack of equal opportunities for women . . . believe me, you have a great lifestyle in Britain, the grass really is greener, and I don't mean just on the hillsides.
(GOOD HOUSEKEEPING, May 1991)

I don't want to give the wrong impression here. Some of my best friends work . . . ;

some of my best friends don't. On the whole, they're all quite happy and wouldn't change places with one another. I obviously work myself, only because I do it from home, I can sit on the fence and study the view. And it seems to me from the fence whereon I sit, that the grass looks extremely green from both sides, and that the working mothers, given the chance . . . would just love to be on the home side at least some of the time.
(GOOD HOUSEKEEPING, October 1991)

The message of this novel is that everyone needs illusions: there is a better world out there where the grass is greener, and miracles do happen.
(GOOD HOUSEKEEPING, November 1991)

This is a recent expression, although the human condition it describes goes back to the beginning of time. What we cannot have has always had that extra spice of attraction. Certainly, Eve in the Garden of Eden wanted the fruit because it was forbidden. (See *Forbidden fruit is the sweetest.*) Similarly, what belongs to someone else or is difficult to reach has a peculiar fascination, as has been recorded down the centuries:

The apples on the other side of the wall are the sweetest.
(George Herbert, JACULA PRUDENTUM, 1640)

The fairest apple hangs on the highest bough.
(John Ray, SCOTTISH PROVERBS, 1678)

Today we look over the fence and into another man's garden or yard (the American version is *The grass is always greener in the next man's yard*) and

believe that what he has got is better than ours. Richard Armour's light verse *The other side of the fence*, plays for its effect on this truth:

My neighbor, Herbert, is so neat
His yard's the show place of our street.
His lawn is freshly trimmed and mowed,
He even sweeps his share of road.
No leaf has dropped but he has raked it,
No plant has drooped but he has staked it.
He digs and delves till late at night,
His garden is a lovely sight.
His thumb is green? Well, so is mine,
And if perchance you see no sign
Of cultivation in my yard,
I must admit (and this comes hard)
He has the kind you plant and glean with –
It's envy that my thumb is green with.

Others' possessions and skills may be enviable but not, perhaps, objectively desirable for, after all, as the American psychologist and marriage guidance counsellor, Dr James Dobson, put it: *The grass may seem greener on the other side but it still needs mowing.*

GREEKS

■ Beware of Greeks bearing gifts

When a kindness comes from a rival scrutinise his motives

Aunt Ursula knew Oswald well enough to be a little suspicious of his Greek gifts, but could not help being flattered by his attention.
(R Aldington, SOFT ANSWERS, 'YES AUNT', 1932)

Names on the map

The shires and towns of England have inspired numerous proverbs over the centuries. Many of them are no longer current but a study of them gives a fascinating glimpse into history.

Not surprisingly, a number of regional sayings comment on the agriculture or industry of an area. Beans were a crop that thrived on Leicestershire soil. Records from the fifteenth century state *Lesterschir, full of benys*. By the mid-seventeenth century this had become *Shake a Leicestershire man by the collar, and you shall hear the beans rattle in his belly*. In Shropshire the hiring of farm hands for the summer season often took place on May Day, giving rise to the proverb *May-day, pay-day, pack rags and go away*. In seventeenth-century Lincolnshire it was said that *Hogs shite sope and cows shite fire*, a reference to the fact that the poor of that county washed their clothes with pig dung and used dried cow-pats for fuel. (See *Where there's muck there's money*.) The town of Northampton was, and still is, well-known for its shoe making industry, which arose because the town was centrally placed and surrounded on all sides by fertile grazing land, so that leather was easily obtainable. In WORTHIES OF ENGLAND (1662) Thomas Fuller refers to the proverb *Northampton stands on other men's legs*, stating that it is the place where *the most and cheapest boots and stockings are bought in England*.

Some places were renowned for the excellence of their produce and others for their notoriety. Sutton was well-known for succulent mutton in the eighteenth and nineteenth centuries and Carshalton for beef. Other towns and villages in Surrey had a less salubrious reputation, which might surprise those who live in this prosperous part of London's commuter belt today. A proverbial jingle runs:

Sutton for mutton, Carshalton for beeves;
Epsom for whores, and Ewell for thieves.

Grose in his PROVINCIAL GLOSSARY (1787) explains it thus: *The downs near Sutton . . . produce delicate small sheep, and the rich meadows about Carshalton are remarkable for fattening oxen. Epsom . . . mineral waters . . . were . . . resorted to . . . particularly by ladies of easy virtue. Ewel is a poor village, about a mile from Epsom.*

The history behind other place proverbs can be somewhat grisly. A Cornish saying from the seventeenth century or earlier refers to the practice that coastal folk had of looting the wrecks of ships that foundered on the rocks: *O Master Vier, we cannot pay you your rent, for we had no grace of God this year; no shipwreck upon our coast.* While in neighbouring Devon it was proverbial that the river Dart, which was liable to swell suddenly, would claim at least one life every year: *River of Dart! O river of Dart! every year thou claimest a heart.* Devon seems to have a particularly watery reputation. An exposed stretch of its coastline is regarded as especially hazardous by sailors and fishermen alike, giving rise to the rhyme: *From Padstow Point to Lundy Light, is a watery grave from day to night.*

It is time, perhaps, to lift the spirits with some proverbial *Gloucestershire kindness,* an antidote for gloom and doom . . . until the realisation dawns that *Gloucestershire kindness* is the giving away of something that is no longer wanted or needed.

As it is, the Waleses are floating round the Ionian Sea in an ostentatious gin palace lent them by the mysterious Latsis. I am sure this Greek bearing gifts is doing so without an ulterior motive in his head, but it is a far cry from the Queen and her Hillman.
(DAILY TELEGRAPH, 12 August 1992)

Beware of scientists bearing beautiful mathematical models. They are not dangerous, but can be misleading unless they describe the real world.
(INDEPENDENT, 4 March 1993)

Are they ready for the Maastricht challenge yet in the Lords? During one late-night sitting in their Lordships' House last week, I am told a group congregated around a video screening of Sharon Stone revealing all in Basic Instinct in an office not unadjacent to the Chief Whip's. Recalcitrant peers considering rebelling over Maastricht should beware of Whips bearing ice picks!
(DAILY EXPRESS, 2 May 1993)

The proverb is a line from Virgil's AENEID (19 BC): *Timeo Danaos et dona ferentes* (I fear the Greeks even when they bring gifts). The reference is to the Trojan horse. The Greeks had lain siege to Troy for ten years in an effort to take back the beautiful Helen of Sparta, but the city was so well fortified that it withstood every assault. Then Odysseus thought of a plan. The Greeks constructed a huge wooden horse which they left outside the city gates before appearing to sail away. The Trojans took the horse to be a gift from the demoralised and vanquished Greeks and brought it into the city thinking it a good omen. But the horse contained soldiers who crept out under the cover of darkness to open the city gates. The Greek ships had returned at nightfall and, when the gates swung open, their troops laid the city waste. Aeneas was the only Trojan prince to escape and he became the founder of Rome.

In modern Britain, however, the eye of suspicion has ceased to fall upon Greek gifts, as an article in the EVENING STANDARD shows:

Will the Greeks set sail with their millions? If proposed new tax laws are passed, a flood of millionaire ship-owners could leave London – taking with them the riches and spending power that greatly benefit Britain. How likely is it, then, that these plutocratic foreigners with their old-fashioned ways will soon be loading their household icons on to tankers bound for Piraeus? Certainly it would be odd for the Government to ignore a handsome gesture like John Latsis's £2 million donation to Tory party funds. Nor is it likely that Mr Latsis is alone in giving so generously . . . 'Beware of Greeks bearing gifts', runs the old proverb. But as with so many proverbs, it is a case of easier said than done. When their gifts reach such colossal proportions, it seems an act of folly to show them the door.
(EVENING STANDARD, 20 October 1992)

What do these proverbs have in common?

- *Paddle your own canoe*
- *Don't kick a man when he's down*
- *It pays to advertise*

They are American in origin. A proverb scholar, Richard Jente, was able to demonstrate in an article of 1931 that only 8 out of 176 claimed coinings from the New World *were* of American origin. Since that time, the numbers have surely increased – see **Business Matters** (page 33) for some modern possibilities.

GRIST

■ **All is grist that comes to the mill**

Everything that comes one's way can be used profitably

See also: All is fish that comes to the net

Everything is transformed by his [the author's] power into material and by writing it he can overcome it. Everything is grist to his mill, from the glimpse of a face in the street to a war that convulses the civilized world, from the scent of a rose to the death of a friend.
(W Somerset Maugham, THE SUMMING UP, 1938)

M Janin had rushed, over-precipitately, to the attack. He didn't seem much

disappointed, however, to discover that this wasn't his legitimate prey. . . . Dutchman or German, it was all grist to the mill.
(Christopher Isherwood, MR NORRIS CHANGES TRAINS, 1938)

Grist was the corn that was brought to the wind or watermill to be ground. The miller needed regular supplies of grain to keep his millstones turning and his business profitable. In the sixteenth century, the idiomatic phrase *to bring grist to the mill* meant 'to turn to advantage': *There is no lykelihoode that those thinges will bring gryst to the mill.* (Golding, CALVIN ON DEUTERONYMY, 1583). The proverb *All's grist that comes to the mill* came into use later in varied forms, with the meaning that everything could be put to use profitably for good or ill: *Your stumble, your fall, your misfortune . . . all is grist to the mill of the mean-minded man* (Alexander Whyte, BIBLE CHARACTERS, 1896).

Usage: These days the proverb is often used to express gratitude for offers of help in the sense of *Every little helps.*

HANDSOME

■ **Handsome is as handsome does**

The mark of a good character is deeds not looks

Variant: Handsome is that handsome does

See also: Actions speak louder than words; Beauty is only skin deep

Miss Trottwood, or Miss Betsey, . . . had been married to a husband younger than herself, who was very handsome, except in the sense of the homely adage, 'handsome is, that handsome does' – for he was strongly suspected of having beaten Miss Betsey, and even of having once, on a disputed question of supplies, made some hasty but determined arrangements to throw her out of a two pair of stairs' window.
(Charles Dickens, DAVID COPPERFIELD, 1849)

'Such a handsome young man.'
   'Handsome is as handsome does. Much too fond of poking fun at people. And a lot of going on with girls, I expect.'
(Agatha Christie, A MURDER IS ANNOUNCED, 1950)

'Handsome is as handsome does,' my father was rather given to saying . . . Handsome is handsome it seemed to me, and still does, straight up and no messing.
(GOOD HOUSEKEEPING, November 1992)

The earliest known formulation is in Chaucer's CANTERBURY TALES: *He is gentil that dooth gentil deedis.* (THE WIFE OF BATH'S TALE, c 1386). The reference is to the polished bearing of a gentleman. *Goodly is he that goodly dooth* is quoted as an *auncient adage* by Anthony Munday in SUNDRY EXAMPLES (1580). In the sixteenth century the adjective 'goodly' meant 'fair and well-proportioned', in other words 'handsome'. 'Goodly' as an adverb meant 'kindly and graciously', a meaning which 'handsome' can also have. The proverb *He is handsome that handsome doth* which John Ray included in his ENGLISH PROVERBS (1670) is, therefore, a variant of this earlier expression and teaches that good looks alone are a bad guide to someone's character. Courteous, kindly and generous behaviour is the hallmark of a handsome nature.

In the nineteenth century, as 'handsome' came to be an adjective more applicable to a man than a woman, an attempt was made to adapt the expression for feminine charms. *Pretty is as pretty does* is quoted by T C Haliburton in his collection of WISE SAWS (1854). It did not catch on. But then women had a similar proverb to contend with already: *Beauty is only skin deep.*
(See **Alcott's moral tales**, page 233)

HANG

- **Give a man enough rope and he'll hang himself**

Permit someone enough freedom and he will eventually bring about his own undoing

Variant: Give a thief enough rope and he'll hang himself

[Within] the next 24 hours, you can anticipate an eye-ball to eye-ball discussion or, more truly, a head-on collision over certain topics. It may again fall upon you to take the accommodating stance – if only to give the other person enough rope to strangle themselves.
(TODAY, 3 March 1993)

The proverb was coined centuries ago when a more brutal attitude towards crime and punishment prevailed. Bartlett traces the saying in literature to the French satirist Rabelais who, speaking of critics, wrote: *Go hang yourselves; you shall never want rope enough* (PANTAGRUEL, 1532). The earliest known record in English was in Fuller's HOLY WAR (1639). The variant *Give a thief enough rope and he'll hang himself*, which is still in popular use today, was recorded by John Ray in his ENGLISH PROVERBS of 1678. It refers to the fact that hanging was the sentence for theft. (See also *You might as well be hanged for a sheep as for a lamb*.)

HARE

■ **First catch your hare**

Plan prudently and do not assume success before it has been confirmed

See also: Don't count your chickens before they are hatched; Don't halloo till you are out of the wood

'To seize wherever I should light upon him –'
'First catch your hare!' . . . exclaimed his *Royal Highness.*
(William Thackeray, ROSE AND RING, 1855)

First shoot your dog then freeze it.
(Advertisement for Sony camcorders, SUNDAY TIMES, 22 November 1992)

First catch your war criminals
Sir: With regard to Bosnian war crimes trials, . . . the criminality is in general evident. Jurisdiction exists. A tribunal may be set up. But first catch your criminal. The Nuremberg and Tokyo trials were possible because there had been a war and total surrender. Not so in this case.
(INDEPENDENT, 4 March 1993)

An old proverb recorded by Bracton in DE LEGIBUS ET CONSUETUDINIBUS ANGLIAE (c 1250) gave similar advice: *It is a common saying that it is best first to catch the stag, and afterwards, when he has been caught, to skin him.* The proverbs are culinary ones. Until the hare or stag has been caught, preparations to skin, cook and eat it are useless.

The year 1747 saw the publication of two cookery books, both containing tasty recipes for hare, both reputedly with a form of the proverb. La Varenne in LE CUISINIER FRANÇAIS offered a hare stew: *Pour faire un civet, prenez un lièvre* (To make a ragout, first catch a hare).

But the proverb is more commonly attributed to Mrs Hannah Glasse in THE ART OF COOKERY MADE PLAIN AND EASY. George Brimley, for example, writing in 1853, says that Mrs Glasse's first instruction in the recipe for hare soup was *first catch your hare*. However, a correspondent in the DAILY NEWS of 20 July 1896 refuted that she had ever written such a thing: *The familiar words, 'First catch your hare', were never to be found in Mrs Glasse's famous volume. What she really said was, 'Take your hare when it is cased, and make a pudding.'*

Proverbs drive you crazy

Idioms are in part defined by having a literal as well as a figurative sense. You can, for example, *spill the beans* by knocking over a can of them or by divulging a secret to others. Some proverbs have a similar dual level of interpretation, a phenomenon which has not escaped psychologists and psychiatrists. In fact it has formed the basis for a series of tests to evaluate mental health. A particularly striking case of this is *Two heads are better than one*, which has been written up in an article by Edward Lehman, appropriately entitled 'The Monster Test' (ARCHIVES OF GENERAL PSYCHIATRY, 1960). When patients aged between six and sixteen were asked to draw a picture interpreting this proverb, some 60 per cent of psychotic children drew various types of two-headed monsters. Their work showed an inability to abstract and see beyond the literal. There has been a considerable subsequent debate in the profession between those who bring forward experimental evidence in support of Lehman's conclusions and those who point to the poor reliability of proverb tests. There exists a large bibliography of articles on the subject.

'Cased' means 'skinned'. Therefore the common ascription of the proverb to Mrs Glasse is quite wrong. Interestingly, the book itself may not be hers, either. Dr John Hill was said to be the real author of THE ART OF COOKERY, to which was added in later editions the name Mrs Glass (not Mrs Glasse).

HAY

■ **Make hay while the sun shines**

Take immediate advantage of an opportunity

See also: Never put off till tomorrow what you can do today; Strike while the iron's hot; Gather ye rosebuds while ye may; Take time by the forelock

The next morning Walter proved at once that he meant to make hay while the sun shone. Charles went across to the kitchen for his breakfast at half-past seven, and already he could see the stocky, overall-clad figure at work.
(John Wain, HURRY ON DOWN, 1953)

We've orders pouring in, just pouring. But, mind you, Smeeth, we've got to get a move on. We've got to pile up the orders now — make hay while the sun shines.
(J B Priestley, ANGEL PAVEMENT, 1930)

It is not surprising that agricultural themes are evident in the vast stock of English proverbs for, until the boom in manufacturing industry, Britain was an agricultural economy and reliant upon the weather. If the hay were ready and the weather good, workers would put in extra hours to bring it in. In a changeable climate the next day might bring heavy rain and the crop be lost with serious implications for the winter ahead. As Barclay wrote in SHIP OF FOOLS (1509):

Who that in July whyle Phebus is shynynge
About his hay is nat besy labourynge . . .
Shall in the wynter his negligence bewayle.

The Anglican archbishop of Dublin, Richard Chenevix Trench, was also a noted philologist and poet. He commented on the very Englishness of the proverb: *Make hay while the sun shines, is truly English, and could have had its birth only under such variable skies as ours* (ON THE LESSONS IN PROVERBS, 1853). This certainly captures a popular perception. However, later philologists did not necessarily agree with him. Richard Jente demonstrated in 1937 that probably the expression reached English (its first recorded use is in John Heywood's PROVERBS of 1546) via a Latin translation of DAS NARRENSCHIFF (1494) by German satirist Sebastian Brant. Variable skies are not an exclusively English prerogative!

HEADS

■ **Two heads are better than one**

It is helpful to have a second person's opinion or advice

Two heads are better than one when deciding what to buy and how much to pay;
they are very much better than one when it comes to justifying your purchases and their prices to a critical audience when you get them home.
(E O Shebbeare, SOONDAR MOONI, 1958)

Very good. We just wanted a bit of confirmation on that there point. Two witnesses are better than one. That'll do. Now, just run along and – see here – don't you get shooting your mouth off.
(Dorothy L Sayers, BUSMAN'S HONEYMOON, 1937)

On Channel 4's Countdown, the celebrity guest and the representative from the Oxford Dictionary nearly always manage to find longer words than the contestants. Do they have a computer under their desk?

'No they don't,' a spokesperson told us, 'but they have other advantages over the contestants. For a start, two heads are better than one – and they do have a dictionary in front of them!'
(WHAT'S ON TV, 20 March 1993)

Two have more wit than one wrote John Gower in CONFESSIO AMANTIS (c 1390). Here 'wit' is to be understood in its old sense of 'reasoning'. *Two wits are (far) better than one* was a common form of the proverb until at least the end of the sixteenth century.

John Heywood records *Two heddis are better then one* in his PROVERBS (1546). It was a slight variant on the other form but, by the seventeenth century had superceded it.

HEART

■ **Cold hands, warm heart**

Icy fingers are a sign of ready affection

Years ago it was considered that a person whose hands were habitually cold was shown thereby to be a person of warm heart. In Derbyshire villages, for example, cold hands indicated not just warmth of heart but were a sure sign of fidelity. If her young man remarked to a girl that her hand was cold, she would reply that it showed her heart was warm and true.

■ **Faint heart ne'er won fair lady**

Courage and enterprise are needed to gain the affections of a girl

See also: Nothing ventured, nothing gained

This proverb is common to other European languages. The French say *Le couard n'aura belle amie* (The coward will not win a fair lady) and Cervantes quotes the Spanish equivalent in DON QUIXOTE (1615), calling it an 'old saying'. The earliest known record of the proverb in English is in John Gower's CONFESSIO AMANTIS (c 1390) where the reference is not to a lady but to a castle:

Bot as men sein, wher herte is failed,
Ther schal no castell ben assailed.

Subsequent uses of the proverb speak of 'fair ladies' but John Lyly in EUPHUES AND HIS ENGLAND (1580) combines the two, perhaps showing that, for a time, both were current: *Faint hart Philautus, neither winneth Castell nor Lady.* And in 1605 William Camden uses the saying in its present day form: *'Faint heart neuer wonne fair lady* (REMAINS).

Possibly the proverb goes back to feudal times when great landowners ruled and protected their vast estates from fortified castles. These castles housed retainers, fighting men pledged to their lord. Ambitious lords might extend their power and influence by laying siege to fortresses and usurping their weaker neighbours. For this a ruthless, not a faint heart, was required. Similar qualities were required, it seems, on the battlefields of the heart.

Medieval times also saw the rise of the French cult of courtly love. This ritualised form of courtship was confined to the aristocracy and had its roots in the adoration of the Virgin, whose perfection was seen reflected in woman. Courtly love was governed by strict rules of conduct in which earthly love was honoured with all the rites accorded to divine love. In France, it was an extramarital platonic relationship, where marriage was usually nothing more than a business contract. In English literature courtly love was seen more as a courtship ritual leading to marriage. A suitor needed courage to approach a lady who had become the subject of his adoration; to be scorned and rejected was the ultimate humiliation.

Usage: Often used to challenge the inhibitions of a shy suitor

HELL

■ **Hell hath no fury like a woman scorned**

When rejected by a man, a woman is ferociously hostile towards him

Variant: Hell has no fury like a woman scorned

See also: Revenge is sweet

The scorned wife of a baronet took amazing revenge on her wayward husband – by playing milkman with his finest vintage wine. . . Sarah, 54, told how she went on her giveaway trip with over 70 bottles of vintage red from Sir Peter's cellar. . . Lady Moon, who calls her 17-stone husband Hippo, added: 'Hell hath no fury like a middle-aged woman scorned . . . '
(DAILY MIRROR, 27 May 1992)

PARIS PUTS THE BOOT IN
Hell hath no fury like a scorned Parisienne shop assistant. 'She's a tall woman, with fairly large feet,' remarked the Chanel boutique shoe manageress when the Princess of Wales left, purchase-less after 15 toe-squeezing minutes.
(DAILY EXPRESS, 6 May 1993)

There seems to be remarkable unanimity down the ages (amongst male writers at least) that the anger of a woman who has been scorned or jilted is uniquely virulent. The Latin proverb has it that *When injured, women are generally implacable.* In English there are various similar comments before the first one in 1696 (by Cibber in LOVE'S LAST SHIFT) that introduces 'hell': *We shall find no fiend in hell can match the fury of a disappointed woman, – scorned, slighted, dismissed without a parting pang.*

Just one year later, in Congreve's THE MOURNING BRIDE, there is the couplet that experts consider the main source:

Heav'n has no rage, like love to hatred turn'd,
Nor Hell a fury like a woman scorn'd.

Surprisingly, the precise formulation that is used today is not recorded till the middle of the twentieth century.

Usage: When the traditional form with 'hath' is used (quite frequently), it gives the impression of a rather self-conscious quotation

■ **The road to hell is paved with good intentions**

Unless good intentions are translated into action they are useless and will never be counted to one's credit

They [those chapters] also contain, by way of warning, descriptions of the way things ought not to be done – recipes for not realizing the ends one professes to desire, recipes for stultifying idealism, recipes for paving hell with good intentions.
(Aldous Huxley, ENDS AND MEANS, 1937)

According to a letter written by St Francis de Sales to Madame de Chantal (1605), the origin of the proverb is to be found in some words of St Bernard of Clairvaux. (See *Love me, love my dog.*) The letter reads: *Do not be troubled by St Bernard's saying that hell is full of good intentions and desires.* St Bernard's comment was well known to seventeenth century writers both in England and abroad. Frequent use in Christian sermons and writings brought it to popular notice. Thomas Adams, in one of his sermons (1629), writes: *One said, that hell is like to be full of good purposes, but heaven of good works.* George Herbert expresses the thought as *Hell is full of good meanings and wishings* (JACULA PRUDENTUM, 1640).

In LIFE OF SAMUEL JOHNSON (14 April 1775) James Boswell gives the form *Hell is paved with good intentions* as one of Johnson's sayings: *No saint . . . was more sensible of the unhappy failure of pious resolves than Johnson. He said one day, . . . 'Sir, hell is paved with good intentions.'* This turn of phrase may have been new to Boswell's ears but it was not Johnson's inspiration. This reworking of St Bernard's thought had been previously used by John Wesley (JOURNAL, 10 July 1736) and he refers to it as a 'true saying'.

The modern form, *The road to hell is paved with good intentions,* changes the proverb yet again. Perhaps John Ruskin was responsible for this. In ETHICS OF DUST (1866) he writes: *Their best intentions merely make the road smooth for them . . . You can't pave the bottomless pit; but you may the road to it.*

HELP

■ **Every little helps**

Every contribution, no matter how small, swells the total

See also: Look after the pennies and the pounds will look after themselves

London is set for a saleroom popfest with the auction of 1,200 lots of memorabilia stardusted by contact with the chart-toppers. The £1m at stake might seem hardly worth the bother when compared with the £2 billion combined drop in turnover at Sotheby's and Christie's during the last 12 months, brought on by recession, war and deflation of the art balloon. Every little helps, however, as the lady at Christie's South Kensington said when she catalogued a tiny corner of toasted Mother's Pride, snatched from the jaws of a Beatle. (SUNDAY TIMES, 11 August 1991)

. . . his initiative means that Britain's trade balance is £30,000 to the good. That may be a drop in the ocean when set against a projected current account deficit of £18.7 billion for 1993. But every little helps. (DAILY EXPRESS, 28 April 1993)

An amusing quotation from Gabriel Meurier's TRÉSOR DES SENTENCES (1590) uses and illustrates the proverb at the same time:

Every little helps, said the ant, weeing in the sea at the height of midday.

Nevertheless the proverb did not come into English until the late eighteenth century.

There is, however, an old financial expression which means the same: *Many a small makes a great* or *Many a little makes a mickle*, 'mickle' being an Old English word for 'a large amount'. Early written references to this go back to the turn of the thirteenth century but the proverb reflects ideas expressed in ancient Greek and Latin texts.

Usage: Usually refers to financial matters but can be applied to other contexts.

HOME

■ **An Englishman's home is his castle**

An Englishman's home is a private place; no one has the right to enter without his agreement

Variant: An Englishman's house is his castle

In the siege of Dordogne, an Englishman's flat is his chateau.
(SUNDAY TIMES, 11 August 1991)

Squatters who broke into a property left to me by my mother caused so much damage that the prospective buyers have pulled out and I am left with a property that is not fit to live in. Who said an Englishman's home was his castle?
(DAILY EXPRESS, 24 September 1991)

An Englishman's home is not only his castle. It is usually his single biggest investment – and a benchmark for his personal worth and significance in life.
(WEST SUSSEX GAZETTE, 3 December 1992)

An Englishman's home is his castle. How safe is yours?
(LEAFLET FOR PREMIUM SECURITY, 1992)

The Englishman's unsaleable home is no longer his castle. It is a dungeon. When the housing market peaked in 1988, there were 2.14m transactions. Last year, there were just 1.14m. I am one of the trapped million. Will my new-born daughter, Persephone, ever experience the wide open spaces of a semi?
(SUNDAY TIMES, 28 February 1993)

Ray defines this expression as *a kind of law proverb* (ENGLISH PROVERBS, 1670). For many centuries the law of the land has said, it is believed, that every Englishman should have the right to absolute freedom within his own house and that no bailiff has the power to infringe this right. A man's home is therefore likened to a castle; a place where he is protected and secure. Staunforde expresses this right in 1567 and Lambard in 1588. The English jurist, Sir Edward Coke, who rose to chief justice of the King's Bench and privy counsellor under James I, fiercely defended the common law even, when necessary, against the attempts of the king himself to change it by authority of divine right. In his summary of Semayne's case he writes: *The house of everyone is to him as his castle and fortress, as well for his defence against injury and violence as for his repose.*

And in the third of his INSTITUTES (influential early textbooks on modern common law, written between 1628 and 1644) he says: *A man's house is his castle, et domus sua cuique tutissimum refugium.* This Latin phrase is quoted from the Roman statement of law, the PANDECTS (II, iv, 18), on which Staunforde, Lambard and Coke rest their assertions of the principle that it is the law, not the massive walls of a castle, that give a man security.

It is not a long step from legal definitions and maxims to a proverb. By Shakespeare's day there are already recorded half a dozen instances of the phrase's use, and from that time on they have proliferated. In a detailed study, Archer Taylor (1965) points out the developing applications of the phrase from Thomas Fuller (1642) to Jack Kerouac (1957). Fuller in his SERMONS goes beyond a strictly legal context and presses man to make his conscience his castle. Kerouac in ON THE ROAD turns the proverb into a description of domestic rather than legal freedom:

Now you see, man, there's real woman for you. Never a harsh word, never a complaint, or modified [sic]; her old man can come in any hour of the night with anybody and have talks in the kitchen and drink the beer and leave any old time. This is a man, and that's his castle. He pointed up at the tenement.

The form of the proverb as well as its contexts of use also changed over the centuries. *A man's house* became *An Englishman's house.* Pitt is reported to have used it as early as 1763 in the House of Commons, but the first written use is in James and Horace Smith's HORACE IN LONDON (1813):

An Englishman's house was his castle till now,
But castles are now and then taken.

Since the 1920s, the variant *An Englishman's home . . .* has crept in, such that today it is the predominant form.

The bad news, however, is that the inviolable Englishman's home is today a myth. One MP calculated that there are as many as 300 categories of public officials who have rights of entry. The slightly better news is that many of these are exactly the same person, but wearing a different hat. Also, in a number of cases, warrants must be obtained first and twenty-four hours' notice given. But there still remains a daunting list of callers that cannot long be kept at bay: the police, gas, water and electricity services, Customs men, VAT and tax officers, and so on. The proverb's claims are a long way wide of the reality.

■ **Home is where the heart is**

Home will always hold one's affections no matter where one may wander

Home is definitely where the heart is in Howard's End . . . Nowhere is Ruth Wilcox happier than in her house in the country, but when she leaves it to her unconventional, cultured friend Margaret Schlegel in her will, the eminently conventional, prosperous Wilcoxes unite to deny her dying wish.
(GOOD HOUSEKEEPING, May 1992)

But have we really lost out? The brain drain should not be regarded as Britain's loss, more as a compliment . . . Once we accept this then the rest will follow. And we can

still take the credit, even if it's not happening back home. Because home is where the heart is.
(DAILY EXPRESS, 24 February 1993)

WHEN HOME IS WHERE THE WORK IS
Anoop Parikh finds out how a landing and a spare bedroom were transformed into nice little earners for their owners.
(WEEKEND TELEGRAPH, 30 May 1992)

The ancients, Plutarch and Cicero amongst them, were wont to write tenderly of home and some authorities consider that this proverb was coined by Pliny. It receives scant attention in English literature, however, until as late as the twentieth century. It does not figure in Walsh's comprehensive entry on proverbs of the home in his HANDY-BOOK OF LITERARY CURIOSITIES of 1892, where one might certainly expect to find it if it were current; the first recorded reference is in Elbert Hubbard's A THOUSAND AND ONE EPIGRAMS of 1914.

Usage: It has a rather sentimental tone

■ **Home, sweet home**

There is nowhere better than the central place of family living, where you find ease, relaxation and identity

See also: There's no place like home

'After my work in the city,' remarks Mr Charles Pooter in Grossmiths' The Diary Of A Nobody, *'I like to be at home. What's the good of a home if you are never in it? "Home Sweet Home", that's my motto.'*
(GOOD HOUSEKEEPING, September 1991)

Home sweet home: The picturesque cottage that you could win
(Photo caption, DAILY MAIL, 25 May 1993)

The expression is first found as the title of a very famous song of John Howard Payne (see *There's no place like home*). It quickly gained international acclaim and recognition. Intriguingly, its author's immediate circumstances were very different from the romantic, emotional image conjured up by the song. Payne writes:

How often have I been in the heart of Paris, Berlin, London, or some other city, and have heard persons singing or heard organs playing 'Home, Sweet Home', without having a shilling to buy myself the next meal or a place to lay my head! The world has literally sung my song till every heart is familiar with its melody, yet I have been a wanderer from my boyhood, and, in my old age, have to submit to humiliation for my bread.

In fact Payne's later career was quite prosperous and successful.

The proverb itself struck a chord in the nineteenth century heart. Along with religious messages, letters of the alphabet and flowers, it is found widely on the needlework samplers of the period. Moral mottoes were part of the skilled handwork that graced the walls of Pennsylvania and New England and of England itself in the Victorian age.

Usage: Can be rather cloyingly sentimental and for that reason should perhaps be avoided. Often said on return home after a trying or tiring time away

■ There's no place like home

Only in one's own home can one feel deep and warm contentment

See also: Home, sweet home

From the Black Baptist Church where his inaugural day began, they were as at ease as the evening before – being never so humble in their new hometown.
(DAILY MAIL, 21 January 1993)

The proverb as we know it today comes from 'Home Sweet Home', a well-known song from the musical play CLARI, THE MAID OF MILAN, which was first performed at Covent Garden in 1823. John Howard Payne, a young American struggling unsuccessfully to make a living in the London theatre, wrote the words, setting them to a tune he overheard being played through a window as he walked by:

Mid pleasures and palaces though we may roam,
Be it ever so humble, there's no place like home!
A charm from the skies seems to hallow us there,
Which, seek through the world, ne'er is met with elsewhere.

An exile from home, splendor dazzles in vain,
Oh, give me my lowly thatched cottage again;
The birds singing gayly, that came at my call,
Give me them, and that peace of mind dearer than all.

But Payne's own inspiration is a re-working of an old well-used proverb: *Home is home (though it be never so homely),* and even the title of the song may have been borrowed from Sir John Harrington's translation of Ariosto's ORLANDO FURIOSO (1591): *For home though homely twere, yet it is sweet.*

The Victorians were very fond of Payne's song which expressed their ideal of hearth, home and family values. Nevertheless, *There's no place like home* did not immediately supplant the old proverb for in DOMBEY AND SON (1848) Dickens still clings to the old adage: *The saying is, that home is home, be it never so homely.* The sense here of *homely* is 'ordinary, simple, unadorned', a sense which is still current in American English today, particularly in the context of plain, not very good-looking women.

The song brought Payne from poverty and obscurity (he was imprisoned for debt in 1820 during his time in London) to recognition and comfort. He collaborated with Washington Irving and for thirty years had a good career as author and adapter of plays. In 1842 he was appointed American Consul in Tunis, where some ten years later he died. Thirty years on, Mr Corocoran of Washington applied to bring his remains back to his home country. As Payne was reinterred at Oak Hill Cemetery, Washington, a thousand mourners sang 'Home Sweet Home'.

HOMER

■ **Even Homer sometimes nods**

Even the most gifted are not at their best all the time

Variant: Even Homer nods

See also: To err is human, to forgive divine

You have to accept the crochets of an author of great parts. Homer sometimes nods and Shakespeare can write passages of empty rhetoric.
(W Somerset Maugham, BOOKS AND YOU, 1940)

A letter may have gone wrong. Depend upon it, that is what has happened. The Post Office is a wonderful institution, but even Homer nods. I am sure you will find Mr Noakes at Broxford safe and sound.
(Dorothy L Sayers, BUSMAN'S HONEYMOON, 1937)

Even the great Greek epic poet, Homer, could not sustain his brilliance at all times. Horace in DE ARTE POETICA (c 20 BC) defends the master's lapses thus: *I, too, am indignant when the worthy Homer nods, but in a long work it is allowable to snatch a little sleep.* Before long *Even Homer sometimes nods* had captured popular imagination and become a common saying. References to it have been found in English literature from the sixteenth century.

Usage: Literary and rather dated

HONESTY

■ **Honesty is the best policy**

Truthfulness and square-dealing are sound foundations for living

I am afraid we must make the world honest before we can honestly say to our children that honesty is the best policy.
(George Bernard Shaw, RADIO ADDRESS, 11 July 1932)

ARIES (Caroline Bone, Robert Snell, Helen Archer): You have a tendency to be a little too frank when dealing with some people. Now although I agree that honesty is the best policy, there are ways and means. So make your 1992 resolution to think before you speak.
(AMBRIDGE VILLAGE VOICE, LAMBING ISSUE, Spring 1992)

Aesop's fable THE WOODMAN AND THE AXE (c 570 BC) tells of a woodcutter who was working beside a river when he lost his axe in the water. The distressed man was sitting on the river bank in tears when Mercury appeared and, upon hearing the sorry tale, dived into the river and brought out a gold axe. Asked if it was his, the woodman said it was not. Diving again Mercury reappeared with a silver axe, but again the man said that it was not his. When Mercury plunged into the river a third time, he brought up an iron axe which the woodcutter claimed as his. Impressed by the man's honesty, Mercury gave him not only his own axe but the other two as well.

On hearing of the woodcutter's remarkable experience, one of his friends went off and tossed his own axe into the river. Again Mercury appeared and, responding to the man's tearfulness, plunged into the river bringing up a golden axe. As soon as he saw it the man, in great excitement, claimed it as his own but Mercury, offended by his base dishonesty, threw the golden prize back into the water and went away without even bothering to retrieve the man's own axe.

The earliest known written appearance of the proverb in English is in Edwin Sandy's EUROPAE SPECULUM of 1599. From the middle of the following century it was commonly used. The saying translates directly into a number of other European languages. Cervantes, for instance, uses it in the second part of DON QUIXOTE (1615).

There is the question whether one should adopt honesty for its own sake, as a moral universal, or whether adopting it as a *best policy* simply turns it into a matter of self-serving expediency. Some would go even further. Honesty may generally be considered to be the best policy, but is it always politic? Washington Irving thinks not: *I am of the opinion that, as to nations, the old maxim that 'honesty is the best policy' is a sheer and ruinous mistake* (KICKERBOCKER HISTORY OF NEW YORK, 1809). *Realpolitik,* it seems, tempers the more wholehearted endorsement given to the proverb in earlier centuries, turning an absolute into a relative mistake.

HONOUR

■ **There is honour among thieves**

Lawbreakers subscribe to a code of practice amongst themselves

See also: Dog does not eat dog

Cicero remarked that even thieves, who did not observe the laws of the land, had a code of their own to live by. The code revolved around loyalty towards others in the underworld. Publilius Syrus summarised it with more than a hint of approval when he wrote that *Even in crime loyalty is rightly displayed* (SENTENTIAE, c 43 BC). Shakespeare took up the theme. When the companions who were to have helped him stage a highway robbery prove unreliable Falstaff is tempted to abandon dishonesty, declaring *A plague on it when thieves cannot be true one to another* (HENRY THE FOURTH, PART ONE, Act 2, scene ii, 1597).

Essayist William Hazlitt attempts to define the nature of that honour:

Their honour consists in the division of the booty, not in the mode of acquiring: they do not (often) betray one another; they may be depended on in giving the alarm when any of their posts are in danger of being surprised; and they will stand together for their ill-gotten gains to the last drop of their blood
(TABLE TALK, 1821)

Many British novelists have drawn attention to the thieves' pact – Defoe, Scott and Dickens among them – and those who enjoy some kinds of modern crime fiction will know that today's thief is as honour-bound as any in ancient Rome. More realistic contemporary writing is, however, brutal in its depiction of when thieves fall out: gangster warfare, Mafia vendettas, triad feuds, etc. Honour among thieves, it seems, is in short supply.

Usage: The expression has a rather dated, Dickensian ring

HOPE

■ **Hope springs eternal in the human breast**

To have optimistic expectations for the future is part of man's nature

See also: Every cloud has a silver lining; Tomorrow is another day; The darkest hour is that before the dawn

The fellow who said hope springs eternal in the human breast should have started probing under my vest next morning.
(R L Gouldman, MURDER BEHIND THE MIKE, 1941)

Despite the legions of female fans and a succession of sexy co-stars, John is still looking for his own leading lady. 'We all hope to meet someone to share our lives with – hope springs eternal!' he sighs.
(INSIDE TV, December 1992)

The proverb is from Pope's ESSAY ON MAN (1732). The poet says that man never experiences complete happiness but is always looking forward to a brighter future:

Hope springs eternal in the human breast:
Man never is, but always to be, blest.
The soul, uneasy and confin'd from home,
Rests and expatiates in a life to come.

Pope may well have been familiar with some famous earlier expressions of a similar theme. Pascal in his PENSÉES (1670) wrote: *Thus we never live, but we hope to live; and always disposing ourselves to be happy, it is inevitable that we never become so.*

Pope, a Roman Catholic, may also have known the work of another French preacher, Massillon, who wrote in his Sermon for St Benedict's Day: *We never enjoy, we always hope.*

A source and influence closer to home was Dryden. His play AURENGZEBE was first performed in 1675. It contains the following lines:

When I consider life, 'tis all a cheat.
Yet, fool'd with hope, men favour the deceit;
Trust on and think to-morrow will repay.
To-morrow's falser than the former day;
Lies worse, and while it says we shall be blest
With some new joys, cuts off what we possest.
Strange cozenage! none would live past years again,
Yet all hope pleasure in what yet remain,
And from the dregs of life think to receive
What the first sprightly running could not give.

HORSE

■ **All lay loads on a willing horse**

Everyone takes advantage of the person who never says 'no'

He was . . . the 'willing horse' upon whom every one of the many duties . . . were laid.
(THE TIMES, 24 April 1926)

The proverb was first recorded early in the seventeenth century and is a variant of a slightly earlier one, *Folke call on the horse that will cary alwey* (John Heywood, PROVERBS, 1546). In past centuries merchandise was transported by teams of pack-horses, these animals being strong and able to negotiate uneven roads and rough, narrow tracks. Naturally any horse which had a docile and willing temperament would be picked to bear the extra load, leaving its mettlesome or stubborn companions to carry the lighter burden.

■ **Don't change horses in mid-stream**

If you must change your mind, choose your moment well; don't change direction or tactics in the middle of a difficult undertaking

Variant: Don't swap horses while crossing a stream

If James were allowed time to introduce enough Irish, he might again trust to the loyalty of his regiments; but meanwhile the morale of his army was in dire confusion. He was swapping horses in midstream, and the Revolution was deliberately timed to catch him in the act.
(G M Trevelyan, THE ENGLISH REVOLUTION, 1938)

The sentence given above, for example, would nowadays often be written: 'not letting a person be aware wherein they had offended.' From the point of view of strict old-fashioned grammar, this is obviously bad; it involves a change from the singular to the plural horse in mid-stream.
(H S Davies, GRAMMAR WITHOUT TEARS, 1951)

By far the safest way to change one's horse, if it is really necessary, is to dismount first. To swap horses while crossing a stream is difficult and hazardous.

The proverb owes its popularity to U S president Abraham Lincoln. Dissatisfaction with Lincoln's handling of the American Civil War mounted until calls came for a change in the presidency. In spite of this the National Union League decided to support his renomination. Lincoln thought it best to accept and, in a reply to the League delivered on 9 June 1864, gave his reasons for doing so:

I do not allow myself to suppose that either the convention or the League have concluded to decide that I am either the greatest or best man in America, but rather they have concluded that it is not best to swap horses while crossing the river, and have further concluded that I am not so poor a horse that they might not make a botch of it in trying to swap.

An alternative version of the same address credits an old Dutch farmer with putting the saying into Lincoln's repertoire.

■ Don't shut the stable door after the horse has bolted

It is no good taking precautionary measures to prevent something unpleasant happening after the event

The horse having apparently bolted, I shall be glad to assist at the ceremony of closing the stable door.
(Ngaio Marsh, DEATH OF A PEER, 1940)

It is simply there to lock a stable door that bureaucrats in Brussels left open in 1968.
(BBC Radio 4, YOU AND YOURS, 23 October 1991)

But didn't all that extra-marital sex irretrievably damage their marriage? Yes it did. But the relationship wasn't on solid ground so the damage involved is difficult to assess. Sex has always been an interest of mine and I had no intention of getting monogamously involved with someone who'd already said they weren't in love with me. It was like trying to take out the insurance before the horse has bolted.
(DAILY MAIL, 14 January 1993)

The Dutchman was exposed, rapidly, as just another eunuch in the heavyweight harem . . . Boxing needed an illustration of the qualities that have made Bruno an authentic folk-hero to raise its tone . . . The British Board, in insisting yesterday that any future opponent will be scrutinised more closely, were merely closing the stable door with a flourish, long after the horse had bolted.
(DAILY TELEGRAPH, 22 November 1991)

This proverb exists in many European languages. The earliest record is in a French text dating back to the late twelfth century. It does not appear in English literature until the middle of the fourteenth century. Early uses of the proverb speak of shutting the stable door after the horse is 'lost' or, more frequently, 'stolen'. 'Bolted' is a twentieth century variant.

Stevenson quotes a quaint alternative from the pen of Thomas Fuller. In WORTHIES: CHESTER (1662) Fuller writes: *When the daughter is stolen, shut Peppergate,* and explains that when the daughter of the mayor of Chester eloped she slipped through Pepper-gate, an obscure side-entrance set in the city wall, whereupon the sorrowful mayor had the gateway blocked up.

Another French proverb with the same message is *After death, the doctor.*

■ Never look a gift horse in the mouth

Don't find fault with something which has been offered as a present

Variant: Don't look a gift horse in the mouth

See also: Beggars can't be choosers

'How good of you!' exclaimed Isabel overwhelmed by the dedication. Then she took thought and at the risk of seeming to look the gift-horse in the mouth, she said: 'But how are we your benefactors?'
(L P Hartley, A PERFECT WOMAN, 1955)

'. . . people who have known me for a long time, and have known of the situation and of Soon-Yi, have said to me take Soon-Yi and run. They say, you're a lucky guy, she's delighted and happy, and you guys have terrific times together. Don't look a gift horse in the mouth.'
(GUARDIAN, 8 June 1993)

The proverb rebukes those rude and ungrateful people who insist on inspecting the gifts they receive and finding fault with their quality. When some of St Jerome's writings met with unkind criticism he chastised his critics, saying that they should *never inspect the teeth of a gift horse.* The carping was uncalled for since the writings had been offered out of generosity of spirit. But perhaps his critics deserve a modicum of sympathy; apparently the scholarly saint had a reputation for being somewhat prickly and cantankerous.

Jerome's use of the expression at the turn of the fifth century may be the earliest record we have but the saint himself refers to it as a common proverb, so its history obviously goes back even further. Nor is it confined to English; the expression can be translated directly into many European languages. Italian has both this proverb and a variant *Don't worry about the colour of a gift horse.*

Never look a gift horse in the mouth alludes to the fact that a horse's age can be assessed by the number and condition of its teeth. From the time a horse's permanent teeth have all come through at about five years old, its molars are gradually being worn down until, in a very old horse, the roots are almost at the surface and some teeth may be lost altogether. The front incisors appear longer with age and protrude further to the front. A glance in the horse's mouth, therefore, would quickly determine whether the animal were a young steed or an old nag. One favourite trick amongst unscrupulous horse dealers was to file down the teeth to make the horse look young. From the eighteenth century this practice was known as bishoping.

A good reason for accepting a horse given as a gift is that it brings with it good luck and healing. At least, so many have believed. In Yorkshire burying a horse alive was a cure for disease. In Ireland, on a horse's death its feet and legs were hung up in the house and even its hoofs held sacred. And most widespread of all these ancient superstitions is the power for good luck and protection of the horseshoe.

All in all, it was a hard-headed character who would turn down the many beneficent associations attached to the horse and subject a gift to too stringent scrutiny.

■ **You can take a horse to water, but you can't make him drink**

You can create opportunities for a person but you can't force him to accept them

Variant: You can lead/bring a horse to water, but you can't make him drink

Well, the next thing was that Fabio should be induced to select her. It had been a matter of bringing the horse to water and making him drink. Oh a most difficult and delicate business! For Fabio prided himself on his

independence; and he was obstinate, like a mule.

(Aldous Huxley, LITTLE MEXICAN, 1957)

Well, you can bring an ass to the water, but you cannot make him drink. The world was the water and Egbert was the ass. And he wasn't having any.

(D H Lawrence, ENGLAND MY ENGLAND, 1922)

The proverb, which speaks of taking the working horse to the trough or stream for refreshment, was included in John Heywood's PROVERBS (1546). This proverb is sometimes found with the variants *but twenty cannot make him drink* (Samuel Johnson) or *a thousand cannot make him drink* (Trollope).

Samuel Johnson made a pertinent use of the proverb in his conversation with Boswell. Boswell was concerned that his father intended him to become a lawyer, to which Johnson replied, *Sir, you need not be afraid of his forcing you to be a laborious practising lawyer; that is not in his power. As the proverb says, 'One man may lead a horse to water, but twenty cannot make him drink'* (Boswell, LIFE OF JOHNSON, 14 July 1763).

More recently, a well-known roadside restaurant chain proposed offering healthier meals as well as the usual burgers and other fast food. Asked if there would be sufficient demand the spokeswoman pointed out, *You can take a consumer to his salad but you can't necessarily make him eat* (BBC Radio 4, WOMAN'S HOUR, 7 January 1993).

HOUR

■ **The darkest hour is that before the dawn**

When circumstances could not be worse a turn for the better will not be long in coming

Variant: The darkest hour is (just) before dawn

As so often happens in the story of England's struggles in India, the darkest hour proved to be that just before the dawn. (Justin McCarthy, HISTORY OF OUR OWN TIMES, 1900)

The blackest hour, claims the proverb, is the one before even the faintest traces of the coming dawn can be discerned. Figuratively, someone in pain will find the last dark hour before relief comes darkest of all. The meaning of the proverb is that when things come to the worst they will mend.

An early record in English literature comes in Thomas Fuller's A PISGAH-SIGHT OF PALESTINE (1650): *It is always darkest just before the day dawneth.*

Of course, the practical difficulty is to know whether the uttering of the constant refrains *Things can't get any worse* and *Things can only get better* really is at the very last hour before dawn. Maybe it's still a little earlier in the night. In any event, the proverb seems to capture the universal sense of *hope that springs eternal in the human breast.* It is found in several synonymous phrases in English, and in various other languages, as this list from Walsh shows:

*When things are at their worst, they soonest
mend
When bale is highest, boot is nighest
The longest day will have an end
After a storm comes a calm
By dint of going wrong all will come right*
(French)
Ill is the eve of well (Italian)
*It is at the narrowest part of the defile that
the valley begins to open* (Persian)
*When the tale of bricks is doubled, Moses
comes* (Hebrew)

HOUSE

■ **A house divided against itself cannot
stand**

Any unit suffering from internal
dissension will not be able to resist
external pressures

See also: United we stand, divided we
fall

*The sister kingdoms of the north – Arabia,
Persia, Ferghana, Turkestan – stretched out
their hands . . . and greeted ridiculous
Chandrapore, where every street and house
was divided against itself, and told her that
she was a continent and a unity.*
(E M Forster, A PASSAGE TO INDIA, 1924)

*It was easy for Claverhouse and his
dragoons to keep down a country thus
divided against itself, so long as there was
no revolution in England.*
(G M Trevelyan, HISTORY OF ENGLAND,
1926)

*Whether this Danegeld would really allow
BA to finish the affair is debatable. The BA
board appears to be deeply divided and, if a
house divided itself [sic] cannot stand, an
airline has no chance.*
(DAILY TELEGRAPH, 19 January 1993)

The origin of the proverb is biblical.
Jesus had healed many people, several
of them possessed by spirits. The stir
that this was causing irritated the
religious authorities. The scribes came
down from Jerusalem and accused Jesus
of being possessed by Satan and of
using satanic power to cast demons out
of others. Jesus pointed out that their
argument was illogical saying: *How can
Satan cast out Satan? And if a kingdom be
divided against itself, that kingdom cannot
stand. And if a house be divided against
itself, that house cannot stand. And if Satan
rise up against himself, and be divided, he
cannot stand, but hath an end* (MARK
3:23–26)

But the argument was not new, even
then. The idea of division causing
weakness had been put forward by
Aesop centuries earlier in THE BUNDLE
OF STICKS (c 570 BC).

■ **People who live in glass houses
shouldn't throw stones**

Beware of criticising someone if you
yourself are vulnerable to the same
criticism

See also: The pot calls the kettle black

Originally the proverb warned against
throwing stones at one's adversary if

one had a glass head. In TROILUS AND CRISEYDE (c 1374) Chaucer writes:

And forthy, who that hath a head of verre,
From cast of stones wave him in the werre.

This saying, which has a Spanish equivalent, was in use up to the end of the eighteenth century. The proverb *People who live in glass houses shouldn't throw stones* is a variant of this earlier expression and was probably invented in the sixteenth century, although some credit James I with the first use. It was coined at a time when the use of glass in domestic architecture was increasing. Glass production had fallen into decline after the Romans and, apart from Venetian glass, which was discovered as an art form in the twelfth century, and stained glass for ecclesiastical purposes, it did not really pick up again until the late 1400s. Even the rougher bluish more utilitarian glass that was produced was not to be taken for granted. In Tudor England glazed windows were still a luxury that only the nobility could afford, poorer people having to content themselves with windows of horn, simple wooden shutters or hovels with no windows at all. Thomas More appreciated the difference glazed windows made and longed for good airy housing for all citizens. In Amaurote, the main city of the fabulous Utopia, all the houses enjoyed this benefit:

But nowe the houses be curiouslye buylded
after a gorgious and gallante sorte, with
three storyes one over another . . . They kepe
the winde oute of their windowes with

glasse, for it is ther much used, and som here
also with fine linnen cloth dipped in oyle or
ambre . . . For by thys meanes more lighte
commeth in, and the winde is better kepte
oute.
(UTOPIA, 1516)

Even in Elizabethan England when the yeomanry eventually began to aspire to glazed windows, they were still regarded as a luxury. The wills of John Tyther of Shropshire and John Butler of Surrey, both yeomen, include their glass windows among other personal effects. A person with the good fortune to live in a glazed house would be foolish indeed if he chose stones as a weapon with which to fight his neighbour.

A story is told that the Duke of Buckingham, favourite of James I of England (James VI of Scotland), mounted a campaign of harassment against some prominent Scotsmen which included hiring mobs to smash their windows. Buckingham's own London residence was popularly called the 'Glass House' because it had a great number of windows. Not surprisingly, it was not long before his victims retaliated in kind. When Buckingham complained to the king, His Majesty simply replied, 'Steenie, Steenie, those who live in glass houses should be carefu' how they fling stanes.'

IGNORANCE

■ Ignorance is bliss

Upsetting news cannot dim your happiness while you remain ignorant of it

Variant: Where ignorance is bliss, 'tis folly to be wise

See also: What the eye doesn't see, the heart doesn't grieve over

Jennie remained blissfully ignorant of his illness and did not even see the heavy-typed headlines of the announcement of his death until Bass came home that evening.
'Look here, Jennie,' he said excitedly, 'Brander's dead!'
(Theodore Dreiser, JENNIE GERHARDT, 1911)

Leave her in ignorance. Ignorance is bliss.
(Tennessee Williams, THE ROSE TATTOO, 1951)

WHEN IGNORANCE IS SHEER BLISS
The tell-tale alloy stains down the mast should have given us a clue but I wrongly diagnosed this as movement in the lower kicker strut attachment. They say ignorance is bliss: the worry and fear after that discovery was greater than any concern in the race to date.
(THE TIMES, 7 January 1993)

Do people really want to see what their favourite characters look like?
That was the warning I received when I told colleagues I'd be working on the Addicts' National Tour.

Ignorance is bliss, or so it seemed.
(AMBRIDGE VILLAGE VOICE, LAMBING ISSUE, February 1993)

Sophocles, writing at the end of the fifth century BC, recognised that a total, cabbage-like ignorance is 'the sweetest life'. From this arose two cognate sayings in classical Latin, which Erasmus in his ADAGIA (1536) rendered as *To know nothing is the happiest life.* Thomas Gray reworked the thought in ODE ON A DISTANT PROSPECT OF ETON COLLEGE (1742), where the poet, looking out over a view of the famous public school, muses in a melancholy way upon the difficulties the future must necessarily hold for its pupils:

Alas! regardless of their doom
The little victims play!
No sense have they of ills to come
Nor care beyond the day. . .
Yet, ah! why should they know their fate,
Since sorrow never comes too late,
And happiness too swiftly flies?
Thought would destroy their paradise!
No more; – where ignorance is bliss,
'Tis folly to be wise.

The last lines rapidly acquired proverbial status, to be regularly quoted in full up to the present day. The saying has also a common abbreviated form *Ignorance is bliss* and has given rise to two idiomatic forms: *blissful ignorance* and *blessed ignorance.*

IMITATION

- **Imitation is the sincerest form of flattery**

Copying someone or something pays an implicit and genuine compliment to that person or thing

They say that imitation is the sincerest form of flattery, but in the magazine world it can also be the quickest route to redundancy. The danger for Blitz in growing up with its readers was always that they might find the same sustenance outside our pages.
(GUARDIAN, 9 September 1991)

Readers loved the fact that editorial was uninterrupted. And the celebrities fell in love with it, too. A star in Hello! can be assured of acres of colour photographs and an interview technique so anodyne it has become a cult. This is the recipe OK! is following, but can it work a second time? OK!'s editor . . . concedes that imitation is the sincerest form of flattery.
(DAILY EXPRESS, 23 March 1993)

Charles Caleb Colton is most famous for his collecting of aphorisms. An early instance of this saying is in Volume 1 of his LACON (1820), where he records the elliptical *Imitation is the sincerest of flattery*. Later addition of the word 'form', to produce the contemporary phrasing, makes the expression clearer.

IRON

- **Strike while the iron's hot**

Make the most of an opportunity, act when circumstances are favourable

See also: Take time by the forelock; Make hay while the sun shines; Never put off till tomorrow what you can do today

When Ashley, striking while the iron was hot, rose in the Commons a month later to introduce a Bill excluding all women and girls from the pits and boys under thirteen, he found himself almost a national hero.
(A Bryant, ENGLISH SAGA, 1940)

Striking while the iron was hot, I reminded them that my means of livelihood had been scattered to atoms by that blasted dog, old Bell, and ventured to say that if another musical instrument weren't forthcoming I'd be on the parish, willy-nilly.
(Eden Phillpotts, WIDECOMBE FAIR, 1913)

The origin of the expression is concerned with the practices of the blacksmith in his smithy. This is acknowledged in the earliest recorded use (c 43 BC) of the Latin proverb in Publilius Syrus's SENTENTIAE *(You should hammer your iron when it is glowing hot)*; Heywood confirms it: *And one good lesson to this purpose I pike/From the smithis forge, whan thyron is hot strike* (PROVERBS, 1546), while Caxton informs us that *Whan the yron is well hoote, hit werketh the better* (THE FOURE SONNES OF AYMON, c 1489).

Chaucer used the proverb back in the fourteenth century in a wider context, urging us to strike while the iron is hot when relationships are at stake: *Right so as whyl that iren is hoot, men sholden smyte, right so, men sholde wreken hir wronges whyle that they been fresshe and newe* (TALE OF MELIBEUS, c 1386).

Since then the saying has developed in meaning and form. It has been applied very generally to any situation where quick action is needed to take advantage of an opportunity; by the second half of the sixteenth century it appeared in the words we know today.

JACK

■ **All work and no play makes Jack a dull boy**

Time for recreation is essential to make a balanced and interesting person

See also: Variety is the spice of life

Life was not all work and no play. True enough, the times when the backwoodsman could play were few and far between, but they did come. The cornhusking frolic was one of these occasions.
(L Huberman, WE, THE PEOPLE, 1932)

There is a number of proverbs about Jack. Jack was 'everyman', 'the man in the street' in past centuries, the equivalent of the present day Joe Bloggs. Other languages have characters who represent the typical man – French has Gros Jean and American John Doe. Other proverbs about Jack include *Jack of all trades is master of none* and *Every Jack must have his Jill.*

An early record of *All work and no play*

makes Jack a dull boy comes in James Howell's ENGLISH PROVERBS (1659). Samuel Smiles shows us the other side of the coin: *All work and no play makes Jack a dull boy; but all play and no work makes him something greatly worse* (SELF-HELP, 1859).

■ **Every Jack has his Jill**

There is a partner in life for everybody

See also: Marriages are made in heaven

Every Jack has his Jill;
If one won't, the other will.
(H W Thompson, BODY, BOOTS AND BRITCHES, 1940)

Everybody enjoys a love story with a happy ending. The Tudor public were no exception. The sixteenth century version of boy meets girl was Jack meets Jill. In Shakespeare's A MIDSUMMER NIGHT'S DREAM (1590), Puck endeavours to undo all the mischief he has wrought and declares:

Jack shall have Jill;
Nought shall go ill;
The man shall have his mare again, and all shall be well.

By the early seventeenth century the proverb in the form we know it had been coined. It is used today to reassure someone who is vainly searching for a life partner that there is someone for everyone. Some people, however, can undo the comfort they offer at a stroke. As Whyte-Melville wrote: *Every Jack has his Gill, if he and she can only find each other out at the propitious moment* (GENERAL BOUNCE, 1855).

■ **Jack of all trades is master of none**

To have a superficial knowledge of many skills means no real skill in any area

Variant: Jack of all trades is of no trade; Jack of all trades, master of none; Jack of all trades and master of none

The term *Jack of all trades*, to describe someone who dabbles in many skills but has no real knowledge of any, has been current since the beginning of the seventeenth century. The first recorded use of the fuller proverbial form *Jack of all trades and master of none* was in Maria Edgeworth's POPULAR TALES (1800). It echoes the French proverb which states that *When one is good at everything, one is good at nothing.* Trench quotes a graphic German proverb: *The master of one trade will support a wife and seven children: the master of seven trades will not support himself.*

There are always people who will make wide-ranging claims for themselves, yet the evidence contradicts them. The spelling and grammar (or 'gramer') of Roger Giles make one wonder about his many other claimed accomplishments in this eighteenth century handbill quoted by Walsh:

Roger Giles, Imperceptible Penetrator, Surgin, Paroch Clarke, &c., Romford, Essex, hinforms Ladis and Gentlemen that he cuts their teeth and draws corns without waiten a moment. Blisturs on the lowest turms, and fysics at a penny a peace. Sells god-fathers cordial and strap-ile, and undertakes to keep a Ladis nales by the year and so on. Young Ladis and Gentlemen tort the heart of rideing, and the gramer language in the natest manner, also grate Kare takein to himprove there morals and spelling, sarm singin and whisseling. Teaches the jewsarp, and instructs young Ladis on the gar-tar, and plays the ho-boy. Shotish, poker and all the other ruls tort at home and abroad. Perfumery in all its branches. Sells all sorts stashionary, barth bricks and all other sorts of sweet-meats, including beeswax postage stamps and lusifers; likewise taturs, roobub, sossages and other garden stuffs, also fruits, such as hard bake, inguns, toothpicks, ile and tinware, and other eatables. Sarve, treacle, winegar, and all other hardware. Further in particular he has laid in a stock of tripe, china, epsom salts, lollipops and other pickels, such as oysters, apples and table beer, also silk, satin and hearthstones, and all kinds of kimistry, including wax-dolls, rasors, dutch cloks, and gridirons, and new laid eggs evry day by me, Roger Giles.
P.S. – I lectures in joggrefy.

Usage: The expression is not always derogatory; in the right context and tone it could be used in the frequent short form *Jack of all trades* of someone who impresses by his range of skills.

JOB

■ **If a job's worth doing, it's worth doing well**

If you think a task merits your attention, then you should do it to the best of your ability

The proverbial cynic

Several writers have taken the sound, usually wholesome and helpful advice of the proverb and given it a cynical and witty turn. In San Francisco in 1904 Ethel Watts Mumford, Oliver Herford and Addison Mizner published THE ENTIRELY NEW CYNIC'S CALENDAR OF REVISED WISDOM for 1905. A few extracts:

January
- *Knowledge is power – if you know it about the right person*
- *Tell the truth and shame the – family*
- *The wages of Gin is Debt*

February
- *Actresses will happen in the best regulated families*
- *Too many hooks spoil the cloth*

March
- *He who owes nothing fears nothing*
- *Money makes the Mayor go*
- *There's a Pen for the wise, but alas! no Pound for the foolish*

April
- *Wild oats make a bad autumn crop*
- *He that is down need not fear plucking*

May
- *Don't take the Will for the Deed – get the Deed*
- *Nothing succeeds like – failure*
- *Charity is the sterilized milk of human kindness*

June
- *The gossip is not always of the swift, nor the tattle of the wrong*
- *Advice to Parents – 'Cast not your girls before swains'*

July
- *Only the young die good*
- *THE DOCTOR'S MOTTO – A fee in the hand is worth two in the book*
- *The wisest reflections are but Vanity*

August
- *The more taste, the less creed*
- *The danger lies not in the big ears of little pitchers, but in the large mouths*

September
- *He who fights and runs away*
  Will live to write about the fray
- *A gentle lie turneth away inquiry*

October
- *Never too old to yearn*
- *The pension is mightier than the sword*

November
- *A fellow failing makes us wondrous unkind*
- *Society covers a multitude of sins*
- *All is not bold that titters*

December
- *THE STEAMER'S MOTTO – You can't eat your cake and have it too*
- *The more waist the less speed*

There is a galaxy of writers whose fame rests on their satirical and acerbic view of life: Fred Allen, Russell Baker, Ambrose Bierce, Gordon Bowker, Leonard Louis Levinson, H L Mencken, Dorothy Parker, E B White and others. In German, Gerhard Uhlenbruck's writings are in the same tradition. In amongst their definitions, quips and witticisms are many based on proverbs. That most prolix of authors, Anon, also has a few mordant messages to his credit, as have some lesser luminaries:

- *A travesty is imitation without flattery*
- *Silence is not always golden. Sometimes it's just plain yellow*
- *Opportunity is something that goes without saying*
- *Home is an Englishman's castle while his wife is at the pictures*
- *Home is a place where you can scratch any place you itch* (Henry Ainsley)
- *Tomorrow is one of the greatest labour-saving inventions of today* (Vincent T Foss)
- *Tomorrow is always the busiest day of the week* (Richard Willis)

Variant: What is worth doing at all, is worth doing well

If a thing's worth doing, it's worth doing late.
(Frederick Oliver)

If a job's worth doing, it's worth doing well. There are a great many jobs which are clearly worth doing, but can be perfectly well botched, or at the very least rushed through. This extends to most household tasks . . . and a good few culinary ones (why anyone should skin, peel and chop tomatoes when they can open a tin is beyond me).
(GOOD HOUSEKEEPING, November, 1992)

If a thing is worth doing, it is worth doing badly. This paradox of G K Chesterton comes to the rescue of the perfectionist intimidated by that word 'well'. If a thing is worth doing, better by far to have a go at it and risk an unsuccessful outcome than not to bother at all.

The proverb itself is reported to have been the favourite motto of Charles Dickens. In the Preface to LETTERS OF CHARLES DICKENS (1893) the people who should know – his sister-in-law and eldest daughter – tell us: *Dickens would take as much pains about the hanging of a picture. . . as . . . about the more serious business of his life; thus carrying out . . . his favourite motto of 'What is worth doing at all is worth doing well'.*

The saying, however, predates the nineteenth century; Lord Chesterfield used it in one of his letters (10 March 1746).

KITCHEN

■ **If you can't stand the heat, get out of the kitchen**

If the pressure is too much for you to bear, get away from it

Not only does medical school not teach them to cope with the stresses and learning difficulties inherent in the work, it actually makes them worse. . . . They come in with a healthy approach. Within weeks they realise that the pressure is such that they must either get down to it or get out. The attitude they get from most of their teachers is 'If you can't stand the heat, get out of the kitchen.'
(GUARDIAN, 4 October 1991)

Planning is hard enough for the year about to start. Mr Lamont has told us what he plans for the year after that, which is really tempting providence. By the time the heat gets too much, he may have left the greenhouse.
(DAILY TELEGRAPH, 17 March 1993)

This expression was coined in the 1950s by US President Truman who used it on a number of occasions in both spoken and written contexts. In his book MR CITIZEN (1960) he writes: *Some men can make decisions and some cannot. Some men fret and delay under criticism. I used to have a saying that applies here, and I note that some people have picked it up.* It may be that the expression was simply picked up and popularised by Truman. TIME magazine of 28 April 1952, according to one contemporary authority, has Truman, quoting Major General Harry Vaughan, use the saying to explain his own forthcoming retirement.

KNOWLEDGE

■ **Knowledge is power**

The more we know, the stronger the influence we can exercise on others

The story of acquiring knowledge, especially forbidden or illicit knowledge, is ages old. In the account of the Garden of Eden, begun in GENESIS 2, God commanded Adam not to eat of the tree of the knowledge of good and evil. The serpent's crafty sales pitch, designed to persuade Eve into eating the tree's fruit, was based on the knowledge she would gain and on its benefits in making her god-like: *And the serpent said unto the woman, Ye shall not surely die; For God doth know that in the day ye eat thereof, then your eyes shall be opened, and ye shall be as God, knowing good and evil* (GENESIS 3:4–5). What an inducement – the omnipotent power of being God as just one benefit of knowledge!

In England, Francis Bacon was well aware of the biblical dimension of knowledge and power: *The desire of power in excess caused the angels to fall: the desire of knowledge in excess caused man to fall* (ESSAYS: OF GOODNESS, 1612). In NOVUM ORGANUM (1620) he expressed the ancient relationship between knowledge and power thus: *Knowledge and human power are synonymous.* And again in MEDITATIONES SACRAE: DE HAERESIBUS (c 1626): *Knowledge itself is power.* Bacon's near contemporary, Hobbes, developed his own view. In his LEVIATHAN (1651), for example, Hobbes entitles Chapter 10 *Of Power, Worth, Dignity, Honour and Worthiness* and argues the case for a rather worldly-wise view of power. The same thread of self-interest and misuse of power runs through succeeding centuries – for example, Ethel Watts Mumford (see **The proverbial cynic**, page 146) said: *Knowledge is power, if you know it about the right person* (1904). A recent instance is this hard, epigrammatic statement from Stanley I Benn: *The more one knows about a person, the greater one's power to destroy him.* Rabelais (c 1495–1553) was much closer to the perspective of the Garden of Eden, however: *Knowledge without conscience is the ruination of the soul.*

LATE

■ **Better late than never**

It is better to turn up (or present a piece of work) after the agreed time than not to bother at all

Oh, Mr Dexter, we have been so anxious, but better late than never. Let me introduce you to Miss Wilbraham and Gräfin von Meyersdorf.
(Graham Greene, THE THIRD MAN, 1950)

I'm sick of these disgusting women I've spent my life with, if you'll forgive my mentioning them, and I'm rather anxious to settle down. A bit late in the day, perhaps, but better late than never.
(George Orwell, A CLERGYMAN'S DAUGHTER, 1935)

Proverbial wallpaper

Graffiti and proverbs have a good deal in common. The relationship between them has even been the subject of academic papers. Suffice it to say that both represent the wit and wisdom of the people, and that graffiti artists often use a well-known proverb as their starting point. But the theorising spoils the fun – here are some to enjoy:

- *Laugh and the world laughs with you. Snore and you sleep alone*
- *Laugh – and the world thinks you're an idiot*
- *He who laughs last doesn't get the joke*
- *A friend in need is a bloody pest!*
- *Give a man enough hope and he'll hang himself*
- *Happiness can't buy money*
- *Everyman reaps what he sows – except the amateur gardener*
- *He who finds fault in his friends has faulty friends*
- *Where there's a will – there's a greedy solicitor getting in on the act*
- *Where there's a will, there's an inheritance tax*
- *All that glitters isn't gold. All that doesn't glitter isn't either*
- *Money is the root of all evil – and a man needs roots!*
- *The money that men make lives after them*
- *He who ploughs a straight furrow is in a rut*
- *Constipation is the thief of time. Diarrhoea waits for no man*
- *All's fear in love and war*
- *Beneath a rough exterior often beats a harlot of gold*
- *Chaste makes waste*
- *Familiarity breeds*
- *The devil finds work for idle glands*
- *'Tis better to have loved and lust,*
  Than never to have lust at all
- *Two's company, three's an orgy*
- *It takes two to tangle*
- *If at first you don't succeed, try a little ardour*
- *A bird in the bed is worth two in the bushes*

Perhaps one should conclude with the old English proverb that *A wall is a fool's paper.*

We have long argued that the Government was misguided in aiming its AIDS warnings at the whole population. Yesterday Health Secretary Virginia Bottomley announced that future publicity would be directed towards the high-risk groups – homosexuals and drug users. Better late than never. It is good to see she has finally taken that message on board.
(DAILY EXPRESS, 4 May 1993)

Bartlett traces the proverb to a Latin expression used by Livy in his HISTORY (c 10 BC). The saying is found in the devotional manual ANCREN RIWLE (c 1200) and the DOUCE MANUSCRIPT (c 1350), as well as in Chaucer's CANTERBURY TALES (c 1386).

thought itself the equal of America and Russia in the war against Germany. Europe has waited longer than it expected for the last laugh.
(SUNDAY TIMES, 17 January 1993)

Sir Walter Scott, writing in PEVERIL OF THE PEAK (1823), calls this a French proverb. It is, in fact, also found in Italian. An early English record of use is in John Vanbrugh's play THE COUNTRY HOUSE of 1706.

The variant He who laughs last laughs longest was coined this century and is even more difficult to say than the original. The idiomatic expression to have the last laugh is based on the proverb.

LAUGH

■ **He laughs best who laughs last**

Don't rejoice too soon. Premature delight at success may turn to disappointment

Variant: He who laughs last laughs longest

He who laughs, lasts.
(Mary Pettibone Poole, A GLASS EYE AT THE KEYHOLE)

A hundred years ago, the clever people in Britain were of two sorts. The radicals, brought up on Richard Cobden, knew the future was going to be American anyway. The conservatives, having read John Seeley, were concerned to put a Greater Britain and its empire together to face America and Russia. A mere 50 years ago, Britain still

LEARNING

■ **A little learning is a dangerous thing**

Relying on a shallow understanding of a topic where deeper knowledge is called for will lead to problems

Variant: A little knowledge is a dangerous thing

A LITTLE LEARNING . . . AND OTHER DANGEROUS THINGS
Miranda brought home more paintings of which she is hugely proud. More colours, more curves, but still all squashed into one extremity of the paper. I began to worry. Could it be her eyesight? Perhaps one side of her body or brain was not functioning. Worse, I've read about children's artwork revealing deep psychological distress . . .

Next day . . . I popped inside [the new playgroup] for a visit . . . Miranda rushed *into a painting overall and straight up to an easel. Tiny as she is, she had to stretch up on tiptoes to reach . . . There was a great deal of paint on the overall and the easel, but only a few of the confident curves made it to the paper . . .*

So much for my little bit of knowledge – a dangerous thing. Still, I expect that like most parents I'm on one of those learning curves, too.
(FAMILY CIRCLE, February 1988)

Home checkup kits are also becoming commonplace, but be careful; a little knowledge can be a dangerous thing. If in doubt, consult your dentist.
(GOOD HOUSEKEEPING, November 1991)

The proverb is a line from Alexander Pope's ESSAY ON CRITICISM (1711):

A little learning is a dang'rous thing;
Drink deep, or taste not the Pierian spring:
There shallow draughts intoxicate the brain,
And drinking largely sobers us again.

The poem expounds the principles of literary taste and style and discusses the rules governing literary criticism. Pope's views follow neoclassical lines, hence the reference to the Pierian spring, the dwelling place of the nine Muses, the goddesses who inspire learning and the arts.

These days the line is quoted widely to refer to any sphere of knowledge where shallow understanding might lead one into difficulties. This is in keeping with earlier expressions of the same thought. Bacon, for example, suggests that *A little philosophy inclineth man's mind to atheism, but depth in philosophy bringeth men's minds about to*

religion (OF ATHEISM, 1598), and Donne formulates the general meaning in a way that might well have become a proverb itself: *Who are a little wise the best fools be* (TRIPLE FOOL, 1633)

LEAVE

■ **Leave well alone**

Don't disturb or try to improve a situation which is acceptable as it is

Variants: Let well alone; Leave well enough alone

See also: Let sleeping dogs lie; If it isn't broken, don't mend it

When she asked him squarely if he meant to request another [dance] from the Countess, he said no, positively. He knew when to let well alone, a knowledge which is more precious than a knowledge of geography.
(Arnold Bennett, THE CARD, 1911)

It's for Holly to let him know about that chap. If she doesn't, it means she doesn't want him told, and I should be sneaking. Anyway, I've stopped it. I'd better leave well alone!
(John Galsworthy, IN CHANCERY, 1920)

Plutarch in his MORALIA: OLD MAN IN PUBLIC AFFAIRS (c AD 95) reminds us of a fable by Aesop which illustrates the proverb well. A hedgehog offered to remove the ticks from the coat of a fox but the fox refused the offer, reasoning that if he removed the well-fed ticks from her back their places would simply be taken up by hungry ones.

Let well alone was quoted as a saying by Terence as early as the second century BC. References to the ancient proverb are found in English from Chaucer's ENVOY TO BUKTON (c 1386) onwards but not until the middle of the eighteenth century do we find it quoted in the familiar form.

An expression much-used over centuries to preserve the *status quo*.

Usage: The form with *let* is more formal and less common

LEOPARD

■ A leopard can't change his spots

A person cannot change his basic nature

Variant: A leopard can't change its spots

But a leopard does not change his spots nor, as Ivy Compton-Burnett once said, his feeling that spots are rather a credit. Osborne's anger remains unabated, though directed nowadays at increasingly soft targets: principally women ...
(WEEKEND TELEGRAPH, 2 November 1991)

Most of the time, McEnroe was chasing shadows of his past. Yet despite his 6-4, 6-4, 6-4 defeat, he seemed happy to have replaced the memory of his default two years ago with something more positive.

'I would rather lose than win a title and behave badly,' he said ... In probably his last visit to Australia, he behaved

impeccably. Maybe the leopard is changing its spots after all.
(THE TIMES, 23 January 1992)

The article by Sir Fred Catherwood ... was very optimistic, but if the European Community's track record so far is anything to go by, it will prove to be fallacious. The rich countries frustrate the poor countries' attempts to develop themselves by restrictions on trade. The worst such restrictions pertain to agriculture. America and the EC ban agricultural imports and dump on the world market their own subsidised surpluses. The impact on poorer countries has been devastating.

If this had been the case so far, why should things be any different beyond 1992? Can the leopard change his spots?
(TEAR TIMES, ISSUE 58, Autumn 1992)

The great danger, of course, is that Lamont will throw it [recovery] away again with a tax-raising budget as he frets about inflation. He has made every wrong call so far in this recession. This budget is likely to be his last, but can he change his spots?
(SUNDAY TIMES, 17 January 1993)

It will be interesting to see what happens before the season's final major championship ends in August. It will be equally revealing to see how Faldo reacts if he does not collect any of the game's star prizes.

If Faldo can still say: 'So what' then he will have changed. Then he really will be able to stick his tongue out at those who said he couldn't change his spots.
(DAILY EXPRESS, 26 May 1992)

The proverb is from the Old Testament. God, through the prophet Jeremiah, was showing his people how far short they were falling of his standards. Sin had become so deeply embedded in their character that change, without God's help, was a near impossibility. JEREMIAH 13:23 asks: *Can the Ethiopian change his skin, or the leopard his spots?*

The proverb is still used in this sense today; some undesirable traits are so ingrained that a person can no more change his behaviour than a leopard the pattern of his skin.

Jeremiah was writing in the seventh century BC when leopards would have been familiar to herdsmen. Even today, all these centuries later, about two dozen still survive, although it was thought at one time that the Sinai leopard was extinct.

Usage: Often used in shortened form, such as *You can't change your spots.*

LIGHTNING

■ **Lightning never strikes twice in the same place**

One is never afflicted twice in the same way

Nowadays scientists can explain how and why lightning occurs and meteorologists give us advance warning of imminent storms but, in ancient times, lightning was a display of immense and terrifying force and was often attributed to the wrath of the gods or evil spirits. In thirteenth century China taxes were not levied on anyone whose crops had been struck by lightning. The phenomenon was considered to be a sign of God's displeasure. Had the ruler connected himself in any way with a man so blighted, he would also have had to share in his misfortune.

In Roman times it was observed that lightning never seemed to strike the bay laurel and so leaves from this plant would be worn on the head for protection during thunderstorms. Later bay laurel bushes were planted near houses to keep them safe. The humble house-leek was another plant supposed to have protective powers. It was thought that house-leeks, planted on a roof and left undisturbed, would repel lightning. In the eighth century Charlemagne decreed that every home in his empire should be protected by the plant. The superstition was still held eight centuries later. In NATURALL AND ARTIFICIALL CONCLUSIONS (1586) Thomas Hill wrote: *If the herb house-leek or syngren do grow on the housetop, the same house is never stricken with lightning or thunder.*

By the middle of the eighteenth century, however, men were facing up to the perils of lightning in a scientific way. In the December 1753 edition of POOR RICHARD'S ALMANACK, Benjamin Franklin includes an article entitled 'How to Secure Houses, etc. from Lightning' and gives comprehensive information on the use of lightning conductors such as are still in use today.

Superstitions about lightning, however, continue. A much more recent belief, which comes from America, is that *lightning never strikes twice in the* same place. This has been proved untrue many times, high structures being especially vulnerable: the Empire State building in New York is struck a dozen times a year on average and the large bronze statue of William Penn on City Hall in Philadelphia is also hit several times a year. Some human beings seem to be exceptionally unlucky. In America Roy C Sullivan of Virginia was struck seven times during his lifetime before dying of self-inflicted gunshot wounds. But then no one had told him about the bay laurel.

LIKE

■ Like it or lump it

The idea may not appeal to you but you will have to put up with it

Variant: If you don't like it, you can/you'll have to lump it

Well, what I always say is, people must take me as they find me, and if they don't like it they can lump it.
(W Somerset Maugham, OF HUMAN BONDAGE, 1915)

He was compelled to learn that various ladies had said once and for all that they were not going to have their salaries slashed like that and that if Mr Fenkel didn't like it he could do the other thing.
(J B Priestley, THE GOOD COMPANIONS, 1929)

I am as I am, people can like my bags, jowls, crow's-feet, laughter lines, incipient pleated lips – or lump it. And if any superficial twit

is smirking behind my back saying 'Old Val's looking her age, she could do with a nip and tuck,' I'll put two fingers up and say that it's they who have a problem, not me.
(GOOD HOUSEKEEPING, June 1991)

'Lump' in this context means 'to accept with bad grace something that has to be endured'. So, according to the proverb, if a plan or state of affairs is not to a person's liking there is the choice of accepting it cheerfully or putting up with it grudgingly. The *Oxford English Dictionary* dates the expression from 1833 when it was used in John Neal's THE DOWN-EASTERS. Dickens, Mark Twain, Shaw and Galsworthy are amongst the authors who have used this common colloquialism since.

Usage: Informal. Often said of something that is unavoidable

LIVE

■ Live and let live

Show the tolerance towards others you would expect them to show towards you

See also: It takes all sorts to make the world

They [English authors] are not inordinately affected by adverse criticism, and with one or two exceptions do not go out of their way to ingratiate themselves with the reviewers. They live and let live.
(W Somerset Maugham, A WRITER'S NOTEBOOK, 'Preface', 1949)

Twice I'd been disappointed waiting for Luciano, and once I'd startled a lady who was sneaking ashore from a muted water-taxi near the great Gesuati church. We'd both recoiled in alarm, then snuck on our respective ways. Live and let live. I was pleased that somebody at least was keeping the exotic carnival days alive.
(Jonathan Gash, THE GONDOLA SCAM, 1984)

I am amazed that people are so naive as to confuse actors with the roles they play. Richard Wilson is an extremely good actor, but people seem to think he is Victor Meldrew. To think that Wilson has led an uneventful life in his 56 years is stupid.

His argument backing legalisation of cannabis was put intelligently and succinctly. Although I would never touch any drug myself, I feel we should live and let live.
(DAILY EXPRESS, 18 March 1993)

Gerard de Malynes, writing in 1622, claims the saying is from Holland: *According to the Dutch Prouerbe . . . Leuen ende laeten leuen. To liue and let others liue.* The proverb may have crossed the Channel but its message travelled unheeded. Throughout the seventeenth century the relationship between Britain and Holland vacillated between latent hostility and uneasy peace. Three savage wars were fuelled by economic rivalry.

The proverb translates directly into other European languages. Perhaps a recognition of an allusion to the proverb increased international sales of LIVE AND LET DIE! Ian Fleming's second novel in

the James Bond series (1954) went on to become an immensely successful film.

LONDON

■ **The streets of London are paved with gold**

The capital city is the best place to make one's fortune

See also: The grass is always greener on the other side of the fence

Famous cities and capitals have always tended to exercise a magnetic appeal. Sometimes the reasons are religious (Mecca or Lourdes); more often they are economic. Today rural inhabitants of developing countries flock to urban centres in the pursuit of a job. Such is the appeal of Mexico City and Sao Paulo that they are amongst the very largest conurbations in the world.

London has attracted people to it for many centuries. Shakespeare expressed this well in HENRY THE FOURTH, PART TWO (1597): *I hope to see London once ere I die.*

The well-known story of Dick Whittington tells how rumour reached the friendless orphan that the streets of London were paved with gold and silver, inspiring him to go and seek his fortune there.

Three correspondents of NOTES AND QUERIES of 1884 comment on the story. The first refers to attractions of London:

O London is a dainty place,
A great and gallant city!
For all the streets are paved with gold,
And all the folks are witty.
And there's your lords and ladies fine,
That ride in coach and six;
That nothing drink but claret wine,
And talk of politicks.

(A NEW ACCOUNT OF COMPLIMENTS; OR, THE COMPLETE ENGLISH SECRETARY, WITH A COLLECTION OF PLAYHOUSE SONGS, 1789)

The attraction of London was felt far and wide – this book with its curious title was published in Glasgow. The second correspondent gives his personal recollection of the rhyme from his nursery soon after the turn of the nineteenth century:

Oh, London is a fine town, a very famous city,
Where all the streets are paved with gold,
And all the maidens pretty.

The third more specifically gives this explanation:

The real origin of this saying appears to have been the golden shower which fell upon Farinelli in 1734 . . . when Handel was deserted and driven away, and 5,000 l a year paid to Charles Broschi, commonly called 'Farinelli'.

Enormous payments to superstars were a feature of eighteenth century life as well as of the twentieth. This case became something of a cause célèbre, with references being made to it in the popular theatre. The fourth stanza of a song in the fourth scene of Henry Carey's ballad opera of THE HONEST YORKSHIREMAN runs:

And there the English Actor goes,
With many a hungry belly,
While heaps of Gold are forc'd, God wot!
On Signior Farinelli.

The opera was played at Drury Lane in 1735, just a matter of months after the enormous pay out to Sr Farinelli.

However, although the story is appealing, it may well be that the saying is better related to the popular story of Dick Whittington, for which there is a much older factual base. Sir Richard Whittington of Pauntley in Gloucestershire became one of the richest London merchants of his day and was Lord Mayor on three occasions before his death in 1423. The first recorded reference to the legend that grew up around him was in 1605 – but it contains no mention of streets paved in gold. Perhaps it was after all Sr Farinelli who was instrumental in adding this element to the myth.

Usage: Usually used somewhat cynically either of someone setting out with high hopes, or of someone whose unrealistic expectations have come to grief

LOOK

■ Look before you leap

Think carefully before acting. Beware of taking sudden, rash decisions

When you feel tempted to marry . . . look twice before you leap.
(Charlotte Brontë, SHIRLEY, 1849)

Certainly he was not a man who was likely to forget to look before he leaped, nor one who, if he happened to know that there was a mattress spread to receive him, would leap with less conviction.
(Lytton Strachey, EMINENT VICTORIANS, 'CARDINAL MANNING', 1918)

However, even though the situation on the work front remains rather volatile, you are still urged to look before you leap. What seems to be an offer you can't refuse could well turn out to be a retrograde step.
(RADIO TIMES, 9 – 15 January 1993)

The trouble is, 'serious' is sometimes the one word which doesn't seem to apply to Ken Clarke. He's likeable, sure, but almost too damned likeable for his own good. Mr Clarke has more friends than enemies in the Tory party. But he seems stuck with the image of a man who leaps before he looks.
(DAILY MAIL, 21 January 1993)

How to do your bidding.
Look before you leap: Get the catalogue and pick what you want to view beforehand.
(DAILY EXPRESS, 3 March 1993)

One of Aesop's fables, THE FOX AND THE GOAT (c 570 BC), illustrates this old proverb and was probably instrumental in its origin. A fox tumbled into a well and was unable to climb out. A thirsty goat passed by and asked the fox if the water was sweet. The fox seized his chance and, extolling the quality of the water, encouraged the goat to join him in the well. When the goat had quenched his thirst he began to fret as to how they would get out of the well. The fox persuaded his companion to stand against the wall so that he might climb

out from on top of his shoulders, promising to pull the goat up after him. Once out of the well, however, the fox ran off remarking that the goat was a stupid creature. 'You should not have gone down without thinking how you were going to get up,' he said.

A similar message is carried by another of Aesop's fables (c 570 BC), that of THE TWO FROGS. When the pool in which the two frogs lived dried up in the summer heat, they left to look for another home and found a well. The foolish frog wanted to jump in but was restrained by his wise friend who pointed out the difficulty they would be in if that well dried up too.

The earliest record of the proverb is in the DOUCE MANUSCRIPT dating back to about 1350:

First loke and aftirward lepe;
Avyse the welle, or thow speke.

By the early sixteenth century it was well known in the form *Look ere thou leap.* Within a hundred years it had assumed the form we know today.

LOVE

■ All's fair in love and war

No moderating rules govern a person's conduct in amatory or military matters

All's fair in love – an' war – an' politics.
(George Ade, COUNTY CHAIRMAN, 1903)

It's love in a manner of speaking, and it's certainly war. Everything dirty goes.
(Stallings and Anderson, WHAT PRICE GLORY?, 1924)

Only love illuminates a woman's eyes with that kind of radiance. Love and all its works. My instant conclusion: lover-boy lives somewhere on Torcello, and we'd presumably bump, accidentally of course, into this rustic cretin which would give her the excuse to leave me stranded. Don't get me wrong. I wasn't narked. I mean all's fair in love and all that. But even gigolos get paid. I'd somehow got myself into the position of unpaid stooge.
(Jonathan Gash, THE GONDOLA SCAM, 1984)

ALL'S ALMOST FAIR IN LOVE AND WAR
Last week's court ruling reinstating a homosexual man to naval duty is the first liberal demonstration of Clinton's presidential promises.
(THE TIMES, 19 November 1992)

The assumption behind this proverb is that the end justifies the means. This has long been recognised in the theatre of war. Livy hinted at it two millennia ago: *To those to whom war is necessary it is just* (HISTORY, c 10 BC). Courtship, too, may entail the use of any means if one is to emerge victorious and take the prize. These excesses of the heart are considered forgiveable because love has long been understood as a force which cannot be restrained: *Both might and mallice, deceyte and treacherye, all periurye, any impietie may lawfully be committed in loue, which is lawlesse* (John Lyly, EUPHUES, 1579).

The link between love and fighting for a kingdom was already established in a proverbial form by 1606: *An old saw hath bin, Faith's breach for love and kingdoms is no sin* (Marston, THE FAWN).

Later in the same century Aphra Behn writes: *Advantages are lawful in love and war* (THE EMPEROR OF THE MOON, 1677). There was also the strong contemporary influence of DON QUIXOTE by Cervantes. Publication of Part One was in 1605 and it was soon translated into English. One passage runs: *Love and war are the same thing, and stratagems and policy are as allowable in the one as in the other.* But the wording that we are familiar with today did not appear until two centuries later.

Nowadays a different kind of war is being waged and the phrase is just as likely to be heard in the boardroom. As Christian N Bovee said: *Formerly when great fortunes were only made in war, war was a business; but now when great fortunes are only made by business, business is war. All's fair in love and war* is a convenient proverb to justify dubious conduct in any situation where self-interest reigns.

Usage: Used as a comment, sometimes as an excuse, on a nasty underhand manoeuvre, perpetrated out of romantic love, out of love for one's country or for business advantage

■ **The course of true love never did run smooth**

A couple will inevitably have to overcome obstacles to and in their relationship before they can settle down together

Variant: The path of true love never runs smooth

The course of true love never did run smooth. And the loves of Saunders Skelp and Jessy Miller were no exception to the rule.
(Michael Scott, THE CRUISE OF THE MIDGE, 1836)

The proverb is a quotation from Shakespeare's A MIDSUMMER NIGHT'S DREAM (1590). In Act 1, scene i, Lysander sighs:

Ay me! for aught that I could ever read,
Could ever hear by tale or history,
The course of true love never did run smooth.

His lament is heartfelt for, just like the young couples in the love stories he has read, his love for Hermia is fraught with difficulty. Hermia's father has ordered her to marry the young nobleman Demetrius. Under the law of Athens she has four days in which to comply before being either put to death or confined to a nunnery.

There is a prolonged silence in the literary record until 1836, when there is an allusion to the saying in Dickens. He reformulates it to take account of contemporary popular interest in the railways: *The course of true love is not a railway* (PICKWICK PAPERS, 1837). In the same period, Michael Scott also used it in THE CRUISE OF THE MIDGE and it was subsequently taken up by other writers.

■ **Love is blind**

All normal standards of judgement cease to operate for those in love

An obvious explanation is that love does indeed blind the sufferer to the faults of the loved one and to all else around. More specifically, amongst the many statues of Cupid, the Roman god of love, there are some that depict him blindfolded. Shakespeare catches this in these lines from A MIDSUMMER NIGHT'S DREAM (1590):

Love looks not with the eyes, but with the mind,
And therefore is winged Cupid painted blind.

A French proverb ruins the high moral tone by putting the reality more flippantly:

Love is blind; that is why he always proceeds by the sense of touch.

So does this gem:

Love is blind – and when you get married you get your eyesight back.

MAN

■ **Manners maketh man**

High standards of social behaviour establish a person's reputation and standing

Variant: Manners make the man

Written records of this old proverb go back to the fourteenth century. In the middle ages there were ceremonies for every occasion, from the freeing of a serf to the creating of a knight, and strict codes of behaviour were laid down for each. Politeness was expected in everyday life too; guests were to be met at the gate and escorted out when they left, children were instructed to be courteous and young ladies were expected to walk rather than run and to sit with their hands demurely folded in their laps, especially when they found themselves beside a personable young man:

If thou sit by a right goode manne,
This lesson look thou think upon.
Under his thigh thy knee not fit,
Thou art full lewd, if thou does it.

Helpful guidance like this was to be found in manuals of etiquette such as the fourteenth century BOKE OF CURTASYE.

Some table manners may have changed over the centuries (see *Fingers were made before forks*), but by no means all. This instruction on how to eat bread would pass for good manners in any classy restaurant today:

Bite not on your bread and lay it down,
That is no curtesy to use in town;
But break as much as you will eat . . .

Some of the rules of etiquette commonly expected at feasts or dinners were laid down in guild statutes for the guidance of the members. In the following code, devised for the guild of masons, the proverb appears:

Good manners maketh a man . . .
Look that thine hands be clean
And that thy knife be sharp and keen . . .
If thou sit by a worthier man
Than thyself art one,
Suffer him first to touch the meat.
In chamber among ladies bright,
Hold thy tongue and spend thy sight.

Good conduct was also clearly expected of the students of New College, Oxford, whose founder William Wickham had *Manners makyth man* cut into the stonework as the college motto in 1380. Indeed, so insistent was he about the importance of good behaviour that two years later he bestowed the same motto upon Winchester College.

Usage: Fixed formulas, such as idioms and proverbs, provide the only homes for old words or grammar. The ending for *maketh* comes into this second category. The advice of the proverb smacks of Victorian values

■ One man's meat is another man's poison

Tastes differ – what one person enjoys, another will dislike

See also: Beauty is in the eye of the beholder

The time, the place, the shifting significations of words, the myriad dispositions of the audience or the reader – all these things are variables which can never be reduced to a single formula. Queen Caroline's meat was Queen Victoria's poison; and perhaps Lord Macaulay's poison was Mr Aldous Huxley's pap.
(Lytton Strachey, LITERARY ESSAYS, 'CONGREVE, COLLIER, MACAULAY, ETC', 1949)

One man's pay rise is another man's redundancy notice.
(DAILY MAIL, 15 September 1992)

Such charts make a nonsense of angling because, when it comes to conditions, one man's meat is another man's poisson. There

is no such thing as an ideal fishing day: the piker likes his frosty morning, and the tarpon freak his still and searing noon; a big curl on the water is grand for the loch, when salmon are your quarry, and mahseer strike during hail.
(WEEKEND TELEGRAPH, 16 January 1993)

A lick of paint will probably improve your chances of a sale, but wallpapering may not. Remember one man's improvement is another man's eyesore. So avoid bright colours and make sure any 'improvement' is in keeping with the look of the property.
(GUARDIAN, 23 January 1993)

The proverb is from DE RERUM NATURA (45 BC), a work by the Roman philosopher and poet Lucretius, who writes: *What is food to one man may be fierce poison to others.* The proverb was in frequent use in the form we know today from at least the seventeenth century onwards. One medical explanation of the proverb that has been put forward is the varying sensitivity people exhibit to different substances. Sufferers of coeliac disease cannot tolerate gluten, those tormented by migraine shun chocolate and almost everyone knows someone who has an allergic reaction to some food or other. As Donald G Cooley puts it in EAT AND GET SLIM (1945): *One man's strawberries are another man's hives.*

Usage: The sense now goes beyond the physical effects of what is consumed to a difference in appreciation of films, politics, the opposite sex, etc.

MARRIAGE

■ **Marriages are made in heaven**

God provides the best partner

Variant: Matches are made in heaven

See also: Marry in haste, repent at leisure

They say marriages are made in heaven; but I doubt, when she married, she had no friend there.
(Jonathan Swift, POLITE CONVERSATION, 1728)

Marriages may, for some, be made in heaven, but for generations of local couples they have been made at the Copthorne Gatwick Sterling Hotel.
(CRAWLEY OBSERVER, 11 September 1991)

Prentice Hall International, the British-based subsidiary of Simon & Schuster, the world's largest educational publisher, has taken over Cassell's ELT.
David Haines of Prentice Hall said, 'This is a merger made in heaven.'
(ENGLISH AS A FOREIGN LANGUAGE GAZETTE, November 1991)

It seems like fate that two such extraordinary people as Sue Ryder and Leonard Cheshire should meet and marry. Was it a marriage made in heaven?
'Yes, it certainly was. I think we were very compatible. We never ever had rows or anything like that,' Lady Ryder says; 'If we didn't agree about something we just didn't talk about it'.
(SUNDAY EXPRESS, 12 December 1992)

. . . it is also an open secret in the media world that the McCarthy–Morrell pairing

has not always been the 'made-in-heaven' match the public would like to imagine. Keenan in his book related how McCarthy had boasted of his Beirut girlfriends, to which he replied: 'I've been running out of women to think about and now I've got all yours to sleep with for the next week or two.' (THE TIMES, 31 March 1993)

The MIDRASH, a collection of rabbinical expositional and homiletical commentaries on the Old Testament set down in approximately AD 550, teaches that *marriages are made in heaven*. The biblical base on which it builds is PROVERBS 19:14: *House and riches are the inheritance of fathers: and a prudent wife is from the Lord.*

An English proverb to this effect appeared in literature towards the end of the sixteenth century (to be frequently repeated thereafter), though a borrowed French proverb *Marriages are made in heaven, and consummated on earth* was in circulation in England a little earlier than this. Another English proverb contemporary to the one under discussion saw marriage partners not as being carefully matched by a benevolent god but being flung together, for good or ill, by destiny: *Weddyng is desteny And hangyng likewise, saith the prouerbe* (John Heywood, PROVERBS, 1546).

This negative view is reflected in the volume of harsh criticism marriage has received from literary pens over the centuries (see *Marry in haste, repent at leisure* for a selection). It has also been a subject for humour:

Marriages are made in Heaven, and if we once set to work to repair celestial mistakes

we shall have our hands full (Henry Arthur Jones, 1851–1929).

But then as Addison so astutely pointed out:

No little scribler is of wit so bare,

But has his fling at the poor wedded pair.

Usage: In these days of common marital disharmony and divorce, the proverb can be used somewhat cynically

MARRY

■ **Marry in haste, repent at leisure**

Those who rush into marriage without thinking will have plenty of time to ponder upon their mistake after the ceremony

See also: Marriages are made in heaven

She had married in haste, and repented, not at leisure, but with equal rapidity (James Payn, THICKER THAN WATER, 1883)

When he was asked whether or not a man should marry, Socrates (469–399 BC) is sagely reported to have said, *Whichever you do you will repent it* (in Diogenes Laertius, LIVES OF THE PHILOSOPHERS: SOCRATES, AD 200–250). Perhaps Montaigne was influenced by his cynicism, for he compared marriage to a cage where *the birds without despair to get in, and those within despair to get out* (ESSAYS, 1595). LIPPINCOTT'S MAGAZINE reiterated the same thought, though in a different form, in an anonymous rhyme from the 1830s:

Marriage is like a flaming candle-light
Placed in the window on a summer's night,
Inviting all the insects of the air
To come and singe their pretty winglets
there:
Those that are out butt heads against the
pane,
Those that are in butt to get out again.

'If in doubt, don't' is the message. Philemon, writing at the turn of the third century BC thought the union would only bring regrets: *He who would marry is on the road t o repentance* (FRAGMENTS, c 300 BC). This wisdom is repeated in French courtly literature. The unknown author of LA CHASTELAINE DE SAINT-GILLE (c 1250) writes: *Nobody marries who doesn't repent of it.* A later French proverb, also echoed in English literature, puts it this way: *Marriage rides in the saddle, and repentence upon the croup.*

By the sixteenth century, however, it is not marriage itself but hasty marriage which brings regret in its wake. In PETITE PALLACE (1579), George Pettie warns that *Bargains made in speed are commonly repented at leisure* and English literature of the period is full of like advice. Shakespeare preaches it more than once. In MUCH ADO ABOUT NOTHING (1599), Beatrice gives the woman's perspective on the union:

Wooing, wedding, and repenting, is as a Scotch jig, a measure, and a cinque-pace: the first suit is hot and hasty, . . . the wedding, mannerly-modest, as a measure, . . . and then comes Repentance, and, with his bad legs, falls into the cinque-pace faster and faster, till he sink into his grave (Act 2, scene i).

The proverb finds its neat expression *Marry in haste and repent at leisure* in John Ray's collection of ENGLISH PROVERBS (1670). This formulation may be Ray's translation of the Italian for, like many proverbs, the saying is found in a number of languages. European opinion concurs that to rush into marriage brings a lifetime of regret. Consider well before you *tie a knot with your tongue that you cannot untie with your teeth.* Gentlemen, let the French dramatist Marivaux (1688–1763) guide your thinking:

I would advise a man to pause
Before he takes a wife:
In fact, I see no earthly cause
He should not pause for life.

Ladies, ponder the fate of Mary Ford:

Here lies the body of Mary Ford,
Whose soul, we trust is with the Lord;
But if for hell she's changed this life,
'Tis better than being John Ford's wife.

MASTER

■ **No man can serve two masters**

You can't give equal allegiance to two conflicting principles

See also: You can't serve God and Mammon

Men cannot serve two masters. If this cant of serving their country once takes hold of them, good-bye to the authority of the Church.

(George Bernard Shaw, SAINT JOAN, 1924)

One has no real human relations: it is the complaint of every artist. The artist's first duty is to his genius, his daimon; he cannot serve two masters.
(Aldous Huxley, THE OLIVE TREE, 1963)

No man can serve two masters. This is the law which prohibits bigamy.
(Anonymous)

This is a biblical proverb. In MATTHEW 6:24 Jesus explains why attempting to serve two masters, in this case God and Mammon, is impossible: *No man can serve two masters: for either he will hate the one, and love the other; or else he will hold to the one, and despise the other.* The proverb made an early appearance in English. It is found in a collection of political songs dating from about 1330: *No man may wel serve tweie lordes.*

MAY

■ **Ne'er cast a clout till May is out**

Do not remove any layers of winter clothing until the end of May. Don't trust any improvement in the weather till June arrives.

Variant: Ne'er cast a clout afore May is out

This could be taken as a very English proverb, deriving from the unpredictability of a climate where, even as late as May, the weather might suddenly turn very chilly and make one regret leaving off one's vest.

Surprisingly, however, the origin probably lies in an old Spanish proverb quoted by Correas in his VOCABULARIO (c 1627): *Do not leave off your coat till May.* There is a corresponding English rhyme: *Who doffs his coat on a winter's day, will gladly put it on in May.* A French proverb explains why it is foolish to be taken in by bourgeoning May: *Mid-May, winter's tail* – even with the year so advanced a cold snap might be expected – while an old English agricultural weather proverb says that *A snowstorm in May is worth a load of hay.* Good reason to keep one's coat on.

Leave not off a Clout, Till May be out appeared in Thomas Fuller's GNOMOLOGIA (1732). A 'clout' was a rag or cloth and so here it means an article of clothing. 'May', besides being the name of the month, is also the name given to hawthorn blossom. (This meaning is found in the old English May Day rhyme *Here We Go Gathering Nuts in May*, which is a corruption of *Here We Go Gathering Knots of May*, or 'posies of May blossom'.) For this reason some authorities consider that the proverb means 'Don't cast off any clothing until the May blossom has come into flower', but most consider that May refers to the month.

The Victorians were ever careful about their health. They thought that colds were caught by getting cold. A proverb quoted by R D Blackmore in CRIPPS CARRIER (1876) reveals why it was so important to keep on those warm winter layers even in May: *This is the worst time of year to take cold, A May cold is a thirty-day cold.* There is evidence to

When there's an 'R' in the month

The British summer months from May to August (with no 'R' in their spellings) have been the focus of considerable folk wisdom and advice. William Harrison in his DESCRIPTION OF ENGLAND (1577) writes that *Our oisters are generallie forborne in the foure hot moneths of the yeare, that is Maie, Iune, Iulie, and August,* adding *'which are void of the letter R'.* Two health manuals of the period, Vaughan's DIRECTIONS FOR HEALTH (1600) and Moufet's HEALTHS IMPROVEMENT (1658), warn against eating oysters in those months *which wante the letter R,* and Buttes says that oysters are *vnseasonable and vnholesome* in these months (DYETS DRY DINNER, 1599).

The advice is sound, although abstaining from an oyster feast is not strictly necessary on the grounds of health but on those of flavour: oysters spawn in this season and are not as tasty. Indeed, a seventeenth century law forbade harvesting oysters in the summer months to protect the spawning shellfish. Later Lord Chesterfield compared the cut and thrust of political life to the oyster season: *Here is no domestic news of changes and chances in the political world, which like oysters, are only in season in the R months, when the Parliament sits* (LETTERS, 1764).

According to proverbial advice, another dish to avoid in months lacking an 'R' is pork. Reasons for this are certainly health-based. Before the advent of refrigeration it was difficult to prevent the meat from spoiling and going off in hot weather and so, in order to guard against nasty bouts of food poisoning, pork was eaten only at cooler times of the year.

A Moroccan proverb follows the same guiding principle: *Eviter les mois en 'R' et vivre en plein air* (Avoid months with an 'R' and live in the open air). In other words, camp out during the summer months and stay sheltered for the rest of the year.

And it seems that the rule may soon be adopted in another context, that of the football club, as this newspaper report shows:

Every League manager, honest to God, is absolutely chuffed to bits when one of his boys is picked for an international squad.

Unless, that is, the lad is required to go away within 60 days of an Autoglass Trophy tie against Scunthorpe.

Or the boy's skills are needed for the club's battle for the Championship, against relegation, for mid-table respectability or to make up the numbers in the card school.

Managers would also rather their players didn't go away when there's an R in the month or when Venus is in the ascendancy. (TODAY, 23 February 1993) suggest that the advice about not casting off clothing until May was over was taken very seriously. Different corners of the country had their own rhyming variants on the proverb:

In Somerset the wisdom was:

If you would the doctor pay,
Leave your flannels off in May
(F T Elworthy, THE WEST SOMERSET WORD-BOOK, 1886)

On the Yorkshire coast the advice was:

The wind at North and East
Was never good for man nor beast,
So never think to cast a clout
Until the month of May be out.
(F V Robinson, WHITBY GLOSSARY, 1855)

Another north country saying foretold the horrors in store for those who scrubbed off the protective layers of winter grime before high summer:

If you bathe in May
You'll soon lie in the clay.

Usage: Centrally heated houses and workplaces, a warming climate and an understanding that viruses and diseases are responsible for most illness are making this proverb redundant. By the middle of the next century it might well have been shelved as a quaint saying for future etymologists and collectors of proverbs to research.

MENDED

■ Least said, soonest mended

Offering explanations for conduct which has given offence will only make the situation worse

If you defend, you'll have to go up to London. In the box, least said is soonest mended. You'll simply say you found you were mistaken, and thought it more honourable to break off at once than to go on.
(John Galsworthy, A FEUD, 1930)

Millwall chairman Reg Burr refused to disclose what offence Harrison had committed. . . . 'I am just sad that he has lost his job in these circumstances. I realise the implications for his England post but that is up to Graham Taylor, the England manager. I am sure Graham knows the reasons. I will not be divulging them myself and I think the less said the soonest mended.'
(DAILY MAIL, 22 October 1991)

. . . a little shoplifting in a supermarket does no harm; rape, in the eyes of some of our judiciary, is not something over which to make heavy weather; least said, soonest mended. To a degree, we have become that which we fight.
(DAILY TELEGRAPH, 7 June 1993)

From the sixteenth to the nineteenth centuries the proverb was *Little said soon amended.* Walter Scott in his novel HEART OF MIDLOTHIAN (1818) uses the proverb in its present day form. Jane Austen uses a similar proverb in SENSE AND SENSIBILITY (1811): *The less said the better.*

MILE

■ **A miss is as good as a mile**

If you miss your goal by an inch or a mile it still counts as a failure

The proverb, which is found in nineteenth century texts, is an elliptical and alliterative form of a saying current since at least the seventeenth century: *An inch in a miss is as good as an ell.* (See *Give him an inch and he'll take a mile.*) There is the same inflationary movement from an ell up to a mile.

■ **Give him an inch and he'll take a mile**

Said of someone who takes advantage of another's kindness or generosity

Variant: Give him an inch and he'll take a yard

Crowned heads may not have had the sense to keep their crowns but they were evidently not too stupid to realize that give Lady Montdore an inch and she would take an ell. (Nancy Mitford, LOVE IN A COLD CLIMATE, 1949)

You have to keep these fellows in their place, don't you know. You have to work the good old iron-hand-in-the-velvet-glove wheeze. If you give them a what's-its-name, they take a thingummy.
(P G Wodehouse, CARRY ON JEEVES, 1925)

Stevenson traces the phrase back to a Latin saying quoted by, amongst others, Publilius Syrus: *He that is permitted more than is right wants more than is permitted* (SENTENTIAE, c 43 BC). Its first appearance in English is in John Heywood's collection of proverbs (1546): *For when I gave you an inch you tooke an ell.*

An ell, like the yard which replaced it in the proverb near the turn of the twentieth century, is an old measurement of length which varied from country to country. The English ell was 45 inches so a person who, on being offered an inch, helped himself to an ell was overstepping the mark indeed.

Proverbs expressing the crime abound in different languages:

Give me a place to sit down, and I'll make a place to lie down (Spanish)
If you give him the length of a finger, he'll take a piece as long as your arm (French)
Call a peasant 'Brother', he'll demand you call him 'Father' (Russian)
If you let them put a calf on your back, before long they'll put on a cow (Italian)

Being taken advantage of obviously arouses strong emotions. The choice of 'mile' in the current English version doubtless echoes this.

MILK

■ **It's no use crying over spilt milk**

What's done is done and getting upset won't change or help matters

Variant: It's no good crying over spilt milk

He was very much annoyed at Blenthorp's escaping him, but as he would have said, a

busy man has no time to waste crying over spilt milk, an ungrateful if common metaphor.

(Richard Aldington, SOFT ANSWERS, 'A GENTLEMAN OF ENGLAND', 1932)

The ordinary Englishman, perhaps because he had more to occupy his mind than the great lords of the political overworld, did not cry for long over the spilt milk of Austerlitz.

(Sir Arthur Bryant, THE YEARS OF VICTORY, 1944)

I wish now I'd thought about the implications, but it's no good crying over spilt milk. Especially when that spilled milk turned out to be Cosima.

(Jonathan Gash, THE GONDOLA SCAM, 1984)

To make sure you don't cry over spilt milk, Miele seal base units all round, including the top and that's before putting your worktop on. Giving total stability and protection against moisture.

(Advertisement for Miele kitchens, GOOD HOUSEKEEPING, April 1991)

Gemma and her second husband . . . would have liked children but [she] doesn't think there's much chance of any now. 'I'm a bit past it. At 42 one tends to give up. I used to think about it a lot but now I don't cry over spilt milk. Life's too short.'

(WHAT'S ON TV, 24–30 April 1993)

In his translation of AESOPE (1484) William Caxton has this to say: *The thyrd [doctrine] is that thow take no sorowe of the thynge lost whiche may not be recouered.* Milk is in this category. If the grain tub is overturned, the contents can be recovered; if a jug of milk is spilt, it can

only be mopped up and is lost forever.

It is difficult to say exactly when the proverb was coined but both James Howell (1659) and John Ray (1678) record it in their collections of English proverbs as *No weeping for shed milk.* The present day wording is from the nineteenth century.

MONEY

■ Money talks

Wealth gets you special treatment and influence

They thought of love in terms of money, not money in terms of love. At least some of them did. Most of George's new friends were men who talked of money, and with whom money talked.

(L P Hartley, TWO FOR THE ROVER, 'A VERY PRESENT HELP', 1961)

Money talks has been current in literature since around the turn of the twentieth century but the idea was not new. In CIVILE CONVERSATION (1586) Stefano Guazzo expresses a piece of proverbial wisdom current in the sixteenth and seventeenth centuries thus: *The tongue hath no force when golde speaketh.* Other writers bear testimony to the eloquence of money. Seventeenth century author Aphra Behn tells us that the language of money is international, while Henry Fielding writes that *Money will say more in one moment than the most eloquent lover can in years* (THE MISER, 1733).

Money, or rather the lack of it, can

provoke a wry, envious humour. Richard Armour writes:

That money talks
I'll not deny.
I heard it once –
It said 'Good-bye'.

■ **The love of money is the root of all evil**

The relentless pursuit of riches dulls the conscience and gives rise to selfish and evil actions

Variant: Money is the root of all evil

See also: You can't serve God and Mammon

'Championships are about earning prestige, not money,' said a scornful Jackson . . . More sweeping in his condemnation is Jon Edwards, the Briton who won the triple jump at the World Cup last year. 'It says in the Bible that the love of money is the root of all evil and that's what is happening in athletics,' he said.
(DAILY MAIL, 12 March 1993)

St Paul, writing to his disciple, Timothy, urges the young man to be content once his basic needs of food and clothing have been met. Possessions, he argues, are of no use in the after-life and the pursuit of riches gives rise to harmful ambitions and hurtful lusts. *For the love of money, he says, is the root of all evil, leading men to flounder in their Christian faith and fall into deep unhappiness* (1 TIMOTHY 6:7–10).

St Paul's words are often misquoted as *money is the root of all evil.* The apostle, however, never condemned money. He himself was happy to put riches to a proper use: to relieve poverty and suffering, or to house an assembly of Christians. What Paul warned against was the accumulation of wealth for self-aggrandisement and self-indulgence.

It is not surprising that such a well-known saying on the topic of money should spawn a crop of witticisms. Mark Twain and George Bernard Shaw are both credited with this telling social comment: *The lack of money is the root of all evil,* while an anonymous and down-to-earth graffito bases itself on the familiar misquotation: *Money is the root of all evil – and a man needs roots.*

MONK

■ **The cowl does not make the monk**

Appearances may belie reality. External trappings are not a guarantee of what they represent

Variant: The habit does not make the monk

See also: Appearances are deceptive

Monasticism flourished in the middle ages. At its best it fostered learning and the arts, founded hospitals and excelled in industry. But, gradually, as royalty and nobility alike salved their consciences with generous gifts of land and money, the monasteries grew wealthy and the light of their example dimmed. Many monks were no longer content to remain within their cloister and observe a simple way of life in accordance with their vows. By the later middle ages they not only kept a rich table but had ceased to labour, assuming a role of overseer to an army of servants. Nor, in many houses, was the vow of celibacy strictly observed. Chaucer gives us a fine portrait of the fourteenth century monk in his CANTERBURY TALES (C 1386). Far from being 'pale like a tormented soul' he liked to feast on swan, wore fur-trimmed clothes, rode a fine horse and had a passion for greyhound racing and hunting.

It is not surprising, then, that this proverb should have medieval roots. The earliest references are French dating back to the thirteenth century. The earliest English use is *Vor the clothinge ne maketh nayght thane monek* in the AYENBITE OF INWIT (1340). This work is a translation by Dan Michel of a French original. This borrowing clearly caught on; a similar thought is found a few years later in Thomas Usk's THE TESTAMENT OF LOVE (c 1387): *For habit maketh no monk; ne weringe of gilte spurres maketh no knight.* Erasmus quotes the medieval Latin versions in his ADAGIA (1523).

The proverb has been a popular one through the centuries. There is always a fascination for those who make high professions and yet fail to meet the standard. In the seventeenth century George Herbert pointed out that *A holy habit cleanseth not a foul soul* (JACULA PRUDENTUM, 1640) and, in the following century, Thomas Fuller observed that *A broad hat does not always cover a venerable head* (GNOMOLOGIA, 1732).

These days the national press serves as watchdog over ecclesiastical indiscretions and, in its zeal to uncover hypocrisy, is swift to publish any hint of scandal, especially of a sexual nature. And Thomas Fuller would not be surprised to know that, even in the twentieth century, broad hats were occasionally set on less than perfect heads, as this diary of Roy Jenkins, in Rome for the coronation of Pope John-Paul II on 22 October 1978, shows:

The Mass began at 10 o'clock and went on until 1.15 . . . Most of the first hour was taken up by the homage of all the cardinals, and I wished I had a key to them. Emilio Colombo wasn't bad and pointed out about 14, but even his knowledge seemed far from perfect. The Duke of Norfolk, in the next row, offered pungent comments about one or two of them.
(THE INDEPENDENT, 22 October 1992).

(See also *The nearer the church the further from God.*)

MOUNTAIN

■ **Don't make a mountain out of a molehill**

Don't exaggerate the size of the problem by making a trifling matter into an insuperable difficulty

The most trivial object or occurrence, when contemplated through the magnifying glass of Dr Johnson's mind, assumed gigantic proportions; he went through life making mountains out of molehills.
(Logan Pearsall Smith, A TREASURY OF APHORISMS, 'INTRODUCTION', 1928)

With one bound he had leapt clear of the tradition of his class and type, which was to see molehills as mountains and mountains themselves as a mere menacing blur on the horizon.
(John Wain, HURRY ON DOWN, 1953)

Scotland's independent whisky distillers are looking to form an alliance to fend off the drinks multinationals. The move follows last week's £286m offer by American Brands' Whyte & Mackay for Invergordon. 'They fit perfectly with us,' said Lunn of Whyte & Mackay. He added: 'Invergordon are in the position we were in before we were bought by Gallaher [a subsidiary of American Brands]. Molehills seem like mountains when you are small and have to think of the short term.'
(THE TIMES, 11 August 1991)

French has a phrase *Faire d'une mouche un éléphant* (to make an elephant out of a fly) to express the idea of a trivial matter which has been exaggerated beyond all proportion. It was originally found in ancient Greek. The English *to make a mountain out of a molehill* is probably a variant. In his CATECHISM (1560) Thomas Becon links the two phrases: *They make of a fly an elephant, and of a molehill a mountain.* This is not the earliest known example of the current form of the proverb, however. It appears in Roper's LIFE OF MORE written some three years earlier.

Usage: Sage counsel, perhaps, but often construed as patronising and intrusive

■ **If the mountain will not go to Mahomet, Mahomet must go to the mountain**

If things cannot be arranged in our favour we must accept the fact and follow an alternative, if less favourable, course of action

Variant: If the mountain will not come to Mahomet, Mahomet must go to the mountain

As the mountain will not come to Mahomet, why Mahomet shall go to the mountain; . . . as you cannot pay me a visit . . . next summer, . . . I shall spend three [weeks] among my friends in Ireland.
(Oliver Goldsmith, LETTER TO D HODSON, 27 December 1757)

Dissembling his chagrin as best he could, he kept on the lookout for Cowperwood at both of the clubs of which he was a member; but Cowperwood had avoided them during this period of excitement, and Mahomet would have to go to the mountain.
(Theodore Dreiser, THE TITAN, 1914)

When in June of 1900 he went to Paris, it was but his third attempt on the centre of civilisation. This time, however, the mountain was going to Mahomet; for he felt by now more deeply civilised than Paris, and perhaps he really was.
(John Galsworthy, IN CHANCERY, 1920)

The proverb takes its origin from an essay of Francis Bacon in which he tells the story of 'Mahomets Miracle':

You shall see a Bold Fellow, many times, doe Mahomets Miracle. Mahomet made the People beleeve, that he would call an Hill to

him; *And from the Top of it, offer up his Praiers, for the Observers of his Law. The People assembled; Mahomet cald the Hill to come to him, againe, and againe; And when the Hill stood still, he was never a whit abashed, but said: If the Hil wil not come to Mahomet, Mahomet will go to the Hil.*
(ESSAYS: OF BOLDNESSE, 1957)

The stubborn mountain was Mount Safa which is situated near the holy city of Mecca. When the mountain did not move, Mahomet is reputed to have told the crowd that it was a sign of God's mercy towards them for, had it moved, it would surely have fallen upon them and crushed them to death.

As to the influences upon Francis Bacon, one of the most learned men of his generation, there appear to be two. Most obviously, Bacon himself quotes in Spanish in PROMUS the internationally known proverb *Si no va el otero a Mahoma, vaya Mahoma al otero* (If the mountain does not go to Mahomet, let Mahomet go to the mountain). A scholar of Bacon's repute may also have been conversant with one version or other of the Arabic ANECDOTES OF CHODJA NAS'REDDIN DSCHOCHA ER RUMI. This has: *If the palm tree does not come to Dschocha, Dschocha will go to the palm tree.* Why Mahomet attempted to call the mountain to himself in the first place is unexplained. One account relates the legend to a prophecy in the KORAN, 52, 10: *On the day the heaven shall be shaken, and shall reel; and the mountains shall walk and pass away.* The New Testament of course, has several passages that might explain Mahomet's action

(1 CORINTHIANS 13:2; MATTHEW 21:21; MARK 11:23) A typical one is: *If ye have faith as a grate of mustard seed, ye shall say unto this mountain, Move from here to yonder place; and it shall move and nothing shall be impossible unto you.* (MATTHEW 17:20). Perhaps Mahomet's faith in the event did not reach the requisite size!

Usage: Shows an acceptability of the inevitable, with a consequent change of plan, and even of heart. There is variation in the spelling of Mahomet.

MUCK

■ **Where there's muck, there's money**

Dirt and the creation of wealth are closely associated.

Variant: Where there's muck, there's brass

Where there's rock there's brass . . . and the top auction houses, suffering from a slump in fine art sales, are cashing in . . . Like importunate groupies camped outside dressing rooms, they are grateful for the cast-offs, throw-outs and giveaways of the popgurus.
(SUNDAY TIMES, 11 August 1991)

In medieval times the dung of cattle was commonly added to the land. Sometimes the manure was spread by natural means. Sheep, for instance, would be penned on the lord's field at night to enrich the soil and scratching posts were put up where growth was sparse to entice the sheep over to that particular spot. As farming methods became more refined there was debate as to which muck made the finest fertilizer. In a book on husbandry (1593), Fitzherbert claims the *Horse-donge is the worste donge that is . . . And the dounge of douues is best, but it must be layde uppon the grounde verye thynne.* However the value of muck to an agricultural economy was undisputed. Writers such a Bullein (1564), Jonson (1599) and others compared the fruitful use of riches with that of manure: *Mr Bettenham . . . used to say, that riches were like muck; when it lay in a heap is gave but a stench . . .; but when it was spread upon the ground, then it was cause of much fruit* (BACON, APOPHTHEGMS NEW AND OLD, 1624).

Increased yields meant greater profits. A new proverb celebrated the source of this developing prosperity: *He hath a good muck-hill at his door* meant 'he is rich' (John Ray, ENGLISH PROVERBS, 1678).

The proverb *Where there's muck there's money* is a variant of a saying from the same period, *Muck and money go together* (John Ray, ENGLISH PROVERBS, 1678).

Later generations have interpreted the word *muck* differently, using it to refer to the grime of the mining and manufacturing industries. Where black smoke belched from factory chimneys, mill and pit owners were becoming rich.

That the proverb was widely used is evident from the number of regional variants it engendered:
The more muck, the more money (East Anglia)

Where there's muck there's brass (Yorkshire – brass being a dialect word for money)
Where there's much ther's luck (Lancashire)
Muck's the mother of money (Cheshire)

Usage: Informal, particularly common form *Where there's muck, there's brass.*

NEWS

■ **Bad news travels fast**

It does not take long for bad news to circulate

Variant: Ill news comes apace

See also: No news is good news

What is news? F P Dunne defined it thus: *What's one man's news is another man's troubles* (MR DOOLEY, JOURNALIST, 1901). In other words news is gossip about another's afflictions. This fascination we have for revelling in other people's misfortunes and hurrying to be the first to break the news to someone else is age-old. Plutarch quotes this ancient Greek saying in MORALIA: ON CURIOSITY (c AD 95): *How much more readily than glad events is mischance carried to the ears of men!* It was echoed in English literature from the second half of the sixteenth century. Originally, as in the Greek, the speed of bad news was contrasted with the slowness of good: *Evil news flies faster still than good*

(Thomas Kyd, SPANISH TRAGEDY, 1594). Poets and dramatists have excelled themselves in expressing the proverb in an original way. *Ill news, madam, Are swallow-wing'd, but what's good walks on crutches*, writes Philip Massinger in his play THE PICTURE (1629) and Milton has *Evil news rides post, while good news bates* (SAMSON AGONISTES, 1671). By the end of the eighteenth century, the proverb had been clipped to its present day form *Ill news travels fast*, 'ill news' becoming 'bad news' during the twentieth century.

■ No news is good news

Without information to the contrary, it is sensible to assume that all is well

See also: Bad news travels fast

Don't believe the proverb: no news probably just means you're being kept in the dark. (MID SUSSEX TIMES, 17 January 1992)

NO MUSE IS BAD NEWS
Contemporary verse has lost its public. It's thought to be difficult, daft and irrelevant. Even poets tend not to read each other's work.
(SUNDAY TIMES, 28 February 1993)

Sir Thomas Overbury seems to have had a talent for being associated with the first recorded uses of proverbs. (See *Beauty is only skin deep*.)

His story is a tragic one. Having upset his patron, the future Earl of Somerset, by speaking out against his forthcoming marriage with the Countess of Essex on the grounds that she was a divorcee, Overbury was imprisoned in the Tower of London on a political pretext. Here

Lady Essex arranged to have him gradually poisoned.

The Earl of Somerset and his new wife the Countess of Somerset were imprisoned for the crime in the Tower of London in the charge of Sir George More. King James I was faced with a problem of great sensitivity. The LOSELEY MANUSCRIPTS of 1616 record two highly secret letters in the King's own hand to Sir George. The first letter of 9 May asks him to urge Somerset to confess, in which case the King will exercise mercy. Sir George's advocacy had no effect. On 13 May, the King wrote once more in the greatest secrecy to Sir George:

Althogh I feare that the laste message I sent to youre infortunate prisoner shall not take the effecte that I wishe it shoulde, yett I can not leave of to use all meanes possible to move him to doe that quhich is both honorable for me, and his owin best. Ye shall thair fore give him assurance in my name, that if he will yett before his tryall confesse cheerlie unto the commissionars his guilteiness of this fact, I will not onlie performe quhat I promeised by my last messinger both towardis him and his wyfe, but I will enlarge it . . . Lett none living knowe of this, and if it take goode effect, move him to sende in haste for the commissioners, to give thaime satisfaction, but if he remaine obstinate, I desyre not that ye shoulde trouble me with an ansoure, for it is to no ende, and no newis is bettir then evill newis, and so fair well, and God blesse youre labours.

This sad story had a tragic end. The King's role is dubious and his motives unclear. He had been duplicitous to Somerset before he was consigned to the Tower; he went to great lengths to keep matters quiet and persuade Somerset to plead guilty; he had a plan ready to put into effect to make out that Somerset was mad, should he suggest that James had had any part in the poisoning. The accomplices to the crime – Weston, Mrs Turner, Sir Gervase Elwes – were all hanged. The Somersets pleaded guilty and were duly pardoned by the King. However, this brought no good end. As Alfred John Kempe put it in 1836, *They became indifferent to each other and lived apart in obscurity and execration. She died before her husband, of a decay so loathsome, that historians have noticed it as a manifest visitation of heaven upon her crimes.*

Although King James is often credited with originating the proverb in his letter of 13 May, it is more likely that he was quoting a saying already in existence. About twenty-nine years later James Howell cites it as an Italian proverb, the translation of which – unlike James I's version – is almost exactly the same as our modern rendering: *I am of the Italians mind that said,* Nulla nuova, buona nuova, *no news, good news* (FAMILIAR LETTERS, c 1650). By the middle of the following century the proverb was established in its present day form and has been in constant use since.

NOBLESSE OBLIGE

■ **Noblesse oblige**

High position brings obligations as well as privileges

Now let me gather together the main threads of this over long letter. They are five . . . THREE: I maintain that it is the duty of the artist to fight for the Walworth Road, however low its taste, as manfully and resolutely as the Walworth Road fights for – Heaven forgive me – its betters. FOUR: That the greater the artist, the greater the obligation. FIVE: Sir Osbert Sitwell's policy of exemption [of artists and intellectuals from military service], if carried to its logical conclusion, must result, though he may not realise it and obviously would not desire it, in the sacrifices of greater numbers of the ordinary man. And sacrifice in a lost war, since no country which exempts the best of its doers as well as thinkers can hope to prevail against a nation fighting as one man. I have no more to add except that it will be a sorry day for this country when for Noblesse Oblige it substitutes ART FORBIDS! (James Agate, NOBLESSE OBLIGE, 1944)

But the 'effer needs an individual name as well, and we have decided on Empress. Em-Press, get it? We shall treat her with all respect due to an animal that bears the proud name Times Empress. Noblesse oblige, of course, and I expect her to undertake a full range of duties. I have mentioned to her that she may expect the occasional invitation to present What the Papers Say, or judge the annual Press Awards. . . . On the other hand, if she gets

above herself and starts misbehaving, I have warned her that she could end up doing duty on the staff canteen menu.
(THE TIMES, 6 March 1993)

This is one of the unusual sayings which are retained in the language from which they are borrowed. The Duc de Levis proposed the saying in MAXIMES ET PRECEPTES (1808), with regard to the establishment of the nobility of the Empire, as the best maxim for the old order and the new. It was not, however, totally original. Aeschylus in PROMETHEUS BOUND (470 BC) had: *Relationships oblige* and Euripides in ALCMENE (c 410 BC): *The nobly born must nobly meet his fate.*

The French maxim soon crossed the Channel and beyond and is found in several nineteenth century writers, including Emerson and Arnold. Nobility and its obligations was a live issue for contemporary debate. As time has gone by, the phrase can now be applied widely to any role or position that carries responsibilities. In some uses, it can have overtones of condescending 'do-gooding' by the higher born.

NOSE

■ **Don't cut off your nose to spite your face**

Beware of indulging in angry or spiteful action which will result in difficulties for yourself

They still pressed him, the Count was particularly insistent, but Eustace shook his head and marched away, his mind full of that sweet soreness which comes of cutting off one's nose to spite one's face.
(L P Hartley, EUSTACE AND HILDA, 1947)

These fellows are simply cutting off their noses to spite their faces. These stock and bond issues are perfectly good investments and no one knows it better than you do. All this hue and cry in the newspapers against Cowperwood doesn't amount to anything. He's perfectly solvent.
(Theodore Dreiser, THE TITAN, 1914)

Peter of Blois mentions this phrase in about 1200 in approximately its current form. Previously the thought of gaining revenge but at significant cost to oneself had been variously expressed. Latin authors referred to burning down their own house or their own corn, hacking their own vines, and sticking an axe into their own legs. After Peter of Blois, there is a developing European tradition of cutting off one's own *nose*. It is a French phrase in the seventeenth century, and Grose in his CLASSICAL DICTIONARY OF THE VULGAR TONGUE (1796) comments: *Said of one who, to be revenged on his neighbour, has materially injured himself.* This same thought is nicely realised in two Chinese proverbs:

Don't thrust your fingers through your own paper lantern
Do not burn down your house even to annoy your chief wife's mother

Usage: This expression is used not simply as a proverbial recommendation but as an idiom in its variety of shorter forms

Contradictions!

If proverbs demonstrate the wisdom of the people, then the people are in two minds and do not know what they want. There are quite a number of proverbs that contradict one another:

You are never too old to learn **vs** *You cannot teach an old dog new tricks*

Look after the pennies and the pounds will look after themselves **vs** *Penny wise, pound foolish*

Nothing ventured, nothing gained **vs** *Better safe than sorry*

Many hands make light work or *The more, the merrier* **vs** *Too many cooks spoil the broth*

Haste makes waste or *More haste, less speed* **vs** *Strike whilst the iron is hot*

Out of sight, out of mind **vs** *Absence makes the heart grow fonder*

Look before you leap **vs** *He who hesitates is lost*

These and other examples perhaps go to show that different people hold very different opinions. Also, the relevance of a proverb can vary in relation to the context in which it is used. Is it true that *The more is always the merrier?* It depends on the situation. Similarly, does *Absence* always *make the heart grow fonder?* Again, it depends.

Proverbs appear to offer a timeless wisdom and truth, but contradictions and the way that contexts condition meaning suggest that their apparent universality is in fact a lot more relative. Building a comprehensive moral system on proverbs, therefore, seems doomed to failure. One early attempt to this end was by Carrión in fourteenth-century Spain. However, later critics have shown his system to be full of contradictions and opposing moral adages.

None the less, contradictory proverbs have their uses. They have formed the basis of psychological tests amongst American college students: when faced with forty-two contrasting pairs, the choices made measured their attitudes on the issues in question. The results showed that black students were more cautious than their white counterparts.

NOTHING

■ **Nothing ventured, nothing gained**

If you aren't prepared to try or to take any risks, you can't expect to meet with success

Variant: Nothing venture, nothing win/have/gain

See also: Faint heart ne'er won fair lady; Throw out a sprat to catch a mackerel

'The only danger I can see is that he may get this pig of yours into a friendly game and take her last bit of potato peel off her. Still, that is a risk that must be faced.'

'Of course.'

'Nothing venture, nothing have, eh?'
(P G Wodehouse, UNCLE FRED IN THE SPRINGTIME, 1939)

Well, here was justification and reward for all he had done! He had had some bad minutes, but it had been worth it. It was like everything else: nothing venture, nothing win.
(F W Crofts, THE 12:30 FROM CROYDON, 1934)

This little bit of wisdom has been expressed in literature since the fourteenth century. In the sixteenth and seventeenth centuries various forms of the proverb were known :

Nought lay downe, nought take up and *Nought venter, nought have*
(John Heywood, PROVERBS, 1546)

Nought stake, nought draw
(Anonymous, MISOGONUS, 1577)

. . . nought venters, nothinge gaynes
(Thomas Heywood, THE CAPTIVES, 1624)

The proverb continues to have different forms, even today. It also has close equivalents in other European languages. The French, for instance, say *He who risks nothing, gains nothing.* And the same idea is variously expressed in many other languages: French and Spanish share *He who will not risk himself will never go to the Indies,* a reference to the fortunes to be made in the sugar plantations of the West Indies in the eighteenth century, where both countries had colonies; Greek refers back to the Trojan horse with *It's through trying that the Greeks took Troy* (see *Beware of Greeks bearing gifts*); and the Moroccans have this exchange between two beggars:

Come on! Let's try and ask for alms, says one.

No! I'm afraid of not getting anything, says the other.

■ **There's nothing new under the sun**

Whatever the novelty, somewhere or other it has been seen, heard or done before

What he called his 'preaching' was at worst a sort of grumbling, ending with the sentiment that boys will be boys and that there's nothing new under the sun.
(G K Chesterton, VICTORIAN AGE IN LITERATURE, 1913)

'They're after something quite new — something that's never been heard of before.'

Country life

Farming was the mainstay of the economy until this century and agricultural proverbs were legion. Many of them were weather sayings, the farmer's attempts to find climatic patterns so that he could plan his activities:

Rain from the east, two wet days at least

When the wind's in the east on Candlemas day (2 February), *there it will stick to the end of May*

A fair day in winter is the mother of a storm

Certain signs gave a more long-term view. A dry March must have brought a sigh of satisfaction to the lips of the arable farmer: *A bushel of March dust is worth a king's ransom*, and a smile of delight when April thunderstorms followed: *When April blows his horn, it's good for hay and corn.* Snow was a sign of fruitfulness: *A snow year's a rich year*, and late snow even more so: *A snowstorm in May is worth a waggonload of hay.* The Kentish weather proverb *Light Christmas, light wheatsheaf, dark Christmas, heavy wheatsheaf* meant that if there was a full moon about Christmas Day, the next year would bring a light harvest. A correspondent with NOTES AND QUERIES quoted a clerical friend who had this to say:

Old W____, now cutting my wood, tells me when he got from church yesterday, he pondered deeply the text, 'Light Christmas, light wheatsheaf,' and wondered whether he should be able to fatten a pig, for he never knew the saying to fail, in sixty years' experience.

Other proverbs guided the farmer through the farming year. On Candlemas Day, for instance, the careful farmer should still have had enough food put by to see his family and livestock through the remaining unproductive months:

A farmer should on Candlemas Day,
have half his corn and half his hay.

And Candlemas was also the season for the sowing of peas and beans:

Sow peas and beans in the wane of the moon;
who soweth them sooner, he soweth too soon.

June was the month when the harvest was set: *If you look at your corn in May, you'll come weeping away; if you look at the same in June, you'll come home in another tune*, while the shepherd was advised: *Shear your sheep in May, and shear them all the way.*

The farmer was advised to sow in plenty for his crop would inevitably attract unwelcome interest: *Sow four beans in a row, one for cowscot and one for crow, one to rot and one to grow*, otherwise it would be a case of *Little sow, little mow.* And there was an abundance of proverbs to help the farmer remember the best conditions for the sowing and reaping of his crop:

Sow beans in the mud, and they'll grow like a wood

Sow in a slop, 'twill be heavy at top (Wheat sown in wet soil will be fruitful)

Sow wheat in dirt, and rye in dust (Wheat likes wet conditions and rye drier ones)

Oats will mow themselves

If you cut oats green, you get both king and queen (If oats are harvested before they appear fully ripe then all the grains will be preserved)

Corn is not to be gathered in the Blade, but in the Ear.

In the last analysis, though, it was all a question of economics – to grow enough for one's own needs and sell the rest for a profit at market. *Corn and horn go together* was an old English proverb meaning that the prices of cattle and corn were linked; when one was dear, so was the other (John Ray, ENGLISH PROVERBS, 1678). But proverbial economists can't agree, just like their modern-day counterparts. A correspondent with NOTES AND QUERIES (1866) quotes the contrary proverb *Up corn, down horn*, with the explanation that when corn was expensive people spent so much on bread that they could not afford beef and the price fell.

'My dear fellow! There is nothing new under the sun.'
(George Orwell, COMING UP FOR AIR, 1939)

This proverb is from the Old Testament of the Bible. ECCLESIASTES 1:9 concludes that *there is no new thing under the sun;* it has all been seen, heard and done before.

OAKS

■ **Great oaks from little acorns grow**

Even that which is most impressive had a modest beginning

It is as if he is unable to resist a mood cue as a dog is a bone, or an actor an entrance. And yet if great presidencies, like great plays, can be said to plant their seeds in their prologue, Bill Clinton came out with a veritable cornucopia of verbal acorns from which to grow great oaks in his inaugural address.
(DAILY MAIL, 21 January 1993)

From little acorns great oaks do spring. In 80 minutes the seeds of self-belief which had begun with an elaborate public Irish warm-up session (the English stayed in their tents) had flourished into a huge tree of pride under whose branches Galwey scored unstoppably at the very death. Looking back it was always coming to this.
(SUNDAY TIMES, 21 March 1993)

There are many examples of the magnificent arising from the insignificant, of great things which *proceede and increase of smaul and obscure begynnynges* (Richard Eden, tr Peter Martyr THE DECADES OF THE NEWE WORLDE, 1555). A Chinese proverb from the sixth century BC tells us that *a journey of a thousand miles began with a single step.* The Bible, in MATTHEW 13:32, reminds us that the minute mustard seed grows into a tree that birds delight to nest in; and Dante describes how *From a little spark may burst a mighty flame* (DIVINA COMMEDIA, PARADISO, c 1300). This idea is encapsulated in the proverb *Magnum in parvo* (A lot in a little), which is still sometimes quoted in the original language today. A related idea which finds expression in Latin and Greek texts is that of the seed or shoot becoming a tree and Erasmus, a scholar of the classical world, marvels that a huge cypress tree is encased in such a small seed (SIMILIA c 1508). It is small wonder, therefore, that the English should develop a comparison with the mighty oak with which they are so familiar. *An acorn one day proves an oak,* writes Richard Corbet (POEMS, c 1640), a thought recorded by Thomas Fuller in GNOMOLOGIA (1732): *The greatest Oaks have been little Acorns.* But it is an American, David Everett, who gives the present day proverb its poetic quality. In 1791 he wrote a verse for seven-year-old Ephraim H Farrar to perform at a school declamation:

You'd scarce expect one of my age
To speak in public on the stage;
And if I chance to fall below
Demosthenes or Cicero,

Don't view me with a critic's eye,
But pass my imperfections by.
Large streams from little fountains flow,
Tall oaks from little acorns grow.

■ **Little strokes fell great oaks**

Great obstacles can be overcome by persistence and effort

See also: Rome wasn't built in a day; Slow but steady wins the race

The earliest recorded version is found in the works of Diogenianus (ADAGIA, c AD 125) and quoted by Erasmus in his ADAGIA (1536). From the sixteenth century onwards *many* strokes were needed to fell an oak but in 1750 Benjamin Franklin included the proverb in POOR RICHARD'S ALMANACK and used the wording in the form we know today: *Little strokes fell great oaks.*

A related proverb also teaches us the value of persistence: *An oak is not felled at a single stroke.* This variant appears first in English in Chaucer's THE ROMAUNT OF THE ROSE (c 1400) and regularly thereafter.

PEARLS

■ **Don't cast your pearls before swine**

Don't lavish valuable or beautiful things upon those who are unable to appreciate their worth

How strange that I should be called a destitute woman! When I have all of these treasures [beauty of the mind and richness of the spirit and tenderness of the heart] locked in my heart. I think of myself as a very, very rich woman! But I have been foolish – casting my pearls before swine.
(Tennessee Williams, A STREETCAR NAMED DESIRE, 1947)

Isabel drove with Goodrich beside her. Happy, but still feeling she was casting swine before pearls, Isabel was painfully conscious of the shortcomings of the scenery; above all its literal flatness.
(L P Hartley, A PERFECT WOMAN, 1955)

The expression comes from the Sermon on the Mount where Jesus says: *Give not that which is holy unto the dogs, neither cast your pearls before swine, lest they trample them under their feet and turn again and rend you* (MATTHEW 7:6). This vivid picture of precious pearls being thrown in the mud before foraging hogs has been open to various interpretations. Some claim *pearls* is a mistranslation for *crumbs*, which would significantly change the sense; others argue that the proverbial saying was a warning against the excessive and ostentatious display of religious rites. Far and away the commonest hermeneutical interpretation, however, is that the truths Christ taught, his 'pearls of great price', should not be made known indiscriminately to those so unwilling to listen that they become aggressively antagonistic. This meaning was plucked from the Bible and used in literature from as early as the fourteenth century. The Chinese have an equivalent proverb cited by Justus Doolittle in his collection of 1872: *Don't play the lute before a donkey.*

An abbreviated form of the expression comes in an old joke:

Man, ushering woman through door before him: Age before beauty.
Woman: Pearls before swine, you mean.

Usage: If used in its basic meaning, the phrase has acquired a superior, patronising tone. Nowadays it may well be jocular

---

PEN

■ **The pen is mightier than the sword**

Words are more effective than weapons

THE ECONOMIST STYLE GUIDE
Because if the sword were mightier than the pen, we'd be selling fencing lessons.
(Advertisement, THE ECONOMIST BOOKS, 1992)

I studied with Vernon Elliott and then I went to Archie Camden, who was the doyen of bassoonists, a very amusing man.

But once I went up to Cambridge the pen proved mightier than the bassoon. Nevertheless I had wonderful fun. I did more playing there than I've done in the rest of my life.
(WEEKEND TELEGRAPH, 9 January 1993)

The influence of the written word has grown in importance over the centuries with the increase in literacy levels and the ready availability of printed materials. Up to the end of the fifteenth century, everything was hand written and necessarily of limited distribution.

From about 1492, there emerged the profession of book publisher, incorporating the trades of the type founder, printer and book seller. The power of the press began to strengthen the power of the pen.

Walsh quotes Claus Petri commenting in 1520 on the prodigious output of King Christian II of Denmark, for whom *letters did more than the sword.* The Portuguese Antonio da Fonseca in the early seventeenth century and the Frenchman Saint-Simon in 1702 both reflected a similar sentiment. In England Martin Parker pointed out the danger of the pen: *More danger comes by th' quill than by the sword* (THE POET'S BLIND MAN'S BOUGH, 1641), a notion reiterated in the following century by William King: *A sword less hurt does, than a pen* (EAGLE AND ROBIN, before 1712).

So feared was the might of the written word that a publisher found guilty of circulating treasonable pamphlets might expect to be nailed to the pillory by his ears, which would later be cut off and left as a warning to others. This was a fate suffered in 1633 by William Prynne, author of a controversial book. Daniel Defoe was a staunch believer in the might of the pen and himself the author of pamphlets and satirical works. In 1703 he was fined, imprisoned and pilloried for the publication of THE SHORTEST WAY WITH THE DISSENTERS, a pamphlet which highlighted the intolerance of the established church.

The form in which we know the proverb today seems to have acquired its definitive statement in Lord Lytton's play RICHELIEU of 1838:

Beneath the rule of men entirely great,
The pen is mightier than the sword.

As society has moved from the quill to the word processor, the saying has had to change with it. The following comes from Lee Thayer's PERSONS UNKNOWN (1941): *The typewriter is so much more to be reckoned with than the sword.*

Usage: A well-used expression, even a cliché

PENNY

■ **A bad penny always turns up (again)**

Undesirable acquaintances have the habit of making unwelcome reappearances. A wayward family member will always turn up again eventually

Variant: A bad penny always comes back

She had not seen him for thirty-six years. He must be over seventy years of age, and he had turned up again like a bad penny, doubtless a disgrace! What had he been doing in those thirty-six years?
(Arnold Bennett, THE OLD WIVES' TALE, 1908)

So here you are again. You're like a bad coin – always turning up.
(Eugene O'Neill, MARCO MILLIONS, 1927)

The proverb speaks of 'bad' or 'counterfeit' money. A common trick when a counterfeit or foreign coin comes into one's possession is to attempt to pass it on to another person

who, naturally, will try to do the same. Invariably, the coin does the rounds until it finds its way back into the pocket from which it started.

When the proverb was used in the early nineteenth century it was a bad shilling which kept coming back but this was subject to devaluation in the twentieth century.

■ **In for a penny, in for a pound**

Once committed to a project or course of action, it is worth giving all possible resources to it

See also: You might as well be hanged for a sheep as for a lamb

Cheyne hesitated. Should he ask for all the information he could get about the sinister quartet and their mysterious activities? He had practically admitted the burglary. Should he not make the most of his opportunity? In for a penny, in for a pound.
(F W Crofts, INSPECTOR FRENCH AND THE CHEYNE MYSTERY, 1926)

' . . . If you saw a lorry carrying a small parcel containing a Verzelini drinking glass accidentally slewed over the wall of the Chelmer canal, what would you do?' . . .

I thought, sensing a trick. Verzelini was a Murano glassmaker from Venice who made it to Good Queen Bess's London and turned out richly valuable Venetian-style glass in his little City factory until the late 1590's. A single glass nowadays would give you enough to retire on. Well, in for a penny . . .
'Okay, I'd try and save it.'
(Jonathan Gash, THE GONDOLA SCAM, 1984)

Okay, I thought. Sod it. In for a penny, in for a pound. I turned the tiny wheel. My great one-speed barge trundled out into the void. I hoped there was water out there.
(Jonathan Gash, THE GONDOLA SCAM, 1984)

The likelihood is that this phrase originated in the gambler's willingness to take greater risks (and so reap greater reward) when convinced of a particular wager. It is used now in much wider contexts where whole-hearted commitment is being pledged, whatever the cost.

The saying has been current since at least the end of the seventeenth century and has been used more recently by many well-known writers including Scott, Dickens, and Somerset Maugham.

■ **Look after the pennies and the pounds will look after themselves**

If you are careful in your management of small amounts of money you will soon amass a larger sum

Variant: Take care of the pennies and the pounds will take care of themselves

See also: Every little helps

Take care of the pence and the pounds will take care of themselves is as true of personal habits as of money.
(George Bernard Shaw, PYGMALION, 1912)

So you're solvent and free of debt at last! The unwanted pounds have disappeared, and you're feeling good. Reward yourself – within your means, of course – perhaps with a meal out, or plans to save for a holiday.

And never forget (drat) that Mother was right. Take care of the pence and the pounds will take care of themselves.
(GOOD HOUSEKEEPING, April 1992)

According to a letter written by Lord Chesterfield to his son on 5 February 1750, the adage was coined by William Lowndes who served three monarchs (King William, Queen Anne and King George I) as Secretary of the Treasury. Mr Lowndes, whom Chesterfield accused of being miserly in an earlier letter, lived rigorously by his maxim. It is to be hoped that he found pleasure in doing so because, since wealth cannot be taken to the grave, it was his two young grandsons who enjoyed the considerable fortune that he had amassed.

Usage: Restricted to financial contexts

PHYSICIAN

■ **Physician, heal thyself**

Before correcting or healing others, first make sure you are not suffering from the same problem yourself

'Check the gases every quarter of an hour, please,' said the specialist in the Intensive Therapy Unit at the Radcliffe Hospital in Oxford to the young nurse on duty. He was played by Julian Mitchell who wrote the script of Twilight Of The Gods, the very last episode in the vastly popular Inspector Morse series. She might have replied 'Physician heal thyself' had she been

Proverbs on the psychologist's couch

Appearances are deceptive indeed. A superficially innocent expression, such as *The pitcher goes so often to the well that it is broken at last*, that tells us literally that a pot that is heavily used for drawing water will eventually break, and proverbially that a sequence of events will one day come to an end, has an entirely different level of analysis.

An example of sexual interpretation is a proverb picture by Greuze, THE BROKEN PITCHER. Early critics of this eighteenth-century painting had noted the hidden sensuality of Greuze's art. More recent commentators trace the symbolism back to the Greek myth of Amymone who, carrying a pot that falls to the ground, was pursued and won by Poseidon. Vinken in a Freudian analysis concludes:

The breaking of the pitcher in Greuze's painting may be interpreted as a defloration. This symbolism brings to mind the peculiar behaviour of one of Freud's patients, a girl with symptoms of obsession, who, before retiring for the night, placed all the pots and vases in her room in the middle of the table to ensure that they would not fall at night. 'Flowerpots and vases,' Freud adds, 'like all vessels, are female symbols. We know the ubiquitous custom that a betrothal is attended with the smashing of a pot or plate. The measures taken against the breaking of pitchers thus denote a rejection of the entire complex that is closely bound up with virginity and defloration.'

There is still more! Another ancient tradition of broken pots goes back to a book of fables in Sanskrit, called the PANCATRANTA, of about AD 500. One of them tells a story that finishes *Engrossed in his fantasies he kicked out, so that his pot broke and he was 'stained white by rice'*. Vinken sees the breaking of the pot in this fable and in subsequent versions found in Europe as representing menstruation, abortion or confinement. The pot is a symbol of the uterus.

There is yet another line of interpretation. In the eighteenth century, Salomon Gessner illustrated his own story entitled THE BROKEN PITCHER. Freudians find in this a strong realisation of the classical imagery of masturbation and impotence.

Who would have thought so much was hidden in so little! A case of *magnum in parvo*, perhaps. But what would the Freudians say about the choice of this proverb here . . . ?

checking the doctor/author's clichés instead. In Twilight Of The Gods they came, you might say, thick and fast, every few minutes. (GUARDIAN, 21 January 1993)

What an angry article. We wonder what happened to Fay Weldon when she spoke to the group of therapists. . . . One of the tenets of Kleinian theory is that what we cannot have, and then envy, we spoil for others. Fay, having had a 'more helpful analysis', is now deriding the process so that readers of the Saturday Review could be discouraged from seeking this form of help. The mentality being: if I am no longer in therapy, nobody else should have it. A classic case of spoiling. (THE TIMES, 6 March 1993)

Jesus chose the synagogue in Nazareth, his home town, to announce that he was the expected Messiah. When the people, dumbfounded at his audacity, started to murmur against him, Jesus said to them: *Ye will surely say to me this proverb, Physician, heal thyself; whatever we have heard done in Capernaum, do also here in thy country* (LUKE 4:23).

Christ's use of the proverb in the gospel popularised it throughout Christian Europe but his words show that the saying was already familiar to his listeners. In the sixth century BC Aesop's fable of THE WORM AND THE FOX had already made the same point. It tells of a worm who boasted to a fox that it was a skilled physician. The fox pointed out that the worm was lame and asked, *How, healing others, have you not healed yourself?*

This theme was reiterated in later classical literature: In PROMETHEUS BOUND (c 470 BC), the Athenian tragic poet Aeschylus writes: *Wretched that I am – such are the inventions I devised for mankind, yet have no cunning wherewith to rid myself of my own sufferings*; Euripedes speaks of one who was *Healer of others, full of sores himself* (FRAGMENTS, c 420 BC); and in AD FAMILIARES, written in the half century before Christ, Cicero warns against imitating bad physicians who claim to be masters of healing but are unable to cure themselves.

PIPER

■ **He who pays the piper calls the tune**

He who finances a project has a right to dictate how the money is spent

He who pays the piper calls the tune is recorded first in its current form in the nineteenth century. It seems to originate in *Those that dance must pay the piper*, a saying from the first half of the seventeenth century.

Country dancing on the green or in a hall was a favourite entertainment for everyone as this traditional rhyme shows:

Much time is wasted now away,
At pigeon-holes, and nine-pin play,
Whilst hob-nail Dick, and simp'ring Frances,
Trip it away in country dances . . .

People danced at festivals, which were numerous, and weddings. The music was provided by travelling musicians who were hired to play their pipes, tambours and fiddles for the merrymaking. Those who wished to dance had to pay for the music and those who paid for the music had the right to name their favourite tune.

Strolling musicians seemed to have had an unerring instinct that their services would be required, for another proverb of the period tells us that *Fiddlers, dogs and flies come to feasts uncalled.* James Kelly explains the proverb thus: *Fiddlers for money, the flies for a sip, and the dogs for a scrap* (SCOTTISH PROVERBS, 1721). An Elizabethan saying specifies what a musician would expect for his services: *Fiddler's fare: meat, drink, and money.* According to James Kelly, this last proverb was later used to refer to an evening's entertainment where the guests themselves had been offered 'fiddler's fare', that is food, drink and the chance to win some money at the card tables.

PITCHER

■ **Little pitchers have big ears**

Be careful what you say in front of the children

Variant: Little pitchers have long / wide ears

Be not angry with the child. Pitchers have ears.
(William Shakespeare, RICHARD III, 1594)

Charley verified the adage about little pitchers, I am sure.
(Charles Dickens, BLEAK HOUSE, 1852)

A pitcher is an earthenware vessel with two ears, or handles, which is generally used for storing or carrying water or other liquids. This proverb, which dates back to at least the sixteenth century, makes a play on the word 'ears': little children may look inattentive but, like little pitchers, their ears are long and they are quite capable of picking up tit-bits of information and gossip their elders would not want them to know.

The wisdom of this proverb is echoed in another: *The child says nothing but what it heard by the fire* (George Herbert, JACULA PRUDENTUM, 1640).

Obviously a safeguard is needed in the event that a parent should be indiscreet. Benjamin Franklin has the answer: *Teach your child to hold his tongue; he'll learn fast enough to speak* (POOR RICHARD'S ALMANACK, 1734).

Usage: Somewhat dated

■ **The pitcher goes so often to the well that it is broken at last**

Continued success will eventually end in failure. Continued dishonesty will eventually be discovered

When – and if – I had my sight back I was going to apply for a transfer to another side of the business. And if that did not go through, I'd quit the job altogether. I had built up a considerable resistance to triffid poison since my first sting in the garden. I could take, and had taken, without very much harm, stings which would have laid an inexperienced man out very cold indeed. But an old saying about a pitcher and a well kept on recurring to me. I was taking my warning.

(John Wyndham, THE DAY OF THE TRIFFIDS, 1951)

This proverb has been one of the most widely used in the European tradition (and beyond), yet it is today relatively infrequent in England. This has not always been the case, however. Early recorded uses go back to the fourteenth century, and it is found in the major proverb collections of subsequent years. In the nineteenth century, it still has life left in it. Walter Scott alludes to it and, intriguingly, the great boxer John L Sullivan is reported to have used it at the moment of his defeat by James J Corbett in 1892. It has a particularly rich and well-documented history in art, literature and psychiatry. (For the last of these, see **Proverbs on the psychiatrist's couch**, page 187.)

Pictures depicting this particular proverb have been the subject of an extensive monograph by Zick, of a section of a book by Pigler and of many shorter articles. It appears that the first pictorial representation is in a French woodcut of about 1485. Subsequently, it features widely in the proverb pictures that became popular with many artists. Of special note are Brueghel's NETHERLANDIC PROVERBS of 1559 and THE BROKEN PITCHER by Greuze (1725–1805). The latter, for example, met with enormous success: even a century after its composition it was still the 'unmistakably most popular painting of Paris, which, in the Louvre, can only be approached through a double barrier of spectators'. Jordaens's (1593–1678)

version of the proverb also inspired Dutch tapestries on this theme.

The proverb has played a significant role in drama. In his play AUTO DA MOFINA MENDES, the major sixteenth century Portuguese dramatist Gil Vicente featured a pot and its subsequent breaking as a vital symbolic representation of Mary's confinement leading to Christ's birth. Much later, Heinrich von Kleist, as a result of a wager with friends, wrote the play THE BROKEN PITCHER (1802). He was inspired to do this by an engraving of Leveau, which itself drew on Debucourt's VILLAGE JUDGE (1781). Debucourt in turn owed a debt to his friend Greuze's very popular depiction of the proverb. Subsequently, Kleist's play gave rise to a story with the same title by Zschokke and a whole series of comic operas in France, between 1818 and 1884.

Usage: Dated

PLACE

■ **A place for everything and everything in its place**

Keep everything neat and tidy, and life will run more smoothly

The twin pillars of the English house, Shoul claims, are privacy and a 'place for everything and everything in its place'. What that means for a start, is no open-plan designs. This American import has a number of sinister features that few home-owners considered while knocking through every wall in sight in the '70s and '80s.
(DAILY TELEGRAPH, 13 March 1993)

Way back in the seventeenth century George Herbert recorded the maxim *All things have their place*, adding rather weakly, *knew we how to place them* (JACULA PRUDENTUM, 1640). This indecisiveness is perhaps one of the reasons why nothing more along these lines is recorded in literature for quite some time. By the nineteenth century, however, the saying is back. Thomas C Haliburton used it in NATURE (1855). A few years later, in THRIFT (1875), Samuel Smiles exemplifies the brisk, businesslike approach of the self-made man. For him tidiness is the basis of sound management. *Order, he says, is most useful in the management of everything . . . Its maxim is, A place for everything and everything in its place.*

Orderliness and neatness are very Victorian values. H W Shaw puts it thus: *As a general thing, an individual who is neat in his person is neat in his morals.* (See *Cleanliness is next to godliness*.) As to how the proverb came about, there is little certainty. Marshall McLuhan claimed in his UNDERSTANDING MEDIA (1964) that the phrase was an allusion to printing and the necessity of returning type to its proper box. This is merely an assertion, without supporting evidence. Archer Taylor (1968), a more reliable guide, suggests that our modern phrase is an extension of the two separate, simpler expressions *There is a place for everything* and *Everything in its place*. It would be quite natural that they should join to form one composite new proverb.

POT

■ A watched pot never boils

Time drags when something is eagerly expected

Variant: A watched pot is long in boiling

'Come, now,' said Mrs Sturgis, 'my master told me to see you to bed, and I mun. What's the use of watching? A watched pot never boils, and I see you are after watching the weather-cock. Why now, I try never to look at it, else I could do nought else. My heart many a time goes sick when the wind rises, but I turn away and work away, and try never to think on the wind, but on what I ha gotten to do.'
'Let me stay up a little,' pleaded Mary, as her hostess seemed so resolute about seeing her to bed. Her looks won her suit.
(Elizabeth Gaskell, MARY BARTON, 1848)

That commonplace object of the kitchen, the *pot*, has spawned quite a number of proverbs over the centuries. Perhaps surprisingly *A watched pot never boils*, one of the most frequent today, is not recorded before the nineteenth century. Since then it has seemed to lend itself to a variety of reformulations, often somewhat humorous in tone. Ogden Nash, for instance, entitles one of his poems A WATCHED EXAMPLE NEVER BOILS. Dorothy Hughes neatly captures the frustration of waiting for a call that does not come: *A watched phone never rang.* (BAMBOO BLONDE, 1931).

But is the proverb true? Two psychologists reported in 1980 on a study that they had carried out. Two groups of people were shown a pot of water on a hotplate. One group was told to say when the water began to boil; the other group was not given this instruction. After this, both groups were left for four minutes, although they were not aware of the duration of the period. Then they were asked to estimate how long the interval had been. The first group's estimated times were appreciably longer than those of the second group. The researchers concluded that the 'watched pot effect' leads to heightened expectancy.

Usage: Occasionally *pan* may be substituted for *pot*

■ **The pot calls the kettle black**

Used of someone who criticises failings in others that he himself possesses

But a very few weeks after Voltaire's arrival, little clouds of discord become visible on the horizon; and one can overhear the pot and the kettle, in strictest privacy calling each other black.
(Lytton Strachey, BIOGRAPHICAL ESSAYS, 'VOLTAIRE AND FREDERICK THE GREAT', 1949)

Pots and kettles may quarrel; but their colour is proverbially much the same. Most of the enemies of romanticism are, in their own way, as extravagant and one-sided (that is to say, as romantic) as the Romantics themselves.
(Aldous Huxley, MUSIC AT NIGHT, 'THE NEW ROMANTICISM', 1949)

The early form of this proverb in the seventeenth century was *The pot calls the kettle burnt-arse* (John Clarke,

PAROEMIOLOGIA, 1639). Cooking was done over an open fire and the saying alludes to the sooty, blackened base of the cooking pots.

The proverb already existed in various forms in Spain and was possibly introduced into English by the publication of Cervantes' DON QUIXOTE (1615) where we find: *The frying pan said to the kettle, get away black-eye.* This version is very close to an Arabic proverb, reminding us that Arab dominion over much of Spain from AD 711 to 1492 left a linguistic heritage behind it.

Quarrels between blackened pots and pans are common to the proverbs of several European languages, but there are also variants. German, for instance, has *One ass nicknames another Long-ears*; French has *Dirty-nosed folk always want to wipe other folks' noses*; and the Scots *'Crooked Carlin,' quoth the cripple to his wife.*

POVERTY

■ **Poverty is no crime**

Being poor in itself is not blameworthy

Variants: Poverty is no sin; Poverty is not a crime

Poverty is no sin was recorded by George Herbert in JACULA PRUDENTUM (1640). It expressed the idea already in circulation that poverty was not a vice but an inconvenience. But while poverty itself is not a crime, it has long been recognised as engendering it. In the first century Cassiodorus wrote that *Poverty is the mother of crime* (VARIAE, c AD 550). The Persian poet Sadi concurred, pointing out that *The needy stain the garment of chastity with sin, as those who are hungry steal bread* (GULISTAN, c 1258). In a letter to James Boswell (7 December 1782), Dr Samuel Johnson considered how poverty prevents even the most determined from leading blameless lives. *Poverty*, he wrote, *is a great enemy to human happiness; it certainly destroys liberty, and it makes some virtues impracticable.*

A further problem is that, while few people would subscribe to the idea that poverty is a crime, its victim is regarded with suspicion or scorned. Menander stated that *A poor man, though he speak the truth, is not believed* (FRAGMENTS, c 330 BC).

The sin is that poverty is permitted to exist. George Bernard Shaw is to the point when he says, *What is the matter with the poor is Poverty: what is the matter with the rich is Uselessness* (MAXIMS FOR REVOLUTIONISTS, 1903). We are all to blame.

PRACTICE

■ **Practice makes perfect**

In order to master any skill you have to repeat it over and over

Hypnotism brought matter for the marvel-mongers, and there followed a long procession of words in limping Greek – a little difficult till practice had made perfect. (George Gissing, THE PRIVATE PAPERS OF HENRY RYECROFT, 'AUTUMN', 1903)

Young birds very frequently make their first flight when their parents are out of sight. Practice of course makes perfect and puts a polish on the somewhat awkward first performance; but there is no elaborate learning needed as with our learning of golf or tennis or figure-skating. (J Huxley, MAN IN THE MODERN WORLD, 'THE INTELLIGENCE OF BIRDS', 1947)

Up to now inspectors have judged schools and teachers according to 'good practice'. But Professor Alexander and Mr Clarke now say that 'good practice' makes far from perfect. The professor's report, based on four years' research, makes 55 recommendations and is a conclusive indictment of modern methods. Teachers fail to stretch pupils arranged in groups with an over-emphasis on project and topic work. (DAILY MAIL, 5 November 1991)

Unfortunately, there are no short cuts to success, even for the talented. Practice makes perfect, says Professor Anders Ericsson of Florida State University, whose study of musicians, chess players and sportsmen showed that the highest achievers practised up to four hours a day for 10 years or more. (GOOD HOUSEKEEPING, June 1993)

The importance of putting theory into practice and learning by experience is an ancient one. For Corinthian tyrant Periander *practice is everything* (APOPHEGM, c 600 BC); *Practice is the best of all instructors* according to Publilius Syrus, (SENTENTIAE, c 43 BC); and Pliny the Younger tells us that *it is difficult to retain the knowledge one has acquired, without putting it in practice* (LETTERS, c AD 108).

Thomas Norton probably drew on Publilius Syrus in his rendering *Use maketh Masterie* in his ORDINALL OF ALCHIMY of 1477, and Heywood records the same form in his collection of proverbs of 1546. Thomas Wilson came very close to our modern form in his ARTE OF RHETORIQUE (1553) where he writes; *Before arte was inuented, eloquence was used, and through practise made perfect.* But the expression was more widely found as *Use maketh perfection* and did not settle into its modern form until the mid-eighteenth century.

At this same period, Dr Johnson communicates the notion of practice making perfect by quoting a Latin proverb in a letter of 16 April 1763: *If at the end of seven years you write good Latin, you will excel most of your contemporaries: Scribendo disces scribere. It is only by writing ill that you can attain to write well.* He is probably continuing a tradition begun over two centuries before. In ADAGIA (1536) Erasmus lists a number of Latin proverbs, variants of the same idea, which teach that learning comes through practice: *By building learn to build, By singing learn to sing*, etc.

The wellerism

Samuel Weller has an unusual claim to fame. Not only was he Pickwick's faithful aide in Dickens' PICKWICK PAPERS but he has had a type of proverb named after him; the wellerism. These expressions have the basic form 'A', *said* B. The quoted words are followed by a mention of the speaker, then usually by an allusion to the context.

One kind involves a reference to ancient fables, in which animals often speak: *'Sour grapes,' said the fox and could not reach them.* Others date back to Anglo-Saxon times: *Things are not well throughout the world,' said he who heard them wailing in Hell.*

Some are probably genuine quotations. Blind Hugh was a noted wit of the sixteenth century: *'That I would fain see,' said blind Hugh.* This may have found more generic expression in the punning saying: *'I see,' said the blind man and picked up his hammer and saw.*

PRICE

■ **Every man has his price**

Everyone is open to bribery if the inducement is sufficient

The popular view is undoubtedly that Sir Robert Walpole is the originator of the phrase. Lord Lytton, for example, wrote a blank-verse comedy entitled WALPOLE; OR, EVERY MAN HAS HIS PRICE (1869), making the minister say both *Every man has his price, I must bribe left and right* and *Every man has his price, my majority's clear.*

However, there has been a long and detailed debate as to whether it was in fact Sir William Wyndham who first used the phrase, and quite what was

There are three things . . .

Three things drive a man out of the house: smoke, rain, and a scolding wife.
This proverb was probably compiled by Pope Innocent III (DE
CONTEMPTU MUNDI, c 1210) from verses in the biblical book of
PROVERBS. The saying came into frequent use, being found in the
works of Langland, Chaucer, George Gascoigne and Shakespeare. It is
an example of a genre of proverb which collects together a set of
subjects which share a common feature, or sets of features that are
attributed to one subject. Other biblical instances can be found in
PROVERBS 30:15 and 18–19.

Such proverbs, which became a feature of a number of European
languages, enjoyed popularity in the middle ages and, during the
Renaissance, collections of these sayings were made, inspiring later
imitators:

Dryve fro your herte three thinges that been contrariouse to good conseil,
that is to seyn, tre, coveiteise, and hastifnesse
(Chaucer, TALE OF MELIBEUS, c 1386)

Three things are unsatiable, priests, monckes, and the sea
(Unknown, PHILIP AND MARY, c 1560)

A ship under sail, a man in complete armour, and a woman with a great
belly are three of the handsomest sights
(James Howell, ENGLISH PROVERBS, 1659)

Some of the earlier instances of these proverbs are quite complex. One
particular example, which is traceable to an eleventh century Arabic
text, gives a long list of qualities that a beautiful woman should
possess – expressed in multiples of three, of course:

And the maiden said: 'The woman is beautiful who possesses eighteen traits
. . . she who is long in three, and small in three, and broad in three, and white
in three, and black in three, and red in three . . . I say long in three, that she
be of great estate, and that she have a long neck and long fingers, and white
in three; her body white, and her teeth white, and the white of her eyes white,
and black in three: black hair and black brows and the black of her eyes black,
and red in three: lips, cheeks, gums, and small in three: small mouth, small
nose and small feet, and broad in three: broad of hips and broad of back and
wide of forehead . . .'

said. The facts appear to be that, in the debate on Bromley's motion to repeal the Septennial Act on 13 March 1734 in the House of Commons, Sir William spoke before Sir Robert, just before the division that rejected the motion, in these words:

Let us suppose, sir, a gentleman at the head of the administration, whose only safety depends upon corrupting the members of this House. This may now be only a supposition, but it is certainly such a one as may happen; and if ever it should, let us see whether such a minister might not promise himself more success in a septennial, than he would in a triennial parliament. It is an old maxim, that every man has his price, if you can but come up to it. This, I hope, does not hold true of every man; but I am afraid it too generally holds true; and that of a great many it may hold true, is what, I believe, was never doubted of; . . . however, let us suppose this distressed minister applying to one of those men who has a price, and is a member of this House.

This account is quoted from THE PARLIAMENTARY HISTORY OF ENGLAND, VOL IX. It is corroborated by the report of this Parliamentary debate which extended from issue 89 to 96 of the contemporary publication THE BEE. Sir William is in veiled parliamentary fashion accusing the Minister, Sir Robert, of 'buying' support, because he knows that *every man has his price.*

It appears, then, that the expression was first given prominence by Sir William, although he himself says it is an old saying and not coined by him. It

may have been a reworking of a remark made by Epictetus in DISCOURSES (c AD 100): *Different men sell themselves at different prices.*

Subsequent to the debate, the attribution to Sir Robert may have come about because his opponents, led by Sir William, obviously considered that such a cynical adage correctly described Sir Robert's beliefs, and his practice towards keeping himself in power. So, through political mud-slinging, a phrase *about* Sir Robert's credo began to be ascribed *to* him. The ascription may have been made all the stronger by Sir Robert himself. Even one of his supporters – John Morley in his book WALPOLE – admits that he said something at least similar:

Walpole has no doubt suffered much in the opinion of posterity, as the supposed author of the shallow and cynical apophthegm, that 'every man has his price' . . . The story is a pure piece of misrepresentation. He never delivered himself of that famous slander on mankind. One day, mocking the flowery and declamatory professions of some of the patriots in opposition, he insisted on finding self-interest or family interest at the bottom of their fine things. 'All these men,' he said, 'have their price.'

Furthermore, Sir Robert seems almost to have accepted the charge himself. Lord Wilmot, in NOT SO BAD AS WE SEEM, gives this account of a discussion with him:

'Sir Robert,' says I, 'we men of the world soon come to the point; 'tis a maxim of yours that all have their price.'

'Not quite that,' says Sir Robert, 'but let us suppose that it is.'

So, popular opinion may be technically wrong in attributing the saying's origin to Walpole, but it seems to be right in substance, in that it describes his political beliefs and practice. All men of power face the same issue – differently expressed, it was reiterated on the other side of the Atlantic at a similar period. *Few men,* wrote George Washington to Robert Howe in 1779, *have virtue to withstand the highest bidder.*

PRIDE

■ Pride goes before a fall

Arrogant people are invariably made to look foolish and ridiculous

Variants: Pride goeth before a fall; Pride comes before a fall

'Pride comes before a fall!' In accordance with this, the greatest of Nature's ironies, the Forsyte family had gathered for a last proud pageant before they fell.
(John Galsworthy, THE MAN OF PROPERTY, 1906)

'I suppose he thinks he'd be mayor himself,' said the people of Blackstable. They pursed their lips. *'Pride goeth before a fall.'*
(W Somerset Maugham, CAKES AND ALE, 1930)

This is from the Old Testament of the Bible. PROVERBS 16:18 reads: *Pride goeth before destruction, and an haughty spirit*

before a fall. From the early sixteenth century the expression was *Pride will have a fall,* and so it continued for over three centuries. The nineteenth century came back to the biblical text. In THE ANTIQUARY (1816), Walter Scott has *Pride goeth before destruction.* Later writers use *Pride goeth before a fall* or *Pride comes before a fall.*

Down the centuries, writers have striven to put into their own telling words and images the wisdom contained in the proverb:

The lofty pine is oftenest agitated by the winds, high towers rush to the earth with a heavier fall, and the lightning most frequently strikes the highest mountains. (Horace)

An avenging God closely follows the haughty. (Seneca)

Like little wanton boys that swim on bladders,
This many summers in a sea of glory,
But far beyond my depth: my high-blown pride
At length broke under me. (Shakespeare)

To lordlings proud I tune my lay,
Who feast in bower or hall;
Though dukes they be, to dukes I say,
That pride will have a fall. (Gay)

When pride and presumption walk before, shame and loss follow very closely. (Louis XI)

What is pride? a whizzing rocket
That would emulate a star. (Wordsworth)

PROCRASTINATION

■ **Procrastination is the thief of time**

Putting off taking action wastes time

See also: Never put off till tomorrow what you can do today; Tomorrow never comes

Never do tomorrow what you can do today. Procrastination is the thief of time.
(Charles Dickens, DAVID COPPERFIELD, 1850)

The proverb is a line from NIGHT THOUGHTS (1742), a poem by Edward Young:

Beware, Lorenzo! a slow, sudden death.
Be wise to-day, 'tis madness to defer;
Next day the fatal precedent will plead;
Thus on, till wisdom is pushed out of life.
Procrastination is the thief of time;
Year after year it steals, till all are fled,
And to the mercies of a moment leaves
The vast concerns of an eternal scene.

Warnings against procrastination have been sounded for centuries. Firstly it wastes time. Back in the first century Seneca wrote that *While we are procrastinating life speeds by* (AD LUCILIUM, c AD 64). Then it is hazardous. Writers in the sixteenth and seventeenth centuries pointed out the dangers of not doing something that really needed to be accomplished. Erasmus alerts us to the fact that *Procrastination brings loss, delay danger* (COLLOQUIA: ADOLESCENS, 1524) and W D Montagu that *There is no*

safetie in procrastinating (AL MONDO, 1633).

Not surprisingly there is an abundance of proverbs in every language that preaches against time wasting and delay:

Delays are dangerous
When the fool has made up his mind the market has gone by (Spanish)
Stay but a while, you lose a mile (Dutch)
When the horse has been stolen the fool shuts the stable (French)
After death the doctor (French)
After the war come the allies (Latin)
A little too late, much too late (Dutch)

And a rich stock of sayings that encourage immediate action:

God keep you from 'It is too late' (Spanish)
Strike while the iron is hot
Make hay while the sun shines
Never put off till tomorrow what you can do today
There's no time like the present
Take time by the forelock
Make hay while the sun shines

For those who find all this insistence on immediate action burdensome there is another side to the coin. When what needs to be done is nothing but a tedious duty, procrastination might be looked upon as saving one's time. This is certainly how Lord Henry looked upon it, for *he was always late on principle, his principle being that punctuality is the thief of time* (Oscar Wilde, THE PICTURE OF DORIAN GRAY, 1891).

PROPHET

■ **A prophet is not without honour save in his own country**

A person's gifts and talents may be recognised by others but rarely appreciated by those close to him

Variants: A prophet is not without honour, except in his own country; A prophet is without honour in his own country

See also: Familiarity breeds contempt

In Florence the Signory thought him an amusing fellow and his letters often made them laugh, but they had no great confidence in his judgment and never followed his advice.
'A prophet is not without honour save in his own country,' he sighed.
(W Somerset Maugham, THEN AND NOW, 1946)

Both Browning and Tennyson seem to me pure poets damaged by being too much honoured as prophets in their own country.
(F L Lucas, EIGHT VICTORIAN POETS, 'BROWNING', 1930)

Matthew's gospel records how Jesus, after travelling around teaching and healing, returned to his own home town, Nazareth, and began to teach in the synagogue. The people there wondered just who he thought he was, trying to tell them what to do. He was, after all, just the son of the local carpenter. Jesus answered their cynicism with these words: *A prophet is not without honour, except in his own country, and in his own house* (MATTHEW 13:58), but was unable to minister to them because of their hostility.

PUDDING

■ **The proof of the pudding is in the eating**

The wisdom of a course of action will be tested when it is put into practice

After all, the proof of the pudding is in the eating: The Eye of the Needle sold thirty-five thousand in England and eighty thousand in America, and for the serial rights of my next book I've got the biggest terms I've ever had yet.
(W Somerset Maugham, CAKES AND ALE, 1930)

In his own heart! The proof of the pudding was in the eating – Bosinney had still to eat his pudding.
(John Galsworthy, THE MAN OF PROPERTY, 1906)

The proof of the pudding is in the eating. Wait for another slice.
(Philip MacDonald, WARRANT FOR X, 1937)

Early medieval puddings were rather like a black pudding or haggis. A length of pig or sheep intestine would be blown open with a reed and filled with a mixture of oatmeal, minced meat, suet and seasoning, then secured at the ends with thin wooden skewers known as pudding-pricks – hence the old sixteenth century proverb *Everything hath an end, and a pudding hath two*. Later, meat or vegetable-based mixtures were encased in a floury dough and boiled or steamed in a cloth, or pudding-poke, instead of a gut and sweet puddings were also eaten.

Recipes for these delicacies were in print at the beginning of the seventeenth century when the proverb was first recorded. One book, HAVEN HEALTH of 1584, had: *Of the inward of beasts are made Puddings, which are best of an hog*. Its author, Cogan, would surely be as much concerned then as we are today with what the pudding tasted like. It may have looked and smelt delicious but have been stodgy in the centre or have had too much salt in it. It had to be subjected to the ultimate test, it had to be tasted before it could be judged good. It had to be 'proved'. The word 'proof' in this proverb is used in its old sense, to mean not 'demonstrate' but 'test', as in *The exception proves the rule*.

PUNCTUALITY

■ **Punctuality is the politeness of kings**

Good time-keeping shows respect to others

Variant: Punctuality is the politeness of princes

This is a translation of the French *L'exactitude est la politesse des rois* and was a favourite saying of Louis XVIII (1755–1824). It is sometimes rendered in English as *Punctuality is the politeness of*

princes. Samuel Smiles, who attributed the maxim to the wrong Louis, also considered punctuality to be *the duty of gentlemen, and the necessity of men of business* (SELF-HELP, 1859), whereas Emile Gaboriau considered it a courtesy to the inner man. *Punctuality*, he wrote, *is a politeness which a man owes to his stomach* (OTHER PEOPLE'S MONEY, 1867).

PURSE

■ **You can't make a silk purse out of a sow's ear**

It is impossible to make something fine and delicate out of materials that are rough and basic

Too late Julia realized that the best and the most-sacrificing of wives cannot make a silk purse out of a sow's ear, an Arnold Bennett out of an Oswald.
(Richard Aldington, SOFT ANSWERS, 'YES AUNT', 1932)

He remembered his uncle's saying that it took three generations to make a gentleman: it was a companion proverb to the silk purse and the sow's ear.
(W Somerset Maugham, OF HUMAN BONDAGE, 1915)

Who says you can't make a silk purse out of a sow's ear? Businessman Michael Timlin has managed to turn a £30 parking fine into a £30,000 sales order from those who fined him. As it was the Amsterdam police, whom he then talked into buying his Halifax company's illuminated signs and flashing

lamps, *his initiative means that Britain's trade balance is £30,000 to the good.*
(DAILY EXPRESS, 28 April 1993)

The New York city school system, largest in the country, has long been known as an educational black hole, swallowing reform plans and school visionaries without trace. It contains a handful of exceptional schools and probably a few thousand wonderful teachers, who continue to make miraculous silk purses out of sow's ears, but the typical city school is a decrepit building in which embattled and often embittered teachers deliver rote learning to disinterested students.
(TIMES EDUCATIONAL SUPPLEMENT, 26 March 1993)

While other domestic animals have coats and their ears are covered with shorter silkier hairs, the sow is blessed with bristles, a rough skin and ears just about the right size and shape for a draw-string purse. Unflattering comparisons between the poor sow's coarse complexion and finer materials have been made since at least the beginning of the seventeenth century. Her ears have proved unsuitable for 'cheverel', 'satin', 'velvet' and finally, in the eighteenth century, 'silk' purses.

The pig's ears were not the only part of its anatomy to be criticised. In the seventeenth and eighteenth centuries its curly tail was pronounced unsuitable for arrow shafts and whistles.

QUART

■ **You can't fit a quart into a pint pot**

You can't do the impossible

It is impossible to do justice to such a work on the stage; it must be mutilated, rearranged, decocted, and in the end, at best, it will hardly do more than produce an impression of confused splendour on an audience. It is the old difficulty of getting a quart into a pint bottle.
(Lytton Strachey, LANDMARKS IN FRENCH LITERATURE, 1912)

There was a noise like a herd of buffaloes coming down the two steps that lead to the bathroom. It was the kids, of course. Two kids in a house the size of ours is like a quart of beer in a pint mug.
(George Orwell, COMING UP FOR AIR, 1939)

A quart is a 'quarter of a gallon,' that is 'two pints'. Therefore it is vain to attempt to get one into a pint pot. This inevitable logic is first recorded in THE LIVING OF CHARLOTTE PERKINS GILMAN (1935), by Gilman herself: *However, one cannot put a quart in a pint cup.*

The scope of application is now very wide – any context where too much is being attempted with too little space, time or resource.

Usage: Informal

QUEEN

■ **Queen Anne is dead**

That's old news, tell me something I don't know

She really must try to forget these things, being away so long had kept them so fresh in her mind. Queen Anne's dead, she said to herself with a grimace, but she knew that she would never really forgive Flo and Edie if they had forgotten that Minnie was an intruder into the family.
(Angus Wilson, THE WRONG SET, 'UNION REUNION', 1949)

Today, when dons stud the Sunday press and impart their mysteries to a million or so television viewers, Pattison, who believed that a University should exist for pure learning and research . . . inevitably seems as dead as Queen Anne.
(J Raymond, THE DOGE OF DOVER, 'DIOGENES IN A FROCK-COAT', 1960)

Queen Anne is dead began as an eighteenth century retort to someone who was reporting stale news as fresh.

Interest in the Queen's death was particularly keen because, in spite of having endured seventeen pregnancies, she was to die childless. This made the question of the succession a complicated one. Would the throne be offered to the Catholic Old Pretender, James Edward, known as the 'warming-pan baby', or would it pass to the Hanoverians? Much parliamentary scheming took place between Whig and Tory members, each considering how best to promote their particular interests. Even on her deathbed Anne was treated to displays of bitter bickering between her senior ministers. Eventually a last-minute ministerial reshuffle eased the situation and two days later the Queen died, having ensured the succession of George I. Once the crisis had passed and the country knew it had a Hanoverian monarch, then the death of the Queen was of no more interest. It was old news.

The French have an equivalent expression, *C'est vieux comme le Pont-Neuf* (That's as old as the Pont-Neuf). The name Pont-Neuf means 'New Bridge' and, of course, once it was just that – the newest bridge to span the Seine. For centuries, however, it has been the oldest bridge in Paris, so a piece of news that is as old as the Pont-Neuf is so old that it dates back to 1607.

Usage: Usually sarcastic in tone. Now rather dated.

QUESTION

■ **There are two sides to every question**

There are two contrasting views to every issue

Variant: There are two sides to every issue

According to Diogenes Laertius (c AD 200–250) it was Protagoras who, in the fifth century BC, first propounded the idea that there are *two sides to every question, exactly opposite each other.* The Greek philosopher was particularly skilled in promoting the less convincing argument to give it equal weight.

The maxim was cited in Charles Kingsley's WATER BABIES (1863) but reference to its wisdom is found in written sources of the previous century. The first comes in THE SPECTATOR (1711–12), a periodical edited and mainly written by Steele and Addison. The magazine purported to be written by members of a club who represented various interests in society. In one article, Sir Roger de Coverley, representative of the country gentry, is asked to settle an argument between the quarrelsome Tom Touchy and Will Wimble. Having patiently listened and carefully deliberated Sir Roger tells them *with the air of a man who would not give his judgement rashly, that much might be said on both sides* (Addison, THE SPECTATOR, No 122, 1711).

Walsh illustrates the proverb with a moral tale written by the Rev Joseph Spence under the name of Sir Harry Beaumont. A prince erected a statue to the goddess of Victory at a crossroads. The goddess held a magnificent shield, one side of which was gold and the other silver. One day two knights, coming to the crossroads from opposite directions, greeted one another and passed the time of day. Then one knight commented on the golden shield. The other corrected him, declaring that it was silver. Before long the knights were in hot dispute and came to blows, each unseating the other from his horse. A peasant, who happened to have seen the incident, approached, patiently explained their error and pleaded with

them *never to enter into any dispute, for the future, till they had fairly considered both sides of the question* (BEAUMONT'S MORALITIES, 1753).

RACE

■ **Slow but sure wins the race**

Patience and perseverance lead to achievement

Variants: Slow but steady wins the race; Slow and sure wins the race

See also: Rome wasn't built in a day; Little strokes fell great oaks

Provided the dunce has persistency and application, he will inevitably head the cleverer fellow without those qualities. Slow but sure wins the race.
(Samuel Smiles, SELF-HELP, 1859)

Patience pays dividends.
Slow but steady is the motto of the Shape Challenge. Don't expect dramatic results within days. Patience will reward you with a gradual, safe and healthy drop in weight.
(DAILY EXPRESS, 29 December 1992)

Hares epitomise speed but they do not always win the race. A slower opponent may reach the line first. To Diogenianus in AD 125 this was the crab. Our current proverb prefers the symbol of the plodding tortoise. The reference is to Aesop's well-known fable of THE HARE AND THE TORTOISE (C 570 BC). The hare was confident that he could beat the slow old tortoise in a race and set off at a great speed. Judging himself to be so far ahead that he could not be caught, the hare sat down and took his ease but had not rested long before he fell asleep. The patient tortoise plodded on and, some time later, passed first the sleeping hare and then the finishing line. *Slow and sure had won the race.* The first recorded use is by Robert Lloyd in his poem THE HARE AND THE TORTOISE (1762):

The bets were won, the Hare awake,
When thus the victor Tortoise spake.
Puss, tho' I own thy quicker parts,
Things are not always done by starts.
You may deride my awkward pace,
But slow and steady wins the race.

It is taken up again a century later – in the quotation above – by Samuel Smiles, in a rather moralising tone that it can still retain today.

Commonly, longer proverbs are reduced in length and the shortened form alludes to the fuller version. In the case of *Slow but sure wins the race*, a shorter form predates Robert Lloyd. *Slow but sure* alone, in a number of related forms, is found at least 150 years earlier. One expression, then, appears to have been fleshed out to form another.

RAIN

■ **It never rains but it pours**

When one thing happens (usually a misfortune), others of a similar kind will inevitably follow

'*It never rains but it pours' might be said . . . of the number of books on Japan* which have appeared in the last few years. (SPECTATOR, 26 April 1913)

IT NEVER RAINS BUT IT POURS
The torrential storm which hit parts of southern Spain recently was not greeted with the enthusiasm you would expect from people who had not seen rain for months. Televised scenes of cars ploughing through streets swamped by floods served only to give Spaniards an ironic reminder of their country's perennial water shortage. (THE EUROPEAN, 4–7 March 1993)

In 1726 *It Cannot Rain but it Pours* was chosen as a book title by Dr John Arbuthnot and, in the same year, was also taken as a title for a paper written by his friends Swift and Pope for inclusion in their PROSE MISCELLANIES. By the time Thomas Gray quoted it in his LETTER TO DR WHARTON (2 February 1771) it had become *It never rains but it pours* and has remained in this form ever since.

REAP

■ **You reap what you sow**

You will eventually have to face up to the consequences of your behaviour

Variant: As you sow, so shall you reap

See also: As you make your bed, so you must lie in it

References to sowing and reaping are plentiful in ancient Greek and Latin literature but this proverb is from the New Testament and can be found in

GALATIANS 6:7. It is a recurrent biblical theme in both the Old and New Testaments that a person, or even a nation, reaps what is sown and is rewarded, for good or ill, according to whether actions are performed in obedience to God. In English, the proverb is found throughout the centuries after its first use in THE PROVERBS OF ALFRED (c 1275): *Hwych so the mon soweth, al swuch he schal mowe.*

It is hardly surprising that a task as fundamental to the sustenance of life should inspire a crop of proverbial comparisons. The success of any harvest depends on the quality of the seed. Sir Walter Raleigh reminds us that *according to the several seeds that we sow we shall reap several sorts of grain* (HISTORY OF THE WORLD, 1614). Some have sown corn cockle and reaped a disastrous harvest:

The cockle of rebellion, insolence, sedition,
Which we ourselves have plough'd for,
sow'd and scatter'd.
(Shakespeare, CORIOLANUS, 1607)

Others need to be warned about the folly of scattering thistles: *He that sows Thistles, shall reap Prickles* (Thomas Fuller, GNOMOLOGIA, 1732).

Thomas Draxe has the answer, advising that *He that soweth good seed shall reap good corn* (BIBLIOTHECA, 1633). But for a really abundant harvest of blessing this needs to be done plentifully. The New Testament reminds us that *he which soweth sparingly shall reap also sparingly; and he which soweth bountifully shall reap also bountifully* (II CORINTHIANS 4:6), advice which is echoed in British proverbs. Ferguson in

his collection of SCOTTISH PROVERBS (1595), tells us *Saw thin, maw thin,* and Randle Cotgrave's DICTIONARY (1611) concurs *Little sow, little mow.*

Perhaps a Persian proverb should have the last word: *If you sow thorns, you cannot reap jasmine.*

RECULER

■ **Reculer pour mieux sauter**

When facing a problem, it is best first to step back and take stock before launching oneself at it

Shares have risen by more than a quarter, virtually in a straight line, in less than five months. After a jump like that, what follows is not so much a bear market, more recueiller [sic] pour mieux sauter.
(DAILY TELEGRAPH, 6 February 1993)

No athlete competing in the high jump, nor any horse attempting to clear a fence, leaps from the foot of the obstacle but takes several steps back and runs at it the better to propel himself over it. The proverb too advises stepping back to take a fresh look at the project before taking off. *Stop when you have begun, draw back a pace,* advised Ovid (ARTIS AMATORIAE, c 1 BC).

From this classical start, the proverb spread into several European cultures. The version in French goes back at least to Montaigne: *They have gone back only that they may leap the better* (ESSAYS, 1580). Herbert in JACULA PRUDENTUM (1640) has the English: *We must recoil a little, to the end we may leap the better.* During later centuries, however, there is a continuing tendency to quote the original French. In the nineteenth century, Hare in GUESSES AT TRUTH (1827) wrote: *We must not overlook the numerous examples which history furnishes in proof that, according to the French proverb, il faut reculer pour mieux sauter.* In the twentieth century, we still quote the original – though it would be nice if the *Telegraph* would get it right!

REMEDY

■ **The remedy may be worse than the disease**

The steps taken to improve a situation may just make it worse

Variant: The remedy is worse than the disease

Rebellion against an unjust and corrupt government may be a remedy worse than the disease
(James Anthony Fronde, THE COUNCIL OF TRENT, 1896)

There are some remedies worse than the disease was one of the maxims of Publilius Syrus in SENTENTIAE (c 43 BC). Gaius Marius would have concurred. According to Plutarch (first century AD), after an operation to have a varicose vein removed, he remarked, *I see the cure is not worth the pain* (PARALLEL LIVES: GAIUS MARIUS). Francis Bacon, in his essay OF SEDITION AND TROUBLES (1597), was perhaps responsible for bringing the proverb *The Remedie is worse than the Disease* into English.

REVENGE

■ **Revenge is sweet**

Getting one's own back is satisfying

See also: Hell hath no fury like a woman scorned; An eye for an eye, and a tooth for a tooth

Homer describes revenge as being *sweeter far than flowing honey* (ILIAD, c 850 BC). William Painter, whose PALACE OF PLEASURE (1566) – translations of ancient and foreign stories into English – influenced English literature by providing contemporary dramatists with a wealth of material upon which to draw, also wrote that *Vengeance is sweet*. The proverb in the form *Revenge is sweet* was later used by Ben Jonson, Milton, Sheridan and Byron, amongst others. Some, like Milton, temper the sweetness with a warning:

Revenge, at first, though sweet,
Bitter 'ere long, back on itself recoils.
(PARADISE LOST, 1667)

Revenge recoiled on the Vachell family of Berkshire. The old story goes that they would not allow the Abbot of Reading to have hay carried through their yard. The abbot sent many messengers to plead with the family, the last being a monk whom Vachell killed in a fit of fury. As a result, he was forced to flee and, in bitter regret for his hasty action, took the motto 'Better suffer than revenge' for himself and his family.

The desire for revenge is certainly a powerful and consuming passion which, according to an old Italian proverb, does not diminish with time. *Revenge of a hundred years*, it says, *hath still its sucking* (milk) *teeth*. Psychologists say that it really does seem sweet since it is providing an outlet for pent up aggression and wounded feelings, and the victim no longer feels helpless. A radio programme reported the case of a young woman who, upset with her boyfriend for seeing another girl behind her back, filled his curtain pole with prawns. The fish rotted, the smell was disgusting but no one could find out where it was coming from. Eventually the boyfriend felt forced to move . . . taking his curtain pole with him.

RIDICULOUS

■ **From the sublime to the ridiculous is but a step**

It only takes a small thing to make the great and important look foolish and absurd

Napoleon Bonaparte, addressing the Abbé du Pradt, used these words to describe his disastrous Russian campaign, which ended in retreat from Moscow in 1812. He is popularly thought to have coined the saying but he was, in fact, condensing a thought from Thomas Paine's THE AGE OF REASON (1793):

The sublime and the ridiculous are often so nearly related that it is difficult to class them separately. One step above the sublime makes the ridiculous, and one step above the ridiculous makes the sublime again.

And again:

When authors and critics talk of the sublime, they see not how nearly it borders on the ridiculous.

Paine, a political radical, was a prominent figure in France during the French Revolution and Bonaparte's ascendancy. He was made an honorary citizen by the republican government and was elected a delegate to the Convention.

Lord Oxford, Coleridge and Deslard had all previously expressed a similar thought in one guise or another, though it is unlikely that Paine was conversant with them. According to a correspondent in NOTES AND QUERIES, Lord Oxford's *The magnificent and the ridiculous are so near neighbours that they touch each other* is found in his manuscript common-place book – hardly a place of easy access to the fiery radical!

Usage: The full proverbial form is now used more idiomatically as *to go from the sublime to the ridiculous,* when something exalted is juxtaposed with something trivial, such as genuine pathos with bathos

ROME

■ **All roads lead to Rome**

There are many different ways of reaching a goal. There are a number of different routes to the same conclusion

Rome has for millennia been a focal point militarily, culturally and spiritually. One suggestion is that all roads literally led to Rome, as the city expanded its control over the Italian peninsula and built roads to itself from its outlying empire.

From its foundation – traditionally by Romulus, the son of Mars – in 753 BC through to the present day, Rome has enjoyed an immense cultural reputation. Much of its monumental grandeur and art stem from its two periods of particular flowering: the Roman Empire up to AD 300, and the Renaissance and the Baroque (1450–1750). The proverb perhaps alludes to its world renown as a centre of culture.

Spiritually, the popes have lived in Rome since the fifth century, except for the period 1309 to 1378 when the papacy moved to Avignon. They enjoyed great temporal as well as spiritual power, especially from the foundation of the Holy Roman Empire in AD 800, directly controlling vast estates and millions of subjects. But it is surely the spiritual, rather than political, centrality of the papacy as head of the Roman Catholic Church that is uppermost. Today, in the world's smallest state of the Vatican, the Pope continues to welcome in St Peter's Square pilgrims who make their way there. For these faithful, all roads do indeed lead to Rome.

Rome's pre-eminence, for whatever reason, has long been recognised throughout Europe. Language reflects that. Certainly this proverb, apparently first in Italian *Tutte le strade conducono a Roma*, is found in many languages. As for English, in 1391 Chaucer wrote a treatise on the Astrolabe, an old instrument used for measuring distances in astronomy. In the PROLOGUE we read that *diverse pathes leden diverse folk the righte way to Rome.* This is the earliest English reference we have to the numerous roads leading to the city.

A similar thought is expressed in non-European contexts, but the focal point is different. In China all roads lead to Peking; in Japan to the Mikado's palace.

■ **Rome wasn't built in a day**

Impressive results are not obtained overnight

See also: Little strokes fell great oaks; Slow but sure wins the race

In truth, diamonds are not made in a day; and, though a Shakespeare or a Coleridge may give you, in a moment, a handful of jewels, who knows how many years of superhuman concentration may have gone to the making of them?
(Lytton Strachey, LITERARY ESSAYS, 'THE FIRST EARL OF LYTTON', 1949)

Early attempts may be frustrating, so let's finish with one last 'take-heart' comment. Rome wasn't built in a day, neither is an ideal science programme for a class!
(Wynne Harlen, DEVELOPING SCIENCE IN THE PRIMARY CLASSROOM, 1989)

Don't be deterred if you do not notice immediate results. Rome wasn't built in a day and miracles are rare. Your arthritis has been developing over many years so it is unreasonable to expect it to improve overnight.
(Leaflet published by the ARTHRITIS FOUNDATION OF NEW ZEALAND, 1992)

Ancient Rome was a great Imperial city. *A city greater than any upon earth*, as Claudian put it in DE CONSOLATU STILICHONIS (c AD 400), *that from one small place extended its power so that upon it the sun never sets*. In the opinion of many experts, probably no other city in history has brought together so many magnificent buildings in one place. Even today, the Pantheon remains virtually complete; there are substantial remains of the Via Appica Antica (the main road to southern Italy of the third century BC), the Colosseum, the Roman Forum, the Palatine Hill, the Arches of Titus and Constantine, and many other monuments. No wonder the Empire and its buildings were not built in a day!

This truth is widely recognised in proverbial form. The earliest known reference comes from a French text written towards the end of the twelfth century. The saying has been in constant use in England since at least the middle of the sixteenth century; John Heywood includes it in his collection of proverbs of 1546.

Stevenson notes that the names of other great cities often replace that of Rome in variants of the expression. The French, for instance, also say *Paris n'a pas été fait en un jour* (Paris was not made in a day). A great local city is perhaps easier to relate to than an even greater one that is more distant but nowhere else can compete with *the grandeur that was Rome* (Edgar Allan Poe, TO HELEN, 1836).

Usage: Regularly used as an encouragement to persevere

■ When in Rome, do as the Romans do

When you are away from home fit in with other people's customs and ways of doing things and don't expect them to change to accommodate yours

Don't put on the sabots again. I told you . . . they were not quite the thing for this country . . . do at Rome as the Romans do. (Charlotte Brontë, SHIRLEY, 1849)

I always do in Rome as Rome does, eat (if I can) whatever is set before me. (W C Baldwin, AFRICAN HUNTING, 1863)

Confucius, Euripides, Sophocles and the rabbis who set down the TALMUD are amongst the wise who have warned travellers to remain sensitive to the different customs and practices they might meet along their way. The proverb *When in Rome do as the Romans do*, however, has a Christian origin.

When St Monica joined her son St Augustine in Milan, she was surprised to find that the church there did not fast on a Saturday as the Roman church was required to do and was perplexed as to which practice she should then follow. St Augustine in turn consulted the wise St Ambrose who gave this sound advice: *When I am here [at Milan] I do not fast on a Saturday; when I am at Rome, I fast on a Saturday. Follow the custom of the church where you are* (St Ambrose, ADVICE TO ST AUGUSTINE, AD 387).

St Ambrose summarised his good counsel: *If you are at Rome, live after the Roman fashion; if you are elsewhere, live as they do there.*

The proverb and variants of it were certainly in common use in the sixteenth century in England and around Europe. Don Diego, Spanish ambassador to the court of Henry VIII, slightly paraphrased the words of St Ambrose to account for his adoption of Protestantism in England: *When you are abroad, live in the manner of the place.*

More widely, a Nigerian author, Ojoade, has shown that there are many parallel proverbs that express the same idea in Chinese, Malay, Russian and Persian. He quotes a large number of similar sayings from language groups in his own country and from other African countries. Remarkable evidence for the universal nature of the relativity of human behaviour!

Usage: Like many proverbs it is not often quoted in its full form except in literature. Leaving the rest to be understood by the listener, spoken and journalistic English commonly reduces it to *When in Rome . . .*

ROSE

■ **A rose by any other name would smell as sweet**

It is the intrinsic quality of a person or thing that matters, not what it is called

The proverb comes from a passage in Shakespeare's ROMEO AND JULIET (1591). The story revolves around two star-crossed lovers who are thwarted by a bitter feud between the Montagu and Capulet households. When Romeo, a Montagu, and Juliet, a Capulet, fall in love they know their relationship will be forbidden by their families. Juliet considers the value of a name:

Tis but thy name which is my enemy . . .
What's in a name? that which we call a rose
By any other name would smell as sweet;
So Romeo would, were he not Romeo called.
(Act 2, scene ii)

Usage: There is a heavily ironical use that applies the phrase to anything evil-smelling or to something of the poorest quality

ROSEBUDS

■ **Gather ye rosebuds while ye may**

Life is passing by so make the most of the opportunities it offers while you can

See also: Make hay while the sun shines; Never put off till tomorrow what you can do today

The proverb is a line from a poem by Robert Herrick who was well known for his love poems and pastoral verses. His poem TO THE VIRGINS, TO MAKE MUCH OF TIME, from which the proverb comes, was popularly known and loved in the seventeenth century. The poem is a wistful exploration of the theme of passing time, of aging and of death. It encourages young women to taste and enjoy the gifts life has to offer while they may be had:

Gather ye Rose-buds while ye may,
Old Time is still a-flying:
And this same flower which smiles today,
Tomorrow will be dying.

The glorious Lamp of Heaven, the Sun,
The higher he's a getting;
The sooner will his Race be run,
And neerer he's to Setting.

That Age is best, which is the first,
When Youth and Blood are warmer;
But being spent, the worse, and worst
Times, still succeed the former.

Then be not coy, but use your time;
And while ye may, goe marry:
For having lost but once your prime,
You may for ever tarry.

The rose as symbol of the fleeting bloom of youth was not a new one in literature, however. Ausonius, the Roman poet of the fourth century, wrote an idyll entreating the virgin to gather fresh roses in her youth, reminding her that life, like the flowers, would quickly fade and pass away. The French poet Ronsard expresses the same idea in LINES TO HIS MISTRESS (1555), as does Spenser in THE FAERIE QUEEN (1596).

Usage: Given its poetic origin and vocabulary, it not surprisingly has an elevated and rather dated flavour

ST SWITHIN

■ **St Swithin's day, if thou dost rain,**
For forty days it will remain

If weather is wet on 15 July, it will continue for forty days afterwards

How, if on Swithin's feast the welkin lours,
And ev'ry penthouse streams with hasty show'rs,
Twice twenty days shall clouds their fleeces drain
And wash the pavement with incessant rain.
(John Gay, TRIVIA, 1716)

St Swithin is christening the apples.
(William Hone, EVERY-DAY BOOK, 1825)

Each year the English eagerly await the weather forecast for St Swithin's Day, 15 July, to determine what the summer weather will be like. According to the old rhyme:

St Swithin's day, gif ye do rain, for forty days it will remain;
St Swithin's day an ye be fair, for forty days twill rain nae mair.

St Swithin, the Bishop of Winchester, was a humble and holy man who was chaplain and trusted advisor to Egbert, King of Wessex, and tutor to his son. He was known for his charitable works and for his building and repairing of churches, which he would dedicate barefoot. When he died in AD 862, he was buried, according to his wishes, in the churchyard just outside the west door of the Old Minster where his grave might be trodden on and the rain might fall upon him. The monks, however, thought his simple grave unworthy of so great a saint and, following a poor labourer's vision of Swithin, arranged to move his remains to the inside of the cathedral. The ceremony was planned for 15 July 971 but was greatly impeded by heavy rain which, according to tradition, continued to pour for a further forty days. Even then St Swithin was not permitted to rest in peace. When the Normans founded a new cathedral church, his relics were moved again on 15 July 1093, but this time without a stormy protest from the saint.

The proverb has been current since the first century, country folk relying upon such lore to plan their activities. The earliest known record in English literature is in Ben Jonson's play EVERY MAN OUT OF HIS HUMOUR (1599): *O, here, 'St. Swithin's, the xv day, variable weather, for the most part rain,' good; for the most part rain: why it should rain forty days after, now, more or less, it was a rule held afore I was able to hold a plough.*

In 1752, England eventually fell into line with her Catholic neighbours and changed from the Julian to the Gregorian Calendar, thus moving the day, if not the date, of St Swithin. Even so, the good saint continues to manifest his displeasure at having his dying wish contradicted as DAILY EXPRESS reports:

Saint Swithun – Bishop of Winchester in AD 852 – did so well with his rain last year that the cathedral roof is now leaking.

David Austen has named a new rose to celebrate the 900th anniversary of the

Cathedral's dedication. Called Saint Swithun, it'll be launched at Chelsea on May 24. It has fragrant pink blooms with all the charm of the old-fashioned rose, plus the modern rose's repeat flowering habit. Ten per cent of receipts go to Winchester Cathedral.
(DAILY EXPRESS, 1 May 1993)

(For more rainy proverbs see **Weather wise,** page 242.)

SEEING

■ **Seeing is believing**

You can believe something is true when you can see the evidence

Seeing is believing . . . only art can make history really credible, or a great name more than a label to an abstraction.
(TLS, 28 May 1909)

Seeing is deceiving. It's eating that's believing.
(James Thurber, FURTHER FABLES FOR OUR TIME, 1956)

Seeing is believing, they say, in a world where we have learned to rely on sight as the dominant sense. But most of us are walking around half-blind and allowing much of life's beauty to pass us by.
(DAILY EXPRESS, 29 December 1992)

There are references to seeing and then believing in both Latin and Greek writings. It has been a proverb in English since at least the seventeenth century and is also commonly found in other European languages. The Italians, for instance, say *Who sees with the eye believes with the heart.*

There appears to be a common source for this proverb and for another less common one, *Men trust their ears less than their eyes*. Variations on the latter are widely found in classical literature and from the sixteenth century onwards in English. A German authority argues that the original story for them both is that of King Kandaules of Lydia who compelled his guard Gyges to admire the naked perfection of his wife. When the Queen realised this, she insisted that Gyges should kill the King and become her husband in his place.

Hundreds of years later, the proverb's development was perhaps influenced by the Bible's story of seeing and believing. Thomas was not with the other disciples when the risen Christ appeared to them and refused to believe unless he could see Jesus and feel his wounds. When Christ appeared to him, Thomas confessed him as God, whereupon Jesus said to him: *Thomas, because thou hast seen me, thou hast believed; blessed are they that have not seen, and yet have believed* (JOHN 20:29).

Modern day anthropologists look at proverbs for the light they cast on society. Dundes, for example, in his book INTERPRETING FOLKLORE (1972) has an essay which argues that *Seeing is believing, I'll believe it when I see it* and *I see, said the blindman*, amongst many other expressions, are all evidences for the primacy of vision in American society. And 'vision' is itself a metaphor for 'understanding'. A perception such as this is important, claims Dundes, because it may well not be shared by the world view of another culture, thus leading to erroneous interpretations in comparative studies. To extend his point, one might legitimately wonder whether *voir, c'est croire* in French and *zobaczyć to uwierzyć* in Polish mean the same to native speakers of those languages as *seeing is believing* to an American.

SHARE

■ **Share and share alike**

In a joint venture any loss or gain should be divided equally

They said that if my sister Susan and myself would join in an attempt to get hold of the secret they would not only cancel the debts, but would offer us a square deal and share and share alike.
(F W Crofts, INSPECTOR FRENCH AND THE CHEYNE MYSTERY, 1926)

He who breaks the unity of our ranks will have to be tossed beyond the pale. The basis for that is already in our tribal life. It is not only a political party that we must organize; it is a brotherhood. We must share and share alike in all things.
(R Wright, WHITE MAN, LISTEN!, 1957)

A fable of Aesop (sixth century BC) illustrates the sharing spirit. Two men were walking down a road when they came upon an axe. One man hurried to pick it up. 'What a piece of luck we've had,' his friend said. 'It's not *we* who have had the luck but *I*,' retorted the other. They had not gone much further when the man who had lost the axe came running along the road to find them. 'We've had it now!' exclaimed the man with the axe. 'It is not *we* who have had it but *you*,' replied his companion, 'since you would not let me share the ownership.'

The proverb is recorded in Cotgrave's DICTIONARY OF THE FRENCH AND ENGLISH TONGUES (1611): *'Escot' Whereat every guest paies his part, or share and share like.* The modern form *Share and share alike* was used by Daniel Defoe ROBINSON CRUSOE (1719) and by Maria Edgeworth in ORMOND (1817): *The woman . . . was dividing the prize among the lawful owners, 'share and share alike'.* The expression is often heard on the lips of exasperated parents trying to cajole their bickering offspring into sharing out sweets or a toy.

SHEEP

■ You might as well be hanged for a sheep as for a lamb

If the penalty is the same whatever the offence, you might as well commit the more serious one

Variant: As good be hanged for a sheep as for a lamb

See also: In for a penny, in for a pound

Others . . . comforted themselves with the homely proverb, that, being hanged at all, they might as well be hanged for a sheep as a lamb.
(Charles Dickens, BARNABY RUDGE, 1841)

It seemed as if she did not like being discovered in her home circumstances.

'I thought it couldn't be your voice,' she said.

But she might as well be hung for a sheep as for a lamb. She invited him out of the mausoleum of a parlour into the kitchen.
(D H Lawrence, SONS AND LOVERS, 1913)

For hundreds of years, death by hanging was the punishment for anyone convicted of stealing. This brutal form of justice was not supported by everyone, however. In the Tudor period, for instance, those with a humanist outlook acknowledged the responsibility of society to provide for the poor. Thomas More shared these views. In UTOPIA (1516) he wrote:

. . . this punyshment of theves passeth the limites of Justice, and is also very hurtefull to the weale publique. For it is to extreame and cruel a punishment for thefte, and yet not sufficient to refrayne and withhold men from thefte. For simple thefte is not so great an offense, that it owght to be punished with death. Neither ther is any punishment so horrible, that it can kepe them from stealynge, which have no other craft, wherby to get their living. Therfore in this poynte, not you onlye, but also the most part of the world, be like evyll scholemaisters, which be readyer to beate, then to teache, their scholers. For great and horrible punishmentes be appointed for theves, whereas much rather provision should have ben made, that there were some meanes, whereby they myght get their livyng, so that no man should be dryven to this extreme necessitie, firste to steale, and then to dye.

In spite of this enlightened outlook, it was not until around 1830 that the death penalty was lifted for theft of any kind. Anyone driven by hardship to steal a lamb, until then, suffered the same fate as one who took a sheep and made off with more valuable spoil. Thieves reasoned that, since they were risking their necks whatever they took, they might as well feast on the larger animal. It is difficult to say just how old the proverb is. The practice of hanging an offender who had stolen livestock certainly predates the earliest record (in John Ray's ENGLISH PROVERBS, 1678) by several hundred years.

Usage: Purists insist on *hanged* but common parlance accepts *hung*. The sense has weakened, such that the proverb may now apply to minor misdemeanours or even be simply a sign of commitment to a project and a willingness to accept any cost, should there be one.

SHIP

■ **Don't spoil the ship for a hap'orth of tar**

Don't risk the failure of an enterprise through small economies of time, effort or money

Variant: Don't lose the ship for a hap'orth of tar

See also: A stitch in time saves nine

The taxi bore him westward through the darkling streets. A three-mile journey – still, he could afford it. Why spoil the ship for a

ha'porth of tar? He had dropped that notion of spending only two pounds tonight.
(George Orwell, KEEP THE ASPIDISTRA FLYING, 1936)

Mrs Owen, the owner of the house she was going to when her time came, had recommended a doctor, and Mildred saw him once a week. He was to charge fifteen guineas.

'Of course I could have got it done cheaper, but Mrs Owen strongly recommended him, and I thought it wasn't worth while to spoil the ship for a coat of tar.'
(W Somerset Maugham, OF HUMAN BONDAGE, 1915)

This is not a nautical proverb and has nothing to do with caulking seams on wooden vessels. Its origins, in fact, are in farming where tar smeared on an animal's sores or open wounds would protect them from flies and deeper infection. Neglecting to treat wounds in order to save on tar was false economy, since the animal might die. This cheap and effective remedy was used on both pigs and sheep. Indeed, in its original form, the proverb was *Ne'er lose a hog for a halfp'north of tar*. Over time, however, either animal found a place in the saying as John Ray reports: *Ne'er lose a hog for a half-penny-worth of tarre. Some have it, lose not a sheep, &c. Indeed tarre is more used about sheep than swine* (ENGLISH PROVERBS, 1678).

Gradually, then, sheep usurped the hogs in the proverb. But further changes were ahead. The rustic pronunciation in many areas of England made 'sheep' sound like 'ship'. By the nineteenth century, when the proverb had become widespread and was divorced from its rural roots, its original meaning was no longer understood and so the written form 'ship' could be adopted without problem. A further shift in form and step away from the original sense took place when the ship was not 'lost' for want of tar but 'spoiled', so that by 1886 E J Hardy was writing: *People are often saving at the wrong place, and spoil the ship for a halfpenny worth of tar* (HOW TO BE HAPPY THOUGH MARRIED).

SIGHT

■ **Out of sight, out of mind**

We soon forget about those people or things we no longer see

He did not actually suggest that she should come home. Evidently it was still necessary that she should remain out of sight and out of mind – a skeleton in a distant and well-locked cupboard.
(George Orwell, A CLERGYMAN'S DAUGHTER, 1935)

As we began to discuss executions, he [a condemned prisoner] used a military metaphor to describe the way the death penalty functions in the US: a 'secret war'.
'As long as they're killing people and they're doing it a hundred miles from any city of any size, and they do it in the middle of the night, it might as well be the boat people in Cambodia, or the Vietnamese. They get rid of us. Out of sight, out of mind. If you're ever going to change that perception, then the execution should be at least televised.

Maybe done at high noon, on Sunday, in downtown St Louis in the square.'
(GUARDIAN, 21 January 1993)

The proverb is an ancient Greek one dating back at least to Homer in the eighth century BC.

Nathaniel Bacon, writing to Lady Cornwallis in the early seventeenth century, rightly calls the saying an 'owlde proverbe' for it appears in English literature in the PROVERBS OF HENDYNG (c 1320) almost three centuries earlier in a slightly different form:

Fer from eze, fer from herte,
Quoth Hendyng.

John Heywood records the proverb exactly as we know it today in his collection of 1546.

Bacon's wife, Anne, however, took issue with the wisdom of the saying. In 1613 she herself wrote to Lady Cornwallis and had this to say: *I do perceive that the old proverbis be not alwaies trew, for I do finde that the absence of my Nath. doth breede in me the more continuall remembrance of him.* Had it been current, the contrary expression, *Absence makes the heart grow fonder*, might have proved a more exact maxim for Lady Bacon.

SILENCE

■ **Silence is golden**

Silence is valuable, wise

See also: Speech is silver, silence is golden

Alas, we shall never know what the duke wanted to say – because he was not allowed to say it. Others rose to condemn this legislation. When he looked as though he was about to rise, attendants moved in to remind him that he had failed to take a minute of his invaluable time to swear his oath of allegiance to the Queen in this parliamentary session.

'So he's not allowed to speak,' an usher explained sternly.

The duke relapsed into a golden silence.

(DAILY EXPRESS, 21 February 1993)

■ **Speech is silver, silence is golden**

Speech is a valuable gift but knowing when to keep quiet is even more so

See also: Silence is golden

The MIDRASH on LEVITICUS (c 600), rabbinical commentaries on the Old Testament book, teaches that *If speech is silvern, then silence is golden*. Since gold is the more precious of the two metals, it follows that it is sometimes better not to speak at all. George Herbert defines the art thus: *Speak fitly, or be silent wisely* (JACULA PRUDENTUM, 1640). It cannot always be assumed, however, that one's silence is creating a good impression. Nevertheless Abraham Lincoln recommends it above speech for, as he points out, it is *better to remain silent and be thought a fool than to speak out and remove all doubt* (EPIGRAM, c 1862). Sadly there will always be those who are *Not able to speak, but unable to be silent* (Epicharmus, FRAGMENTS, c 550 BC). For people thus afflicted there is both comfort and warning in Benjamin Franklin's maxim: *Silence is not always a sign of Wisdom, but Babbling is ever a Folly* (POOR RICHARD'S ALMANACK, 1758). It seems that the path between wise speech and wise silence is a difficult one to tread.

In spite of the early origin of the proverb *Speech is silver, silence is golden*, its use in English is relatively recent. Thomas Carlyle quotes it as a *Swiss Inscription* in SARTOR RESARTUS (1836), which may have been its introduction into the English language. Indeed, Carlyle seems to have had something of a fixation about the maxim. John Morley, commenting on a collected edition of Carlyle's works says, *The canon is definitely made up and the whole of the golden gospel of silence effectively compressed in thirty-five volumes* (LITERARY MISCELLANIES, vol ii). Since then the proverb has often appeared in its full form but, even more frequently, shortened to *Silence is golden*, which gained the ultimate accolade of becoming the title of a pop record in the 1960s.

SMALL

■ **Small is beautiful**

Greater benefits accrue to units and activities of limited scale

See also: Big is beautiful

SMALL IS BEAUTIFUL – AGAIN
Small public companies are back in vogue. After under-performing the FTA All-Share index for the past four years, the share prices of smaller companies are taking off as

investors hunt for neglected value, writes Andrew Lorenz.
(SUNDAY TIMES, 17 January 1993)

SMALL CAN BE BEAUTIFUL WHEN RESEARCH IS BIG
Keele is small in comparison with most institutions – the student population is 4,500 with plans for expansion to no more than 7,500 by the year 2000. Dr Fender believes smallness combined with originality of research programmes places it in a very flexible position.
(INDEPENDENT, 4 March 1993)

Mr Toogood says everybody thinks small is easy as well as beautiful. There are few disciplinary problems, enviable teacher-child ratios, close parental involvement and low overheads . . .
(DAILY TELEGRAPH, 19 March 1993)

Smallness has always had its champions. Early English proverb collections followed Greek and Latin originals in their renderings:

Vnto lyttle thynges is a certayne grace annexed.
(Richard Taverner, PROVERBS, 1539)

Little things are pretty.
(John Ray, ENGLISH PROVERBS, 1678)

Edmund Spenser at the same period put the thought into verse:

*Hereby I learned have, not to despise
What ever thing seemes small in common eyes.*
(VISIONS OF THE WORLDS VANITIE, 1591)

But the virtue of smallness today is acknowledged in a very different arena. One of the most influential books of the second half of the twentieth century was Professor E F Schumacher's SMALL IS BEAUTIFUL (1971). It became a widespread catchphrase, used to support the burgeoning movement for human scale and human values in big business and government. Interestingly, Schumacher wanted to call his book THE HOMECOMERS. His publisher Anthony Blond came up with SMALLNESS IS BEAUTIFUL, then finally an associate Desmond Briggs coined the watchword of a new generation.

SMOKE

■ **There's no smoke without fire**

Rumours are not groundless, they have some truth in them

Variant: Where there's smoke there's fire

Of course, these implications would be sly and groundless, and the opposition would realize it. But the voters might not. They would say where there's smoke there's fire.
(B Benson, LILY IN HER COFFIN, 1954)

Mrs Carter protested that it was merely nervous reaction, but to Berenice it seemed that where there was so much smoke there must be some fire.
(Theodore Dreiser, THE TITAN, 1914)

*At last the secret is out, as it always must come in the end,
The delicious story is ripe to tell to the intimate friend;
Over the tea-cups and in the square the tongue has its desire;*

Still waters run deep, my friend, there's never smoke without fire.
(W H Auden, THE ASCENT OF F6, 1936)

In THE TALE OF MELIBEUS (c 1386), Chaucer attributes this proverb of fire and smoke to the first century philosopher Seneca (c 4 BC–AD 65): *'It may nat be' seith he [Seneca] 'that, where greet fyr hath longe tyme endured, that ther ne dwellth som vapour of warmnesse.'* Stevenson, however, traces the same phrase back still earlier to Publilius Syrus' SENTENTIAE (c 43 BC). In any event, the image of smoke spreading from a fire has for two millennia been the symbol of gossip, rumour and even scandal issuing from at least a spark of truth. It has been recorded in many European languages and in all the great proverb collections in English. It has also proved a productive image – authors such as George Eliot have reinterpreted it in their own fashion:

Gossip is a sort of smoke that comes from the dirty tobacco-pipes of those who diffuse it; it proves nothing but the bad taste of the smoker.
(DANIEL DERONDA, 1874)

SPEAK

■ **Speak when you're spoken to**

Respond when you are addressed. Do not talk when you are not addressed

See also: Children should be seen and not heard

A child should always say what's true
And speak when he is spoken to,
And behave mannerly at table;
At least as far as he is able.
(Robert Louis Stevenson, WHOLE DUTY OF CHILDREN, 1885)

This is another of the rules by which British children have traditionally been brought up. Model children do not gaze in mute embarrassment at their shoes or glare insolently into the distance when addressed by their elders and betters but *speak when they are spoken to,* answering clearly and politely. Children have been brought up along these lines for many centuries. Thomas Fuller gives two helpful maxims in GNOMOLOGIA (1732): *Speak, when you are spoke to; come, when you are called.* And seventy-two years later the advice was repeated by Maria Edgeworth:

Come when you're called,
And do as you're bid;
Shut the door after you,
And you'll never be chid.
(THE CONTRAST, 1804)

Usage: The phrase today could be used to anyone, child or adult, where the

Play up, play up and play the game

Play is one of the defining characteristics of humanity. It has certainly been recognised at least as far back as Plato's proverbial phrase *We must play the game* (c 375 BC). Proverbs themselves allow an expression of this playfulness. Here are some games to try out in an idle moment.

● Make a paraphrase of a list of well-known proverbs. For example, 'consumption constitutes dessert's testing'; 'self-esteem precedes degradation'; 'dormant canines should remain in repose'; etc. Then, one by one, have the other players guess the original proverb (*The proof of the pudding is in the eating; Pride goes before a fall; Let sleeping dogs lie*).

● One of the party is sent out of the room: the rest think of a proverb that he or she must guess through asking questions.

● A variation is to have the questioner solicit a response from the circle of players in turn. The first to respond must include the first word of the proverb once (or twice, or even three times) in the answer; the second the second word; and so on.

● Players look through the OLD TESTAMENT BOOK OF PROVERBS and reformulate selected ones in modern wording.

● An old game, referred to in Shakespeare's HENRY V, is Proverb-Capping. The aim is to outlast a fellow player in quoting proverbs related to an agreed theme.

● A chain game of proverbs entails the second person beginning a proverb with the last letter of the one selected by the first person. The third person starts with the last letter of the second person's, and so on.

● The common party game Charades can be restricted to proverbs (rather than films, novels, etc). Each player has to act out a proverb within a limited time for the others to guess. To make this easier the, say, twenty proverbs that are to be mimed could be distributed to the players beforehand with some of the key words deleted in each one.

● Cryptic drawings and clues, each hiding a well-known proverb, are shown to teams in turn. The goal is to work out within a time limit which saying is alluded to. The team that finishes with the largest number of correct answers is the winner. A commercial version of this game is Dingbats.

Commercial versions of proverb games have long been available. In the late nineteenth century, Parker Brothers updated an earlier game, marketing it as The Good Old Game of Proverbs. Ten years later there was appropriately enough The New Century Game of Proverbs. Both games involved the use of cards depicting common proverbs.

contribution was felt to be completely out of place. However, it would be an aggressive thing to say.

SPEED

■ **More haste, less speed**

The faster you attempt to go, the less progress you will actually make

See also: Festina lente

AQUARIUS: Once again it seems to be a case of more haste less speed or Mars might trip you up. That's a pity since there are no limits to what can be achieved now.
(SUN, 3 March 1993)

It was proverbial in ancient Greek that too much haste meant tasks were performed badly and not on time. This passed into English, the earliest known record being in the DOUCE MANUSCRIPT (c 1350). *The more haste, the worse speed* was a common form from the fourteenth to the early twentieth century.

There was in earlier years a play on words in the proverb, as etymologist W W Skeat points out. There is the sense of 'rapidity' for *speed* that we understand today; it also meant 'profit' or 'success'. This thus gave the additional meaning, 'The faster you work, the less successful your enterprise will be.'

Usage: Often used as a rather smug and extremely annoying comment to someone in a desperate hurry

SPIRIT

■ **The spirit is willing but the flesh is weak**

Good intentions are often stifled by one's human inability to fulfil them. It is difficult to overcome one's bodily cravings with good intentions

The spirit is willing but the flesh is weak. Weak in pain, but weaker still, he thought, more inexcusably weak, in pleasure. For under the torments of pleasure, what cowardices, what betrayals of self and of others will it not commit!
(Aldous Huxley, THOSE BARREN LEAVES, 1925)

'I really must apologize for my short-comings as a correspondent. I've been so very busy!'
'We're neither of us much good at letter-writing, I'm afraid.'
'The spirit was willing, dear boy. I hope you'll believe that. You were ever present in my thoughts . . . '
(Christopher Isherwood, MR NORRIS CHANGES TRAINS, 1935)

Chapter 26 of MATTHEW'S gospel tells how, after their last supper together, Jesus takes his disciples out to the garden of Gethsemane. Knowing his death is imminent, Jesus takes Peter, James and John further into the garden, where he explains how heavy his heart is and asks them to watch with him while he goes to pray. When he returns he finds them asleep. Rousing Peter, Jesus says to him: *What, could ye not watch with me one hour? Watch and pray, that ye enter not into temptation; the spirit indeed is willing, but the flesh is weak* (verse 41).

Use of the verse as a proverb is mainly from the twentieth century and is often used as an excuse for submitting to temptation.

SPRAT

■ **Throw out a sprat to catch a mackerel**

It is worth taking a small risk to make a large profit

See also: Nothing ventured, nothing gained

I concluded that she had probably not understood how large her overdraft had become, or how many sprats she had had to throw to catch a mackerel that now looked like not being caught.
(William Plomer, MUSEUM PIECES, 1950)

She gave a small dinner to the four most influential critics obtainable, and during the evening scores of people dropped in for drinks, and were given signed copies of the great work. These were bread upon the waters, which would be returned a hundred fold – sprats to catch whales of circulation.
(Richard Aldington, SOFT ANSWERS, 'YES AUNT', 1932)

Fishing is a risky business; you have to be prepared to *venture a small fish to catch a great one* (John Clarke, PAROEMIOLOGIA, 1639), or perhaps to *lose a fly to catch a trout* (Herbert, JACULA PRUDENTUM, 1640). Even the French are willing to *lose a minnow to catch a salmon.*

Sometimes, however, things don't go as planned. Throughout the seventeenth century, disappointed fishermen *fish'd for a herring and catcht a sprat.* William Hone came along a little late in the day and inverted the existing proverb in order to put them right: *It is but 'giving a Sprat to catch a Herring,' as a body might say* (EVERY-DAY BOOK, 1827). And Captain Marryat seemed to have the right idea, too, when he spoke of a plan as *a sprat to catch a mackerel* (NEWTON FORSTER, 1832). Dickens' characters expected large returns for their small stakes: *It was their custom . . . never to throw away sprats, but as bait for whales* (MARTIN CHUZZLEWIT, 1844). The idea of such a sizeable haul caught on and by 1869 W C Hazlitt was listing *Set a herring to catch a whale* amongst his collection of English proverbs. This optimism was short-lived, however. It was replaced by realism in the twentieth century when, for most people, the risk of throwing out a sprat was again expected to yield no greater return than Captain Marryat's modest mackerel.

STICKS

■ **Sticks and stones may break my bones but names will never hurt me**

A defiant chant shouted at school bullies; physical violence may wound a victim but taunts will not

The popular rhyming proverb, probably dating back no further than the nineteenth century, has its roots in an older saying. An unknown fifteenth century writer tells us that *fayre wordis brake neuer bone* (HOW THE GOOD WYF TAUGTE HIS DOUGHTIR, c 1450), but the same is true of harsher language as Robert Greene points out: *Wordes breake no bones, so we cared the lesse for his scolding* (WORKS, 1584).

The modern rhyme is a show of defensive bravado and its wisdom is unsound; names and harsh criticism may not harm physically but certainly leave deep emotional scars. An old English rhyme from the thirteenth century PROVERBS OF ALFRED, paraphrased in later English by John Skelton (1460?–1529), acknowledges the destructive power of the spoken word:

Malicious tunges, though they have no bones,
Are sharper then swordes, sturdier then stones
(AGAINST VENEMOUS TONGUES)

Sir Henry Sidney, in a letter (c 1560) to his son, Sir Philip Sidney, wrote: *A wound given by a word is oftentimes harder to be cured than that which is given with the sword.*

Let John Lyly summarise the whole with this neat analogy: *Nettells haue no prickells yet they sting, and wordes haue no points, yet they pearce* (EUPHUES, 1580).

STONE

▪ A rolling stone gathers no moss

A person who is constantly moving from place to place will never amass wealth (or affection)

We keep repeating the silly proverb that rolling stones gather no moss, as if moss were a desirable parasite.
(George Bernard Shaw, 'PREFACE', MISALLIANCE, 1914)

You have been, I fancy, in essence, a disappointed man all your life. You have been the rolling stone – and you have gathered very little moss. You were bitterly jealous of your brother's wealth.
(Agatha Christie, THE ABC MURDERS, 1936)

STONE'S NEW HOMES GATHER MOSS
The chairman of the McCarthy & Stone retirement homes group, has stumbled on a Catch-22 obstacle to sales, which is linked to the recovery in the housing market. The backbone of John McCarthy's business is the part-exchange which allows people to swap their family homes for M&S's sheltered housing – and invest the capital sum from the residue. Much depends on the homeowners accepting the valuation of their property – a system which works well except when people's expectations change. 'We found that when prices were dropping, people wanted to hold on, hoping for a recovery – and now prices look like picking up, they don't want to sell in the hope of getting a better price later,' he said.
(DAILY EXPRESS, 1 May 1993)

Changing with the times

The meaning of a proverb is not immutable. It changes in relation to how people understand it, which is determined in part by the contemporary values of the society. An interesting case in point is *A rolling stone gathers no moss*.

Traditionally this expression has been advice to avoid excessive mobility. This is very understandable in the settled agricultural communities of previous centuries, where the wanderer had a generally bad reputation. The entry for this saying traces this interpretation (see page 223).

However, there has always been at least a small element of ambiguity in its meaning. Horatio Alger (1832–99) fled to Paris from America as a bohemian rebel, ultimately returning to become a minister of the church and influential author of boys' books. Many of them are on the theme of a footloose youngster who in the end makes good. One in particular is entitled THE ROLLING STONE, in which the hero gains riches and success. So the life of a 'rolling stone' could have positive connotations. Dialectal proverbs also were questioning the wisdom of the adage. In CHESHIRE PROVERBS (1917), J C Bridge notes that over the years two English regional tags have been added to the proverb which contradict it. A Cheshire saying is *A rolling stone gathers no moss but a tethered sheep winna get fat*, whilst in Surrey and Sussex the tag is *and a sitting hen never grows fat*.

In the twentieth century, fundamental social changes were taking place that sharpened what had previously only been hints of ambiguity of meaning. The rise of urban patterns of life and, especially, the demands for mobility in order to follow jobs and careers became more insistent. Consequently, being a 'rolling stone' was a positive virtue, not a handicap. This perception was perhaps strengthened in minor ways. From the early 1960s onwards, the Rolling Stones pop group exercised an enormous influence on young people, being the focus of adulation and imitation on an almost unprecedented scale. With teens and twenties at least, this popularity could only have improved the image of the phrase 'rolling stone'.

Another reason for questioning the original meaning of the proverb is also connected with connotations. 'Moss' is seen in the adage as something desirable. However, more generally this may not be the case. George Bernard Shaw puts it well in his Preface to MISALLIANCE (1914): *We keep repeating the silly proverb that rolling stones gather no moss, as if moss were a desirable parasite.* The last thing a gardener wants is moss in his lawn!

By the second half of the twentieth century, then, the proverb remained extremely common (97 per cent of the 162 respondents in Lundgren's survey knew it). Yet there is major uncertainty as to what it means. Lundgren found in his group of 1957 American undergraduates that two-thirds of them believed the expression meant 'If you want to succeed, be on the move, for fear you become an old moss-back.'

For nearly three thousand years, and across endless cultures and languages, *A rolling stone gathers no moss* has reflected society's view that stability is a virtue. In the last hundred years, mobility is in the ascendant. Language has responded, not by introducing a new proverb for the new perceptions but by offering a reinterpretation of the old adage. The two senses now run side by side. The social conditions of the twenty-first century may decide which one will win out.

In his FIVE HUNDRED POINTS OF GOOD HUSBANDRIE (1573), THOMAS TUSSER quotes the proverb, still relatively new to English, along with an explanation of its meaning:

The stone that is rolling can gather no moss,
For master and servant oft changing is loss.

The original form of this ancient Greek proverb was *A rolling stone gathers no seaweed* and probably refers to the action of the tides rubbing the stones on a Greek seashore against one another, so that no weed could begin to cling to their surface. According to Stevenson, we owe the change from seaweed to moss to Erasmus, when he included his new and definitive rendering in his ADAGIA (1523). Twenty-three years later it was well-known enough to be recorded in this form by Heywood: *The rollyng stone neuer gatherth mosse* (PROVERBS, 1546).

Not surprisingly, the saying is common to many European languages, where there are direct analogues. There are also a good number of kindred proverbs that express the same idea:

A tree often transplanted does not thrive (Quintilian*)*
Selden moseth the marble-stone that men often treden (Langland, PIERS PLOWMAN, 1362)
The still hog gets the swill (American)

(See **Changing with the times**, page 224.)

STOOLS

■ Between two stools you fall to the ground

Dithering between two courses of action brings disaster or the loss of both opportunities

The modern world, in fact, had fallen between two stools. It had fallen between that austere old three-legged stool which was the tripod of the cold priestess of Apollo; and that other mystical and mediaeval stool that may well be called the Stool of Repentance.
(G K Chesterton, VICTORIAN AGE IN LITERATURE, 1913)

The others [two plays] fell between two stools. One portrayed the narrow, hidebound life of country gentlefolk; the other, the political and financial world; . . . They were neither frankly realistic nor frankly theatrical. My indecision was fatal.
(W Somerset Maugham, THE SUMMING UP, 1938)

The proverb *to sit down between two stools* has ancient origins. Seneca, for instance, uses it in CONTROVERSIA (c 60 BC). LI PROVERBE AU VILAIN, a French text from the late twelfth century, has: *Between two stools one falls bum to the ground,* and over three centuries later Rabelais in GARGANTUA (1534) says: *He would sit between two stools with his bum to the ground.* The earliest recorded uses of the saying in English, both in John Gower's CONFESSIO AMANTIS (c 1390), speak only of the fall and going to ground. That is the case today. In the intervening centuries, there has been some concentration on the part of the anatomy that actually hits the ground. It was described first as the arse and later as the tail. The eighteenth century seems to have been particularly delicate. Witness first Fielding :

While the two stools her sitting-part confound,
Between 'em both fall squat upon the ground
(TOM THUMB, 1730)

Then Jephson: Between two stools they say a certain part of a man comes to the ground (TWO STRINGS TO YOUR BOW, 1791).

That people should be described as falling between stools is not strange for, as late as the Elizabethan era, chairs were rare; people sat on stools or chests.

STORM

■ After a storm comes a calm

Difficult circumstances will inevitably give way to more peaceful ones

Variant: After the storm comes the calm

See also: The darkest hour is that before the dawn

Try topic for your balm,
Try storm,
And after storm, calm.
Try snow of heaven, heavy soft, and slow,
Brilliant and warm.
Nothing will help, and nothing do much harm.
(Genevieve Taggard, OF THE PROPERTIES OF NATURE FOR HEALING AN ILLNESS)

The earliest recorded use is in the devotional text, ANCREN RIWLE of c 1200. Later, William Langland used the notion of sunshine after inclement weather in PIERS PLOWMAN (1377): After sharpe shoures moste shene is the sonne. Thereafter the theme recurred but always differently expressed. Sometimes the idea was reversed to give the pessimist's view: Calm continueth not long without a storm (George Pettie, PETITE PALLACE, 1576). It was William Camden who first used the phrase in the form familiar today: After black clouds clear weather. After a storm comes a calm (REMAINS, 1605).

A quiet period after a particularly trying experience is often referred to idiomatically as the calm after the storm. There is also the similar expression the calm before the storm.

A parallel proverb is After rain comes sunshine. One authority gives a French origin for this, though it may have evolved independently in the different European cultures in which it is recorded. It may be that there is a connection with a proverb that is spread throughout the world (but little used in English): When it rains and the sun shines, the devil is beating his grandmother.

■ Any port in a storm

In times of want or need any haven will suffice. A last resort

See also: Half a loaf is better than no bread

'Any port in a storm' was the principle on which I was prepared to act.
(Robert Louis Stevenson, ST IVES, 1894)

I have understood that there is a little feeling between you and Mr Hand and the other gentlemen I have mentioned. But, as I say – and I'm talking perfectly frankly now – I'm in a corner, and it's any port in a storm. If you want to help me I'll make the best terms I can, and I won't forget the favor.
(Theodore Dreiser, THE TITAN, 1914)

The dangers of a storm at sea are self-evident to any sailor. In such circumstances it is imperative to find a sheltered anchorage, often in a port, to await better weather. In days gone by, it was common to winter in a port in order to escape the rigours of that season. Wherever you happened to be, providing it offered protection, was better than exposure to the elements.

Because of Britain's sea-faring traditions, many expressions which were first used on board ship found their way into the everyday speech of folk who never left dry land. This is one such proverb. An early use is in James Cobb's play THE FIRST FLOOR written around 1780, since when it has developed much wider applications. Help of any kind, even if not normally acceptable, constitutes *any port in a storm*.

STRAW

■ **A drowning man will clutch at a straw**

A person facing overwhelming difficulty will grasp at any fleeting opportunity to save himself

A drowning man will catch at a straw and Ravenna is but twenty miles from Imola. Can you believe that our friend would hesitate to make so short a journey to achieve a result he so much desires?
(W Somerset Maugham, THEN AND NOW, 1946)

She had been starting to walk away, when that fearful yell had brought her back to get the news bulletin. Eggy was clutching at her arm, like a drowning man at a straw.
(P G Wodehouse, LAUGHING GAS, 1936)

The proverb first appeared in written language at the beginning of the seventeenth century. During the first hundred and thirty years or so, the various forms of the proverb had drowning men clutching at 'twigs', 'helpless things', 'reeds', 'thorns' and 'rushes' before finally settling down in its present form around the middle of the eighteenth century. The picture of a drowning man hoping against hope that the straw will bear his weight and save him is vivid enough but the Italians take his desperation even further. They have a proverb which says A *drowning man will catch at razors.*

Usage: The proverb is often shortened to form the idiom *to clutch at a straw* or *at straws*.

■ **It's the last straw which breaks the camel's back**

The final, often insignificant, event which makes hardship too burdensome to endure further

Variant: It's the final straw which breaks the camel's back

Cook arrived with coffee, and put down the tray with the air of a camel exhibiting the last straw.

(J B Priestley, ANGEL PAVEMENT, 1930)

But if things go badly and they [the French rugby team] are hanging on with faint hope against England when, with 10 minutes to go, Dooley goes over for a try to put England 15 points ahead, then it will be regarded as un coup de Trafalgar – *a Trafalgar hit.*

As opposed to the straw that broke the camel's back, a Trafalgar hit is a cannonball that blows the camel clean out of existence. The big hit that kills off the whole project.

(DAILY TELEGRAPH, 3 February 1992)

A variety of metaphors have been used in a number of languages to express the idea of breakdown resulting from a final tiny stroke. A chord may be finally broken by the feeblest of pulls (sixteenth century Spanish), a cup may overflow with the last tiny drop (seventeenth century English; French has 'glass') and a single grain is charged with making the balance heavier (Arabic). Archbishop John Bramhall, writing in 1677, said that, *it is the last feather that breaks the horse's back,* an expression also recorded by Thomas Fuller in his GNOMOLOGIA in 1732. This proverb was seized upon by Dickens who appears to be responsible for rewording it into the form we are familiar with today: *The last straw breaks the laden camel's back* (DOMBEY AND SON, 1848).

The proverb has been the occasion for several examples of humour and light

verse. Harry Graham writes in MORE RUTHLESS RHYMES FOR HEARTLESS HOMES (1930):

THE LAST STRAW
Oh, gloomy, gloomy was the day
When poor Aunty Bertha ran away!
But Uncle finds today more black:
Aunty Bertha's threatening to run back!

Usage: The last/final straw is often used idiomatically without the rest of the proverb

SUN

■ **Don't let the sun go down on your anger**

Deal with anger and disagreements promptly and don't let them drag on into a new day

Variant: Let not the sun go down on your wrath

He's one of those kids who never let the sun go down on their wrath, if you know what I mean. I mean to say, do something to annoy or offend or upset this juvenile thug, and he will proceed at the earliest possible opp. to wreak a hideous vengeance upon you.

(P G Wodehouse, VERY GOOD, JEEVES, 1930)

The proverb is a biblical one. In his letter to the church at Ephesus Saint Paul writes: *Be ye angry, and sin not; let not the sun go down upon your wrath* (EPHESIANS 4:26). If believers should become angry with one another they are not to fall into sin by bearing a grudge but are to resolve the matter quickly.

The injunction seems sound. A newspaper article giving advice on how to maintain a good marriage relationship quoted the example of a couple who had been happily married for 60 years: *The reason for their enduring love, they said, was because they both refused to go to bed without making up first* (DAILY MAIL, 14 January 1993).

SWALLOW

■ **One swallow doesn't make a summer**

A single indicator of something is not in itself significant

Royal anecdotes, like all others, must make some attempt at 'punch'. Ideally they should be attached to an event or happening.

King William III was said to have been too small to offer his arm to his massive wife Queen Mary. Instead he dangled from hers 'like an amulet from a bracelet'. One simile does not make an anecdote. The simile about the amulet, however, provides a good analogy for the royal anecdote and its event. The anecdote should hang like an amulet from the arm, so to speak, of the greater event.

(Elizabeth Longford, THE OXFORD BOOK OF ROYAL ANECDOTES, 1989)

In ancient Greece the swallow was the herald of spring and such a welcome sight that schoolchildren in Attica were given a day's holiday when the first one was seen. Aesop (sixth century BC) told a fable about a spendthrift who spied a swallow which had been tempted back from its winter migration by some fine sunny weather. 'Spring is here,' thought the young man, and promptly sold his warm cloak, spending the money on carousing in the town. But when the winter weather returned a few days later, the young man learned to his cost that one swallow does not make a spring.

The ancient Greek proverb was *One swallow does not make a spring* (it still is so in Spain and Italy) and, strictly, the English should be the same since this migratory visitor to Europe appears in April after wintering in Africa. However, perhaps the swallow is associated in the English mind with better weather, which comes later in more northerly climes. Hence the change, since the proverb's first appearance in English in the sixteenth century, of spring to summer.

The form of the proverb makes it easy to add on clauses and the saying has been tampered with considerably over the years. These are just a few examples:

Nay, soft (said the widow) one swallow makes not a summer, nor one meeting a marriage.
(Thomas Deloney, JACKE OF NEWBERY, 1597)

One Swallow makes ('tis true) no Summer, Yet one Tongue may create a Rumour.
(Thomas D'Urfey, COLLIN'S WALK THROUGH LONDON, 1690)

*One swallow does not make a summer, nor
one goose a farmyard.*
(C F Rogers, Verify Your References,
1938)

Usage: This ancient proverb is still
applied figuratively in a range of
contexts, from one good quality not
making a good man to one good
economic indicator not meaning an end
to recession

SWINGS

■ **What you lose on the swings you
gain on the roundabouts**

Gains and losses balance out

Variant: What you lose on the
roundabouts you gain on the swings

*A great many things in this universe are
rather depressing. Others, fortunately, are
not. What we lose in the swings of pain,
pointlessness, and evil, we gain on a variety
of aesthetic, sensuous, intellectual, and
moral roundabouts.*
(Aldous Huxley, Music at Night,
'Squeak and Gibber', 1931)

*If it is a wet summer the firm making
mackintoshes will find good markets, if there
is a heat wave there will be a specially big
demand for bathing suits. If we have shares
in both we need not feel unduly anxious
about the weather, for what we lose on the
swings we shall gain on the roundabouts.*
(G Williams, The Economics of
Everyday Life, 1950)

I am blessed with a wonderful marriage too
*and realise how lucky I am. I think the secret
is probably never to take each other for
granted. That way, you can foster a sense of
loyalty and help each other on life's swings
and roundabouts.*
(Archer's Addicts, 1992)

*What you gain on the swings . . .
Tom Rowland compares house-purchase
costs throughout the EC. Britain does well –
but here the bricks and mortar are usually
dearer.*
(Daily Telegraph, 20 January 1993)

*Lawyers are by nature averse to risk. So far,
the hourly-rate system has encouraged them
in that regard. Clients have been expected to
pay for the work done, irrespective of success
or failure. . . . Conversely, lawyers were only
too keen to charge a premium over and above
hourly rates for the success of their
endeavours. There was some measure of the
swings and roundabouts principle, but in
the new economic climate power has
devolved to the clients.*
(The Times, 24 March 1993)

A Latin proverb tells us that what is lost
in one way may be recouped in another.
An old English proverb from the fishing
industry, current in the sixteenth
century, expressed the same idea: *The
hakes . . . haunted the coast in great
abundance; but now, being deprived of their
wonted bait, are much diminished; verifying
the proverb,'What we lose in hake, we shall
have in herring'* (Richard Carew, The
Survey of Cornwall, 1602).

The modern proverb is another
variant, the allusion being to a
fairground where the proprietor might
one day make a loss on running the

roundabouts but a profit on working the swings. Possibly the development of the saying was influenced by Patrick Chalmers' verse ROUNDABOUTS AND SWINGS (1910), part of which reads:

'I find,' said 'e, 'things very much as 'ow I've always found,
For mostly they goes up and down or else goes round and round . . .
What's lost upon the roundabouts we pulls up on the swings!'

The expression has been quoted by Somerset Maugham and Shaw amongst others. There is some variation as to the word order in the proverb. Sometimes writers make the swings gain and other times the roundabouts are in profit. Since it doesn't alter the sense of the saying then either would seem acceptable.

Usage: Often abbreviated to a comment such as *It's swings and roundabouts,* meaning it is 'six of one, half a dozen of the other', so the options open are of equal standing

TAKE

■ **You can't take it with you (when you go)**

Make use of your money while you are alive, you can't spend it when you are dead

St Paul, writing to his disciple, Timothy, reminds him that contentment and a blameless life are true riches, reinforcing his argument with the words *for we brought nothing into the world, and it is certain we can carry nothing out* (TIMOTHY 6:7). These words have become familiar through the Church of England funeral rites. They are amongst those recited by the priest at the start of the service as he enters the church walking in front of the coffin.

THIEF

■ **Set a thief to catch a thief**

Someone with experience of wrong-doing is the best person to catch others at it

No one knows the ins and outs of his business as thoroughly as the thief himself, so who better to arrest or deter another of his kind? When Robert Howard used the proverb in a play in 1665 he called it an 'old saying'. And, indeed, like advice has been around for centuries. Cato the Younger worked upon the premise that *The authors of great evils know best how to remove them* (49 BC) when, in spite of stiff opposition, he recommended that Senate business should be entrusted to the Roman general, Pompey. On a more domestic note, in the PHYSICIAN'S TALE (c 1386) Chaucer reminds us of the old theory that a poacher is the best man to watch over the deer, advice that eventually took the modern form *An old poacher makes the best keeper.* In his CHURCH-HISTORY OF BRITAIN (1655) Thomas Fuller combines the proverbs: *Many were his lime-twigs to this purpose*

Alcott's moral tales

Louisa M Alcott (1832–88) was an American novelist and poet. Her father, Bronson Alcott, kept the family poor by his philanthropic and educational enterprises, so Louisa had to work to help support the family. She wrote her first book in 1848 when she was just sixteen and became particularly famous for LITTLE WOMEN in 1869. Just one year before, she had published LOUISA M ALCOTT'S PROVERB STORIES, in which three stories centre around a different proverb. 'Kitty's Class-Day' is based on *A stitch in time saves nine*; 'Psyche's Art' on *Handsome is as handsome does*; and 'Aunt Kipp' on *Children and fools speak the truth*. Alcott uses some thirty proverbs in her three stories.

In later editions the collection expands to include: 'A Country Christmas' – *A handful of good life is worth a bushel of learning*; 'On Picket Duty' – *Better late than never*; 'The Baron's Gloves or, Amy's Romance' – *All is fair in love and war*; 'My Red Cap' – *He who serves well need not fear to ask his wages*; 'What the Bells saw and said' – *Bells ring others to church but go not in themselves*.

In the brief preface of the final edition, Alcott displays a curious attitude to her work and her readers:

. . . I have collected various waifs and strays to appease young people who clamor for more, forgetting that mortal brains need rest.

As many girls have asked to see what sort of tales Jo Marsh wrote at the beginning of her career, I have added The Baron's Gloves, as a sample of the romantic rubbish which paid so well once upon a time. If it shows what not to write it will not have been preserved from oblivion in vain.

. . . Always set a thief to catch a thief; and the greatest deer-stealers make the best park-keepers.

Our European neighbours have equivalent expressions. French is especially rich, covering all eventualities: *A fripon, fripon et demi* (To a rogue, a rogue and a half). And similarly: *To a deceiver, a deceiver and a half; To a pirate, a pirate and a half; To a Norman, a Norman and a half;* and so on.

TIME

■ A stitch in time saves nine

See to a problem as soon as it starts and you will save yourself a lot of work

See also: Don't spoil the ship for a hap'orth of tar

He intended to take an opportunity this afternoon of speaking to Irene. A word in time saved nine; and now that she was going to live in the country there was a chance for her to turn over a new leaf! He could see that Soames wouldn't stand very much more of her goings on!
(John Galsworthy, THE MAN OF PROPERTY, 1906)

. . . there are worse forms of punishment from a child's point of view than the quick slap. Verbal lashings or sarcasm can be far more unpleasant and enduringly hurtful.

Family discipline is the basis of social order and must be preserved. A smack in time can stave off crime.
(DAILY MAIL, 8 May 1992)

It is only since the advent of the throw-away society after the Second World War that clothes and linen are often discarded if they are torn, showing wear or even just unfashionable. Before this garments were carefully mended, shirt collars replaced and sheets turned edges to middle to prolong their useful lives. The proverb, recorded by Thomas Fuller in GNOMOLOGIA (1732) as *A Stitch in Time may save nine*, pointed out that prompt action at the first sign of a hole would make mending it easier and the darn less visible.

Louisa M Alcott, the nineteenth century American writer, lived in genteel poverty and was no stranger to good stewardship and the well-stocked workbox. *A stitch in time saves nine* was one of the proverbs she chose to illustrate in her PROVERB TALES. (See **Alcott's moral tales**, page 233.)

■ **Take time by the forelock**

Make the most of the present moment and the opportunities it lends

Variants: Take occasion by the forelock; Seize time by the forelock

See also: Make hay while the sun shines; Never put off till tomorrow what you can do today; Strike while the iron's hot

According to Posidippus (c 290 BC) an ancient statue of Time by Lysippus is said to have represented him in the guise of Opportunity, with his hair hanging over his face and the back of his head bald. This was so that he might be seized by the forelock should anyone

meet him but he could never be grasped from behind once he had sped by.

Pittacus of Mitylene, one of the Wise Men of Greece from the sixth century BC, is also credited with this particular piece of wisdom.

Uses in English are frequent from the late sixteenth century onwards, literary imaginations obviously caught by the vivid allegory. There is variation in the form of the expression as to whether 'time' or 'occasion' should be seized by the forelock. This is because the original Greek can be rendered equally in English as 'time', 'occasion' or 'opportunity'. Mulcaster, for instance, in his POSITIONS (1581) alludes to the saying as follows:

Wherfore I must once for all, warne those parentes, which may not do as they would, upon these same lettes which I have recited, or any other like, that they take their oportunitie, when so ever it is offered, bycause occasion is verie bald behinde, and seldome comes the better.

Usage: Now somewhat dated

■ **There's a time for everything**

Everything has its appointed time or season to happen

There's time for everything except the things worth doing. Think of something you really care about. Then add hour to hour and calculate the fraction of your life that you've actually spent in doing it.
(George Orwell, COMING UP FOR AIR, 1939)

The proverb is a biblical one. ECCLESIASTES 3:1 reads: *To everything there is a season, and a time to every purpose under the heaven.*

The expression has been in use since at least the fourteenth century. Chaucer makes frequent use of it in his various writings and William Langland used it in RICHARD THE REDELESS (1399).

■ **There's no time like the present**

Don't put that task off, do it now while you can

See also: Make hay while the sun shines; Never put off till tomorrow what you can do today

'Mind if I ask,' I started up, thinking no time like the present, 'if that Christ Conversing With Law Doctors *is the one nicked from Lausanne?' The thieves had done a simple switch, with copies made from an art book. The curators said the stolen originals were so famous they would be unsaleable, which is a laugh. The antiques game is in a right state, but you still don't have to give Rembrandts away.*
(Jonathan Gash, THE SLEEPERS OF ERIN, 1983)

The proverb appeared in the play THE LOST LOVER by Mrs Mary de la Rivière Manley in 1696, and in Tobias Smollett's HUMPHREY CLINKER in 1771 and has been in frequent use ever since.

■ **Time and tide wait for no man**

Don't hesitate or delay before making a decision or an opportunity might be lost

Variant: Time and tide stay for no man

Time and tide will wait for no man, saith the adage.

But all men have to wait for time and tide.
(Charles Dickens, MARTIN CHUZZLEWIT, 1844)

The proverb was current in the late sixteenth century. It is mentioned in Robert Greene's A DISPUTATION BETWEEN A HEE CONNY-CATCHER AND A SHEE CONNY-CATCHER (1592). No one whose livelihood depends upon the sea can afford to miss the tide whether he be a ship's captain wanting to set sail or a vendor of shell-fish who searches the sands at low tide. Neither the tide nor time will accommodate any delays. Opportunities have to be grasped while the time is ripe. Another meaning of *tide* reinforces the idea of seizing the chance that is presented. It once meant 'season' or 'opportunity', a sense today only extant in Christmastide, Whitsuntide, etc. Therefore, the proverb very early had the meaning 'Time and season or opportunity wait for no man'. Before long, however, the focus shifted to the inexorable predictability of the sea tide since favoured in the expression.

■ **Time flies**

Time passes quickly

This is a translation of a Latin proverb, *Tempus fugit.* Man is much preoccupied by the passing of time, probably because it reminds him of his own mortality.

With the ancients, the relentless passing of time was a recurrent theme. *Alas the years glide swiftly by,* sighs Horace (ODES, 23 BC), while Ovid laments, *Time slips by, and we grow old with the silent years; there is no bridle can curb the flying days* (FASTI, c AD 8).

Modern writers are no more cheerful. Albert Fox Jr has obviously been spending rather too many hours pondering the Latin poets:

Just while we talk the jealous hours
Are bringing near the hearse and flowers.
(TIME, c 1900)

while Sir Osbert Sitwell meditates on the fact that Time always manages to have the last laugh:

In reality, killing time
Is only the name for another of the
multifarious ways
By which Time kills us.
(MILORDO INGLESE)

Sadly, by the time this entry has been read, the reader will be one or two minutes closer to eternity.

■ **Time is a great healer**

All hurts, whether physical or emotional, heal over in time

Variant: Time is the great healer

By the banks of the Leem, rapidly coming to
an accord, less rapidly overcoming mutual
shyness, the two men stammer, sigh, nod
heads sagely and agree that enough is
enough of anything, it can't go on, and that
Time, after all, is the great reconciler.
(Graham Swift, WATERLAND, 1983)

Jill used her work at a library to help her
with the grieving process. She was trying to
prove the old saying 'Time is a great healer.'
(BBC Radio 4, TWO PEOPLE, 22 January 1993)

Time will bring healing, Euripides tells us (ALCESTIS, c 438 BC) and Menander concurs, saying that time is a healer of all ills (FRAGMENTS, c 300 BC). Seneca calls time *Nature's great healer* (AD MARCIAM DE CONSOLATIONE, c AD 40).

Surprisingly, there are few recorded uses of the expression from the classical authors until recent times. Disraeli mentions that *Time is the great physician* in HENRIETTA TEMPLE (1836); otherwise it seems to be the beginning of the twentieth century before the expression gains a common currency.

■ **Time is money**

Time is as much of an asset and resource as money

Time is money and many people pay their
debts with it.
(Josh Billings)

To reverse-engineer a chip, a company must
produce something that achieves exactly the
same effects by wholly different means. With
a chip as complex as the 486, this could take
a great deal of time, and that time is money
to Intel.
(INDEPENDENT, 27 November 1992)

In an age when directors of large companies earn vast salaries and fortunes can be made on the exchange markets, this proverb has a very modern ring. It is, in fact, very ancient. As early as 430 BC Antiphon informs us that *the most costly outlay is the outlay of time* (MAXIM), a maxim repeated just over a century later by Theophrastus (MAXIM, c 320 BC). Montaigne referred to the proverb as an old saying when he quoted it in his ESSAYS of 1580 but perhaps it was Benjamin Franklin's use of it in ADVICE TO A YOUNG TRADESMAN

(1748) which brought it resoundingly into the English language and the fact that Dickens twice favoured it that made it stay there.

TOMORROW

■ **Never put off till tomorrow what you can do today**

If a job needs to be done, get on and do it straight away

See also: Make hay while the sun shines; There's no time like the present; Tomorrow never comes; Procrastination is the thief of time

Never do today what you can
Put off till to-morrow.
(Matthew Browne, ·THE CHILD'S WORLD, c 1866)

'Never put off till tomorrow what you can do today' is familiar to us all; I learnt the folly of that one early in my life as a housewife, when it became clear that I could save myself at least 50 per cent of my labours; a room tidied today simply needs tidying, cleaning and/or scrubbing again tomorrow . . .
(GOOD HOUSEKEEPING, November 1992)

Meanwhile, the limpet-like Lamont clings on resourcefully to his job as Chancellor of the Exchequer, even writing large chunks of the Budget after this and the Budget after that . . . Maybe Mr Lamont has got the balance right. We very much hope so. But we fear, we very much fear, he had put off till tomorrow some of the things he should have done today.
(DAILY MAIL, 17 March 1993)

An ancient proverb warns against putting off work until tomorrow. He who does, it goes on to say, is always at hand-grips with ruin. In Chaucer's day it was not work but well-doing that should not be deferred. In TALE OF MELIBEUS (c 1386) he writes: *Ther is an old proverbe seith: that 'the goodnesse that thou mayst do this day, do it; and abyde nat ne delaye it nat till to-morwe.*

Addison, writing in the SPECTATOR (1712), pronounces that *the maxim . . . should be inviolable with a man in office, never to think of doing that to-morrow which may be done to-day.* And indeed, the proverb has been the axiom of many men of importance.

According to James Howell *Secretary Cecil . . . would oftimes speak of himself, 'It shall never be said of me that I will defer till to-morrow what I can do to-day'* (LETTER, 5 September 1633). Robert Cecil, Earl of Salisbury, was Secretary of State under Elizabeth and James I, rising to the position of Lord Treasurer in 1608 and remaining James's chief minister until his death. Lord Chesterfield, the eighteenth century statesman and man of letters, extolled the import of the saying and the proverb was chosen by US president Thomas Jefferson as one of ten 'canons of conduct' (1817).

Let him who would be great pay heed.

■ **Tomorrow is another day**

Do not allow your present troubles to defeat you, for tomorrow brings the hope of better things

See also: Sufficient unto the day is the evil thereof; Hope springs eternal in the human breast; Don't cross a bridge until you come to it

King Hassan, well Beloved, was wont to say
When aught went wrong, or any project failed;
'Tomorrow, friends, will be another day!'
And in that faith he slept and so prevailed.
(James Buckham (1858–1908),
TOMORROW)

At this precise moment Donna isn't worrying. She can think about it tomorrow. After all, tomorrow is always another date.
(TELEGRAPH MAGAZINE, 13 March 1993)

It is quite likely that we are indebted to Spanish for this expression. In English, until the last century, the proverb was *Tomorrow is a new day.* Spanish still has a similar saying *Tomorrow will be a new day.* The first recorded use in English dates back to 1520, in a play with the title CALISTO AND MELIBOEA. Its source lies in Fernando de Rojas' LA TRAGICOMEDIA DE CALISTO Y MELIBEA, more commonly known as LA CELESTINA, of 1499. The play had a considerable vogue and was widely translated into English, or copied. Another significant Spanish influence is Cervantes' DON QUIXOTE (1605), in which the proverb is also used and which similarly was widely translated into English.

More recently Margaret Mitchell used the proverb to close her well known book, GONE WITH THE WIND (1936), as the willful heroine, Scarlett O'Hara, turned her back on the ruins of her life, and looked to the future with misplaced optimism.

■ **Tomorrow never comes**

A warning not to put things off till later, since they will never get done

See also: Never put of till tomorrow what you can do today; Make hay while the sun shines; Procrastination is the thief of time

The form of the proverb has changed over the centuries. Taverner (1539) says *Tomorrow is never present*, Chamberlain (1602) has *Tomorrow comes not yet* and Ray (1678) records *Tomorrow come never*, a form still current in the first half of the nineteenth century.

The dawn of every new day brings the dawn of a new tomorrow. It is impossible to catch up with the future, as Martial's cryptic epigram shows: *Tell me, Postumus, when does that tomorrow of yours come?* (c AD 90). The proverb is often used as a retort to those who put off tasks or plans 'until tomorrow' for, as Benjamin Franklin noted: *To-morrow every fault is to be amended; but that To-morrow never comes* (POOR RICHARD'S ALMANACK, 1756) or, as a Spanish proverb puts it, *Tomorrow is often the busiest day of the year.*

TRUTH

■ **Truth is stranger than fiction**

Real life happenings are more unbelievable than the wildest imaginings of writers of fiction

The two aircraftmen . . . adopt dumb-struck expressions, inwardly revising perhaps those

guide-books issued to U.S. servicemen in which they are officially advised that the inhabitants of rural England are reserved and unexcitable. No one rushes to fetch the police. No one believes him. The truth is so much stranger than –
(Graham Swift, WATERLAND, 1983)

The close relationship between truth and fiction has been a source of comment over millennia. Horace insisted that convincing fiction should be close to truth: *Fictions meant to please should be very close to truth* (DE ARTE POETICA, c 20 BC); Lowell emphasised the paradox that fiction might be more 'true' than fact: *There is a truth of fiction more veracious than the truth of fact* (THE BIGLOW PAPERS, 1848). Byron quoted the proverb in his DON JUAN (1823):

Tis strange – but true; for truth is always strange,–
Stranger than fiction.

and references to it can be found throughout nineteenth century literature.

At times, as the proverb claims, true stories seem so improbable as to stretch one's credulity. One such is told about Dr Thomas Young who was amongst those attempting to decipher the Rosetta Stone. He had been given an ancient Egyptian papyrus manuscript which he was struggling to make sense of. Amongst the hieroglyphics he made out three names written in Greek characters, Apollonius, Antigonus and Antimachus. A short time afterwards a friend gave him a number of papyrus documents which he had just procured. Dr Young turned with interest to one of these, a manuscript in Greek. Suddenly he noticed with excitement the words Antimachus, Antigensis and then Portis Apollonii. He was looking at nothing other than a Greek translation of the very document which was causing him so much difficulty and frustration. 'A most extraordinary chance,' Dr Young said, 'had brought into my possession a document which was not very likely, in the first place, ever to have existed, still less to have been preserved uninjured, for my information, through a period of near two thousand years; but that this very extraordinary translation should have been brought safely to Europe, to England, and to me, at the very moment when it was most of all desirable to me to possess it, as the illustration of an original which I was then studying, but without any other reasonable hope of comprehending it, – this combination would, in other times, have been considered as affording ample evidence of my having become an Egyptian sorcerer.' The strange coincidence proved a key to unlocking the whole mystery of hieroglyphics.

Remarkable as this incident is, it is not totally exceptional. Yet who, on coming across such a story in a work of fiction, would not accuse the author of an unlikely and contrived plot – a thought expressed by Shakespeare in TWELFTH NIGHT (1601): *If this were played upon a stage now, I could condemn it as an improbable fiction.*

TUNE

■ **There's many a good tune played on an old fiddle**

Age can bring improved, not diminished, performance

This saying is listed in a book of Cheshire proverbs compiled in 1917 but an earlier literary use was in Samuel Butler's THE WAY OF ALL FLESH (1903).

UNITED

■ **United we stand, divided we fall**

Strength lies in unity, division causes weakness

See also: A house divided against itself cannot stand

The Earl of Carnarvon, the Queen's racing manager, has warned enthusiasts of hunting and shooting to be wary of being picked off one by one by their opposition.
'We all stand together or fall together,' Lord Carnarvon told a London meeting of the Standing Conference on Countryside Sports, of which he is chairman.
(DAILY TELEGRAPH, 22 November 1991)

The maxim, which became the motto of the state of Kentucky, is American. It originated in the patriotic LIBERTY SONG written by John Dickinson, published in the BOSTON GAZETTE, 18 July 1768:

Then join hand in hand, brave Americans all.
By uniting we stand, by dividing we fall!

It became a rallying cry in the American War of Independence (1775–1783), a fact acknowledged by George Pope Morris in THE FLAG OF OUR UNION (1849):

A song for our banner! The watchword recall
Which gave the Republic her station:
'United we stand, divided we fall!'
It made and preserved us a nation!

There is nothing American about the idea behind the maxim, however. It was expressed centuries earlier in Aesop's fables and in the Bible. (See *A house divided against itself cannot stand.*) Nor is the range of uses to which the phrase has been put limited to America. It has been used as a rallying cry throughout the English-speaking world in trade unions, churches and armies.

VARIETY

■ **Variety is the spice of life**

What makes life interesting is constant variation and change

See also: All work and no play makes Jack a dull boy

If variety is the spice of life, then that of Mrs Susan Pyper, of West Chiltington, can only be described as highly-seasoned.
(WEST SUSSEX GAZETTE, 3 December 1992)

CLAIRE CLIFTON DISCOVERS CURRY POWDER IS THE SPICE OF VARIETY
There is a bewildering selection of curry powders in supermarkets and oriental groceries, but it wasn't until I started testing and tasting a selection of 20 of them

that I began to realise just how varied they are.
(GUARDIAN, 23 January 1993)

The proverb comes from THE TASK (1784), a poem by William Cowper. Among lines about dress, where Cowper mocks all the excesses and caprices of ever-changing fashion, we find:

Variety's the very spice of life,
That gives it all its flavour. We have run
Through every change that fancy at the loom,
Exhausted, has had genius to supply.
(THE TASK, Book II)

VIRTUE

■ **Virtue is its own reward**

The satisfaction of having acted properly is sufficient recompense in itself

And here I leave it, hoping that I have been helpful. You need not thank me. This sort of writing is its own reward.
(A A Milne, YEAR IN, YEAR OUT, 'JANUARY', 1952)

We are not a people for whom art is just a natural and congenial aspect of existence. The very 'uselessness' of it – the fact that art, like virtue, is its own reward – is a reason for mystification and distrust.
(L Kronenberger, COMPANY MANNERS, 'AMERICA AND ART', 1954)

My grandmother was also very fond of telling me that virtue brings its own reward.

All I can say is that it takes its time about it. I still seethe at the memory of going out of my way to be nice to the unpopular new girl with the greasy hair and BO and finding myself excluded from the in-crowd and losing my place on the roster for Lady Chatterley's Lover for my pains.
(GOOD HOUSEKEEPING, November 1992)

Stoicism was an important and widespread school of philosophy of the ancient world. It was founded by Zeno around 310 BC and its influence is felt in the works of Seneca, Epictetus and others. One of its tenets was that *Virtue is its own reward*, which is widely quoted in many classical writers. Because of their high status in England, this moral maxim has been regularly quoted. It first settled into the form we know today in Dryden's play THE ASSIGNATION of 1673.

Usage: It has an elevated and pious tone

Cornelius Theunissen is a Dutch wood carver. In about 1527 he produced eight woodcuts that illustrated proverbs and is a likely precursor of the many Dutch painters who chose proverbs as the subject of their canvases. One of the earliest and most famous, Pieter Brueghel, was born in about 1520 and died in 1569.

Weather wise

Traditionally, when the British meet, conversation turns to the weather. This preoccupation, however, is not peculiarly British. Many languages have a fund of proverbs which, before the days of more scientific methods of forecasting, reflected the concern with the weather of those in agriculture and fishing.

Scores of proverbs related to the saints' days observed in past centuries, by which the country dweller measured out his year. They foretold weather conditions and harvest yields. Here are just a few:

If it does rain on St Michael (29 September) *and Gallus* (16 October), *the following spring will be dry and propitious*

If it rains on Corpus Christi Day (Thursday after Trinity Sunday) *there will be little rye to put away*

Remember on St Vincent's Day (22 January)
if that the sun his beams display;
be sure to mark his transient beam
which through the casement sheds a gleam,
for 'tis a token bright and clear
of prosperous weather all the year

If it's cold on St Peter's Day (22 February), *then the cold is here for a lengthy stay*

If at Christmas ice hangs on the willow, clover may be cut at Easter

As at St Bartholomew's Day (24 August) *so will all the autumn stay*

Clear on St Jacob (20 July) *plenty of fruit.*

According to this fourteenth-century rhyme, a fair St Paul's day (25 January) was crucial to the happiness and stability of the realm:

If St Paul's Day be faire and cleare,
It doth betide a happy yeare;
But if by chance it then should raine,
It will make deare all kindes of graine.
And if ye clouds make dark ye skye,
Then meate and fowles this year shall die;
If blustering winds do blow aloft,
Then wars shall trouble ye realme full oft.

Other weather predictions were made by observing the sky. These were only sometimes reliable. *When clouds appear like rocks and towers, the earth's refreshed by frequent showers,* for instance, is an accurate description of shower-bearing cumulonimbus clouds. But the well-known saying *Red sky at night, shepherd's delight; red sky in the morning, shepherd's warning* is less dependable, although a glowing sunset does indicate clear skies to the west from where many of the weather systems that affect Britain come.

Sometimes, even in our changeable climate, certain prevailing conditions make prediction certain. The saying *Dew in the night, the day will be bright* is reliable since dew forms on still nights when skies are clear, an indication of high-pressure which brings sunny weather. The direction of the wind, shown by the weathervane on the church steeple, gave an indication of how cold it would be:

When the wind is in the east, it is neither good for man nor beast;
When the wind is in the west, then 'tis at its very best

An east wind is a lazy wind because . . . it will go through you before it will go round you

The west wind is a gentleman and goes to bed (that is, it drops in the evening).

Another well-known proverb *Rain before seven, dry before eleven* often proves correct. A band of rain does not usually last longer than a few hours, so if it sets in early a dry spell before eleven is probable.

Observation of plant life was also relied upon. This proverb about the budding of the oak and the ash was found to be 'generally correct' by a correspondent with NOTES AND QUERIES (1852):

If the oak's before the ash,
Then you'll only get a splash.
But if the ash precedes the oak,
Then you may expect a soak.

But an article in the TIMES LITERARY SUPPLEMENT (4 August 1911) cast doubt on its reliablity, stating that *In North Germany the signs are exactly inverted, and also in Cornwall.*

Heavy crops of berries foretold a hard winter, the fruit being needed to feed the birds:

Holly berries shining red,
Mean a long winter, 'tis said

Mony haws, mony snaws;
Mony slaes, mony cauld taes
(Scottish)

However, the abundance of any crop depends on weather conditions in its embryonic stage and not those prevailing when it comes to maturity. And the same applies to the humble onion:

Onion skin, very thin, Mild winter coming in;
Onion skin thick and tough, Winter coming cold and rough.

The behaviour of animals and birds was also held to be significant:

When a cow tries to scratch its ear,
It means a shower be very near.
When it begins to thump its ribs with its tail,
Look out for thunder, lightning and hail.

Does a cow's ear really only itch when a shower is expected? And, surely, the angry swishing of its tail has more to do with bothersome flies than storms? Here are a few more:

When harvest flies hum, there's warm weather to come.

If the birds begin to whistle in January, there are frosts to come

When sheep and lambs do gambol and fight, the weather will change before the night

When the peacock loudly calls, then look out for storms and squalls

When you hear the asses bray, we shall have rain on that day

If bees stay at home, rain will soon come; if they fly away, fine will be the day

Seagull, seagull, sit on the sand. It's never fine weather while you're on the land.

Weather forecasting has come a long way since Aristotle wrote his METEOROLOGICA in the third century BC but, even with the sophisticated help of satellites and computers, weathermen can still get it wrong. They failed, for instance, to warn of the hurricane that hit the south of England in 1987. So perhaps it is unfair to pour too much scorn on our forebears who, by searching for signs and weather patterns in the world about them, attempted to stay one step ahead of the elements.

For those with an academic bent and a command of German, entries in the Bibliography under Helm and Hellmann provide substantial analysis, with an international perspective, of weather proverbs. Hellmann's own bibliography is seven pages long, showing how important climate has been over many centuries. For readers of French, Legros analyses many weather proverbs from Walloon in southern Belgium.

WALLS

■ Walls have ears

Be careful how and where you disclose your private affairs for, even when it is not apparent, someone may be listening

'She's told me. She's very particular' – *he looked around to see if walls had ears.*
(Arnold Bennett, THE OLD WIVES' TALE, 1908)

'Not so loud,' said Lord Ickenham warningly, *'stations have ears.'*

He led his nephew away down the platform apologizing with a charming affability to the various travellers with whom the latter collided from time to time in his preoccupation.
(P G Wodehouse, UNCLE FRED IN THE SPRINGTIME, 1939)

The proverb advises that, though people may think they are alone when they share their secrets, there may well be someone concealed behind a nearby wall listening to every word. In the middle ages it was the countryside which conspired not only to eavesdrop but also to spy. A medieval Latin proverb (See *The devil sick would be a monk*) from at least the turn of the thirteenth century warns that *Field hath eye and the wood hath the keenness of an ear.* Chaucer used it in THE KNIGHTES TALE (c 1386) and there are several references to it in sixteenth century literature. Ray recorded the expression in his collection of proverbs of 1670. In the following centuries Swift and Scott were amongst those writers who used the saying.

Walls have ears would appear to be a variant for the increasing number of urban dwellers, intent on disclosing their secret affairs not in the open fields but in a quiet room. It appears in French, which also has the countryside proverb, around the turn of the sixteenth century and in English in the following century. Swift mixes the proverbs to good effect in POLITE CONVERSATION (1738): *Hedges have eyes, and walls have ears.*

Precautions against being overheard are obviously important during wartime. *Walls have ears* gained a new lease of life during the Second World War when it was a slogan of government propaganda to make people aware that *Enemy ears are listening* and *Careless talk costs lives.*

WASTE

■ Waste not, want not

If you do not squander your money or resources, you will never be in need

This makes an apt proverb for the age of conservation and recycling. The proverb is found in literature from the end of the eighteenth century. Maria Edgeworth writes thus: *The following words were written . . . over the mantelpiece in his uncle's spacious kitchen, 'Waste not, want not.'* (THE PARENT'S ASSISTANT, 1796).

WATERS

■ **Still waters run deep**

A quiet and composed manner may hide an undesirable quality or some deep troublesome emotion

Variant: Silent waters run deep

To the dwellers in the mountain the smooth river may seem at first unimpressive. But still waters run deep; and the proverb applies with peculiar truth to the poetry of Racine.
(Lytton Strachey, LANDMARKS IN FRENCH LITERATURE, 1912)

You know how Laura is. So quiet but – still water runs deep! She notices things and I think she – broods about them.
(Tennessee Williams, THE GLASS MENAGERIE, 1945)

Still waters are deep. No ripple on the surface betrays the dangers that may lurk beneath. The notion is found in DISTICHA (c 175 BC) which some attribute to Cato: *Though the stream is placid, perchance it hides the deeper wave.* An early English reference to this comes in the CURSOR MUNDI, an anonymous poem of the early fourteenth century written in northern Middle English: *Ther the flode is deppist the water standis stillist.* Those who brood in silence without betraying their emotion are to be feared, for *the stillest humours are the worst* (John Ray, ENGLISH PROVERBS, 1670).

Still waters are silent. Another Latin writer, Quintus Curtius says: *The deepest rivers run with the least sound* (DE REBUS ALEXANDRI MAGNI, c AD 50), a statement echoed in Seneca's HIPPOLYTUS: *Light griefs are loquacious, but the great are dumb.* Sir Walter Raleigh found inspiration in both in a poem he wrote for Queen Elizabeth I:

Our passions are most like to floods and streams,
The shallow murmur but the deep are dumb.
(SIR WALTER RALEIGH TO THE QUEEN, c 1599)

Still water is almost motionless. Shallow water is swift; grudges are noisily expressed and quickly over. The brooding resentment symbolised by deep water scarcely slides by: *Take heed of still waters, the quick pass away* (George Herbert, JACULA PRUDENTUM, 1640).

Still waters run deep indeed, causing Thomas Fuller to cry *God defend me from the still Water, and I'll keep myself from the Rough* (GNOMOLOGIA, 1732)

Usage: Silence in others may hide meditation and reflection and hidden depths. It may hide unforeseen skills, even dubious practices. It may arouse emotions from admiration through to fear. The proverb is used as a comment in situations such as these, and many others.

WEAR

■ **It is better to wear out than to rust out**

It is better to die from being too busy than from sitting about all day

This proverb is usually the retort of a vigorous elderly person upon being told to take things more slowly. Plutarch shared this attitude. Speaking of the elderly he says that their worth is *extinguished by idleness as iron is destroyed by rust* (MORALIA: OLD MEN IN PUBLIC AFFAIRS, c AD 95). A favourite maxim of Martin Luther (1483–1546) was *If I rest, I rust*, and German has other proverbs linking rust and inactivity.

The English proverb comes from a remark made by Bishop Cumberland (c 1700) who, upon being told by a concerned friend that he was over-working and would wear himself out, replied *It is better to wear out than to rust out*. The anecdote has been given several airings, one of them in Horne's SERMON ON THE DUTY OF CONTENDING FOR THE TRUTH. It impressed fiery evangelical George Whitefield who quoted Cumberland as he toiled for the gospel (c 1770): *I had rather wear out than rust out*.

Some people who are getting on in years, however, feel justified in winding down a little. Shakespeare's Falstaff has a word for those who would really rather just rust out in peace:

If ye will needs say I am an old man, you should give me rest. I would to God my name were not so terrible to the enemy as it is. I were better to be eaten to death with a rust than to be scoured to nothing with perpetual motion (HENRY THE FOURTH PART TWO, Act 1, scene ii, 1597).

WIND

■ **It's an ill wind that blows nobody any good**

In every difficulty or loss there is usually someone who benefits by it

Kenneth Clarke, predictably enough, avoids blame for his party by pointing to 'trendy teaching methods' as being the cause. Of course, it is true that some children suffer from ineffective teaching, but there is no evidence that particular methods are to blame. They can all fail if taught badly, and all succeed if used well. Indeed, Professor Clay's success is partly based on the fact that her teachers are taught to start from where the child is . . . a thoroughly child-centred approach . . . So Kenneth Clarke has found himself backing a scheme which proves that a child-centred approach works. It's an ill wind.
(TIMES EDUCATIONAL SUPPLEMENT, 10 January 1992)

The proverb was known in the sixteenth century, being recorded by John Heywood in his PROVERBS (1546). The expression is a nautical one and refers to sailing ships. Where sailors travelling east would have to work hard to tack against an easterly wind, the same wind would be considered advantageous by a ship travelling in the opposite direction, with the wind behind it filling the sails. Somebody will benefit, whatever the direction of the wind. Tusser makes this point in his *Description of the Properties of Wind* in FIVE HUNDRETH POINTES OF GOOD HUSBANDRIE (1573):

Except wind stands as never it stood,
It is an ill wind turns none to good.

The expression figures in all the proverb collections and in major authors such as Shakespeare: *Ill blows the wind that profits nobody.* (HENRY THE SIXTH, PART THREE, 1593)

WINE

■ **Good wine needs no bush**

There is no need to advertise good quality merchandise since the public will soon track it down for themselves. Quality sells itself

For the origin of this proverb we need to look to Bacchus, the Roman god of wine. Images of the god show him wearing the garland of ivy and vine leaves sacred to him. Roman taverns advertised their trade by displaying a bush-like arrangement of vine and ivy outside the door by way of an inn sign, a custom which the Romans took with them to England and other countries they invaded. It is not clear exactly when the proverb this practice inspired was coined but it was certainly in circulation by the early sixteenth century.

The custom of hanging out a bush of ivy lingered in England until quite recently. According to an 1854 edition of NOTES AND QUERIES, it was still the practice on fair days for villagers in Brompton Brian, Herefordshire *either under the impression that upon those particular days anybody may sell beer or cyder without, or a licence is granted for those days only.*

Similarly at the Michaelmas Barton Fair at Gloucester ale, beer and cider were sold from private houses displaying garlands of leaves, the inhabitants claiming an ancient privilege to sell alcoholic refreshment without a licence during a fair.

The presence of ivy leaves in the bush may well have had another signification, a hint that good wine will hurt nobody. The suggestion comes from a late nineteenth century edition of the ATHENAEUM. Writers from Pliny through Cato to Culpepper and Coles have recognised the efficacy of ivy leaves to ward off or cure excessive drinking: *If one has got a surfeit by drinking wine, his speediest cure is to drink a draught of the same wine wherein a handful of [ivy] leaves, being first bruised, have been boiled* (Culpepper). So the sign of the bush not only signals the sale of wine but also suggests it will not bring any harm.

Equivalents in other languages are many, through widespread Roman influence and from the writings of scholars such as Erasmus. His ADAGIA of 1536 has *Vino vendibili suspensa hedera nihil opus,* translated by Taverner as *Wyne that is saleable and goode nedeth no bushe or garland of vyne to be hanged before.* Italian has *Al buon vino non bisogna frasca* (Good wine needs no bush); French *A bon vin ne faut point d'enseigne* (Good wine does not need a signboard) and *Le bon vin n'a point besoin bucheron* (Good wine needs no bush);

Spanish *El vino que es bueno, no ha menester pregonero* (Wine that is good needs no herald); and the Germans say *Guter Wein verkauft sich selbst* (Good wine sells itself).

Usage: As the practice of hanging out a bush to advertise the sale of strong drink has died out, so has the proverb itself. Now not frequently used.

WOMAN

■ **A man is as old as he feels, and a woman as old as she looks**

Women are judged by external appearance, men by their inner youthfulness

The adage that a man is as old as he feels, and a woman as old as she looks, may be said to contain much inherent truth.
(ILLUSTRATED LONDON NEWS, 25 May 1907)

This saying, also known in Italian, appeared in a poem by Mortimer Collins entitled HOW OLD ARE YOU? (1855):

O wherefore our age be revealing?
Leave that to the registry books!
A man is as old as he's feeling,
A woman as old as she looks.

It focuses on the aging process and on the fact that women have always been judged by their outward appearance; men less so. It is principally the woman who is the butt of the sometimes spiteful, sometimes wry comments that are made about aging, and this proverb is no exception. But is it true?

In spite of all the creams and potions available today, it is usually possible to tell a woman's age by the condition of her skin and the shape of her figure. Farmyard similes pour scorn on any attempt she might make to hide her advancing years. If she tries to stay young-at-heart a detractor might say of her *She has many good nicks in her horn*, a cow being said to have a wrinkle in its horn for every year of its life. If she dresses fashionably she is accused of being *mutton dressed as lamb*, and if she should do anything to betray her age she is reminded that she is *no spring chicken*. Understandably, the aging process is resented by many women. As Ninon de Lenclos (1620–1705) wrote: *If God had to give a woman wrinkles, He might at least have put them on the soles of her feet.* Some of the damage can be smoothed over temporarily:

Little dabs of powder,
Little smears of paint,
Make a woman's wrinkles
Look as if they ain't.
(Helen May)

But if this fails then there is nothing for a woman to do but to lurk in the shadows and appear constantly *in the dusk with a light behind her* in the hope of passing permanently for forty-three (W S Gilbert, TRIAL BY JURY, 1875).

Men, on the other hand, are supposed to mellow physically with age, achieving a distinguished but still handsome appearance. Provided they have no aches and pains and keep a youthful outlook, the proverb suggests that they can laugh at the advancing years. The experiences of those who have gone before suggests this is not so, however. Aches and pains are inevitable and drag a man's mind into old age. For Martin Luther, middle age suddenly struct at thirty-eight: *One's thirty-eighth year is an evil and dangerous year, bringing many evils and great sicknesses* (TABLE-TALK, 1521). By forty-three the prime of life is well past if Esaias Tegnér is to be believed: *Today is my forty-third birthday. I have thus long passed the peak of life where the waters divide* (LETTER TO M F FRANZEN, 13 November 1825). Perhaps he would agree with the anonymous comment that *middle age is when we can do just as much as ever – but would rather not*. By the time a man reaches his sixties, it's uphill, or downhill, all the way. *It's only in going uphill that one realises how fast one is going downhill*, says George Du Maurier at 62, and the poet, Longfellow, finds that *to be seventy years old is like climbing the Alps* (LETTER TO G W CHILDS, 13 March 1877). In truth a man's spirit seems to age at the same rate as his body. Dr Johnson laments to Boswell that his diseases are *an asthma and a dropsy, and what is less curable, seventy-five* (1786) and Bob Hope is the voice of the lively octogenarian male: *I don't feel eighty, in fact I don't feel anything till noon, and then it's time for my nap.*

So whether you are male or female, as old as you feel or as old as you look, you are the age you are.

Proverbial genres

The *sottie* is a late fifteenth and early sixteenth century French dramatic genre, based on proverbs. The plays were usually a few hundred lines long and similar to farces and morality plays.

There is also the later and more widely known *proverbe*, in which a proverb is taken as the foundation of the plot. Alfred de Musset in France is the best known writer in this style, although Carmantelli was perhaps the most successful, at the time of their highest popularity.

There's many a lip 'twixt cup and slip

Some writers have a genius for getting things wrong, yet still they manage to make a perverse kind of sense.

Fractured phrases and mangled metaphors have earned Don Edwards a small place in history. A collection of his gems includes:

- *Never a true word spoken in jest*
- *I've got a ton and half to fit into a pint and a quart*
- *The mountain goes into a molehill*
- *We'd better let sleeping ducks lie*
- *It's like chasing the horse after the stable door has been left open*

Samuel Goldwyn is much more famous internationally for similar verbal infelicity. Perhaps part of his fame in this regard is that English was not his native language – he was born in Poland in 1882.

Don't halloa till you are out of the wood. This is a night for praying rather than boasting.
(Charles Kingsley, HEREWARD THE WAKE, 1866)

Manning was an Archdeacon; but he was not yet out of the wood. His relations with the Tractarians had leaked out, and the Record was beginning to be suspicious.
(Lytton Strachey, EMINENT VICTORIANS, 'CARDINAL MANNING', 1918)

Even when the market does pick up, more Farm Street dramas cannot be ruled out. 'I don't think WPP is out of the woods yet,' says Lorna Tilbian, analyst at Warburg Securities.
(THE TIMES, 11 August 1991)

To 'halloo' means to shout aloud. The proverb warns against crying out with joy or relief until danger is certainly past. Sometimes 'halloo' is replaced by 'whistle'. Both the proverb and the shorter idiom *to be out of the woods*, meaning 'to be out of difficulty or danger', were current from at least the end of the eighteenth century. These days the latter is more commonly heard.

WOOD

■ **Don't halloo till you are out of the wood**

Don't assume the difficulty or danger is passed before you have proof that it really is

See also: Don't count your chickens before they are hatched; First catch your hare

WORD

■ **There's many a true word spoken in jest**

A humorous, joking remark may hide a profound insight or a serious criticism. An unintended comment may turn out to be true

Chaucer's Cook and Monk, characters from his CANTERBURY TALES (c 1386), both testify to the truth behind the proverb. The cook, for example, says: *A man may seye full sooth in game and pley.* Chaucer probably related this expression to *True jest, no jest* which he uses in the same work (in the form *Sooth pley, quaad pley*) and explicitly attributes it to the Flemish. It is likely he had in mind *Waer spot, quaet spot.*

At the end of the sixteenth century Ferguson recorded a Scottish saying which, although expressed in archaic vocabulary, is identical in word order and meaning to the modern expression: *There are many sooth words spoken in bourding* (ROXBURGHE BALLADS, c 1665). Both French and Italian have equivalent adages.

International wits have over centuries taken advantage of punching home their point – with a smile:

The Romans would never have had time to conquer the world if they had been obliged first to learn Latin (Heinrich Heine)
If the art of conversation stood a little higher, we would have a lower birthrate (Stanislaw Lec).
One more word out of you and I'll paint you as you are (Berlin artist Max Liebermann to a talkative sitter).
Very nice, though there are dull stretches (Antoine de Rivarol, on reading a couplet).
You have Van Gogh's ear for music (Billy Wilder on hearing Cliff Osmond sing).

These particular examples are taken from Brandreth's excellent THE JOY OF LEX, though the list could be endlessly extended.

Usage: There are two currently different senses. One use is in appreciation of a home truth or particularly apposite remark that has been made, sometimes on purpose and sometimes not, as a joke. The other use is when a humorous remark that was never intended to be taken seriously turns out to be prophetic and comes true.

WORDS

■ **Fine words butter no parsnips**

Fine words (such as flattery or lavish but empty promises) are powerless to change things

Variant: Fair words butter no parsnips

See also: Actions speak louder than words

It perhaps helped to sustain her in an environment of unchanging mediocrity to remember that the d'Arfeys had had, for nearly six centuries, the right to bear the royal lilies of France as part of their arms – a proceeding which, as I had heard Toby slightingly observe, would butter no parsnips whatsoever.
(W Plomer, MUSEUM PIECES, 1950)

A few southern orators continued to protest against the sacrilegious conduct of the deserters. But such reproofs buttered no parsnips. Survivors among the planting aristocracy and their children now moved into the towns as leaders of business

enterprise or strove to place their estates on a money-making basis.
(Charles and Mary Beard, THE RISE OF AMERICAN CIVILIZATION, 1927)

Over the centuries one way to make a dish of plain food more palatable has been to add a knob of butter to it. Since the proverb was coined during the seventeenth century, fair words have been unable to lend appeal to fish, cabbage or turnips, as well as the humble parsnip. The phrase finally settled into its present day form in the second half of the eighteenth century.

Not everyone subscribes to the theory that fine words are ineffective, however. Thackeray puts up a robust argument to the contrary: *Who . . . said that 'fine words butter no parsnips'? Half the parsnips of society are served and rendered palatable with no other sauce* (VANITY FAIR, 1847). But for Ogden Nash, once a parsnip, always a parsnip: *Parsnips are unbutterable* (MY DEAR, HOW EVER DID YOU THINK UP THIS DELICIOUS SALAD? 1935).

General Bildering . . . says it is only a bad workman who quarrels with his tools and repudiates Kuropatkin's criticism of the rank and file.
(JAPAN TIMES, 26 February 1907)

Every workman needs the tools appropriate to his trade to do his work. According to Rabelais in GARGANTUA (1534) *a good workman can use any kind of tools.* In spite of this, there is a class of workmen who seems unable to find tools to his liking and who blames the poor standard of his finished work upon this fact. He is the 'bundler' whom we have all had the misfortune to hire at one time or another. *A bundler,* says Randle Cotgrave, *cannot find good tooles* (DICTIONARY, 1611).

The old form of the proverb was *An ill workman quarrels with his tools.* It is found in literature from the first half of the seventeenth century and is still sometimes heard today, although the twentieth century variant *A bad workman blames his tools* is the current form.

WORKMAN

■ **A bad workman blames his tools**

Someone who has produced a shoddy piece of work will not admit that he is at fault but will seek to lay the blame elsewhere

Variant: An ill workman quarrels with his tools

WORLD

■ **Half the world doesn't know how the other half lives**

One half of society cannot begin to imagine the problems, or pleasures, that the other half faces

Variant: Half the world don't know how the other half live

It is an old proverb that 'one half of the world do not know how the other half live'. Add to it, 'nor where they live'.
(Captain Marryat, THE KING'S OWN, 1830)

The Cambridge experience does turn out a more rounded individual. Cambridge gave me an academic bent in my eventual choice of profession. It did teach me how the other half – or the other 90 per cent – lived, and that's helped me as a restaurateur a lot. It made me aware of all the social nuances.
(CAMBRIDGE UNIVERSITY ALUMNI MAGAZINE, Lent Term 1993)

A form of the proverb is found in the work of Philippe de Commines, courtier of Louis XI of France, who was acclaimed as the first historian since ancient times to present his subject critically and philosophically. In his MEMOIRES (1509) de Commines writes: *This confirms the old saying, One half the world does not know what the other half is doing.* Also in French, Rabelais quotes the form with which we are familiar in his PANTAGRUEL of 1532. The proverb makes a later appearance in English. It was noted by George Herbert in JACULA PRUDENTUM (1640).

The saying is usually applied to those who, from their position of social advantage, are unable to imagine the misery of the disadvantaged. James Kelly explains the proverb thus: *One half of the world kens not how the other lives. Men bred to ease and luxury are not sensible of the mean condition of a great many* (SCOTTISH PROVERBS, 1721).

By contrast, the proverb today might also be used by someone lower in the social scale who takes a privileged glimpse into a more glamorous or socially superior lifestyle. Usage since at least 1890 regularly reduces the full proverb to the idiomatic expression *how the other half live*, as in the extract from the Cambridge University Alumni Magazine.

■ **It takes all sorts to make the world**
The vast variety of humankind entails the need for tolerance

Variant: It takes all sorts to make a world

See also: Live and let live

'Hines was not exactly a weak sister, but he was sort of nondescript. I can't imagine his appealing to your wife.'
   'It takes all sorts of people to make a world. You can never tell who is going to appeal to whom.'
(Erle Stanley Gardner, THE CASE OF THE BORROWED BRUNETTE, 1946)

Live and let live, I always say; but I don't care myself to see a young fellow wasting himself like that. Particularly when he's a parson's son. Still, it takes all sorts, as they say.
(Rose Macaulay, I WOULD BE PRIVATE, 1937)

The expression was used by Cervantes in DON QUIXOTE (1615). Philosopher John Locke, writing early in the eighteenth century, echoed Cervantes' thought and was later credited with its coinage by Samuel Johnson in BOSWELL'S

LIFE OF JOHNSON (17 November 1767): *Some lady surely might be found . . . in whose fidelity you might repose. The World, says Locke, has people of all sorts.* Sometime during the first half of the nineteenth century the proverb was moulded into the present day form and has been in constant use since.

Usage: Can be said as an appeal for tolerance in the face of diversity, or as a resigned comment when faced with behaviour that goes beyond the normal

WORM

■ **Even a worm will turn**

Even the meekest or humblest person will eventually be goaded into retaliation

'Of course you'll generally find us here about six o'clock and we shall always be glad to see you,' he said graciously, but with the evident intention of putting me, as an author, in my humble place. But the worm sometimes turns.
(W Somerset Maugham, THE RAZOR'S EDGE, 1944)

As for all the types about him, the little bowler-hatted worms who never turned, and the go-getters, the American business-college gutter-crawlers, they rather amused him than not.
(George Orwell, KEEP THE ASPIDISTRA FLYING, 1936)

In America, the worm who turns, turns not to the courts but to his six-gun. The fastest growing form of murder there is what they call workplace homicide. A typical scenario, according to police, is when an employee pushed beyond reason or sanity, takes his revenge by shooting his former boss.
(DAILY TELEGRAPH, 24 September 1992)

A correspondent in NOTES AND QUERIES (1853) denied that a worm would turn in anger when stepped upon. He preferred to think that the proverb was coined in the days when the word 'worm' could be applied equally to a viper, a creature much better equipped to round upon its enemy. What the proverb meant, he argued, was that those who had the ability to fight back would certainly do so and so people should take care how they treated them.

The proverb, however, means just what it says and draws the lesson that even the meekest person can be roused to retaliate from the keenly observed natural fact that, when a lowly earthworm is dug up or its tail trodden on, it instinctively writhes, turning back upon itself and appearing to threaten its attacker. This was certainly how Shakespeare understood the already current analogy when he wrote: *The smallest worm will turn, being trodden on* (HENRY THE SIXTH, PART THREE, Act 2, scene ii, 1593).

The proverb is alluded to extensively in English literature from the sixteenth century onwards, thanks to the influence of Shakespeare. It is not, however, exclusive to English; the

French, for instance, say *Un ver se recoquille quand on marche dessus* (A worm recoils when you step on it).

The figurative use of *worm* to mean 'a lowly, despised person' was current even in Old English. Wycliffe, the great Christian reformer, was described as one in 1402, for introducing the seeds of schism in the earth. The term certainly pre-dates the proverb itself.

WRONG

■ **Two wrongs don't make a right**

Copying someone else is no justification for committing a wrong action. Paying someone back in kind is unacceptable

See also: Two blacks don't make a white

Of parallel construction and meaning to *Two blacks don't make a white*, this version is first recorded in the latter part of the nineteenth century in a collection of proverbial folklore.

BIBLIOGRAPHY

This is a selective list of some of the books to which reference has been made. Details of major historical proverb collections can be found in **An accumulation of wisdom** (page 108) and **Erasmus's Adagia** (page 8). For an extremely valuable and comprehensive bibliography of proverbs, Mieder (1982) and (1990) are incomparable.

(1849–1935). *Notes and Queries for readers and writers, collectors and librarians.* London: Oxford University Press.

(1967). *Diccionario de Aforismos, Proverbios y Refranes* (4th ed.). Barcelona: Sintes.

Abel, A. (1977). *Make Hay While the Sun Shines: A Book of Proverbs.*

Anand, C. (no date). *3,000 Proverbs.* New Delhi: New Light.

Andreason, N. C. (1977). Reliability and Validity of Proverb Interpretation to Assess Mental Status. *Comprehensive Psychiatry, 18,* pp 465–472.

Apperson, G. L. (1929). *English Proverbs and Proverbial Phrases: A Historical Dictionary.* London: J M Dent.

Bar-Sela, A., & Hoff, H. E. (1963). Maimonides' Interpretation of the First Aphorism of Hippocrates. *Bulletin of the History of Medicine, 37,* pp 347–354.

Bartlett, J. (1992). *Familiar Quotations* (16th ed.). Boston: Little, Brown.

Benham, W. G. (1948). *Benham's Book of Quotations, Proverbs and Household Words* (3rd ed.). London: Ward, Lock.

Bombaugh, C. C. (1905). *Facts and fancies for the Curious from the Harvest Fields of Literature: A Melange of Excerpta.* Philadelphia & London.

Bonser, W. (1930). *A Bibliography of Works relating to Proverbs.*

Brewer, E. C. (1991). *Brewer's Dictionary of 20th Century Phrase and Fable.* London: Cassell.

Brewer, E. C. (1993). *Brewer's Dictionary of Phrase and Fable* (14th revised ed.). London: Cassell.

Browning, D. C. (1951). *Everyman's Dictionary of Quotations and Proverbs.* London: Dent.

Cahoon, D., & Edmonds, E. M. (1980). The Watched Pot Still Won't Boil: Expectancy as a Variable in Estimating the Passage of Time. *Bulletin of Psychonomic Society, 16* (No. 2), pp 115–116.

Dane, J. A. (1980). Linguistic Trumpery: Notes on a French 'Sottie' (Recueil Trepperel, No. 10). *The Romantic Review, 71*, pp 114–121.

de Dony, Y. P. (1951). *Léxico del Lenguaje Figurado comparado en cuatro idiomas.* Buenos Aires: Desclee, De Brouwer.

Dent, R. W. (1981). *Shakespeare's Proverbial Languages: An Index.* Berkeley: University of California Press.

Dixon, J. M. (1941). *Dictionary of Idiomatic English Phrases* (3rd ed.). London: Nelson.

Dournons, J. Y. (1986). *Dictionnaire des Proverbes et Dictons de France.*

Doyle, C. C. (1972). Smoke and Fire: Spenser's Counter-Proverb. *Proverbium, 18,* pp 683–685.

Doyle, C. C. (1975). On Some Paremiological Verses. *Proverbium, 25,* pp 979–982.

Dundes, A. (1972). Seeing is Believing. *Natural History* (No. 5), pp 8–14 and 86.

Ewart, N. (1983). *Everyday Phrases.* Poole: Blandford.

Fergusson, R. (1983). *Penguin Dictionary of Proverbs.* London: Penguin.

Gillmeister, H. (1978). Chaucer's 'Kan Ke Dort' (Troilus, II, 1725) and the 'Sleeping Dogs' of the Trouveres. *English Studies, 59,* pp 310–323.

Gish, R. (1972). Forster as Fabulist: Proverbs and Parables in 'A Passage to India'. *English Literature in Translation (1880–1920), 15,* pp 245–256.

Halliwell, J. O. (1850). *Dictionary of Archaic Words.* London: John Russell Smith.

Heidel, W. A. (1909). Charity that Begins at Home. *American Journal of Philology, 30,* 196–198.

Hellmann, G. (1923). Über den Ursprung der volkstülichen Wetteregeln (Bauernregeln). *Sitzungsberichte der Preussischen Akademie der Wissenschaften,* pp 148–170.

Helm, K. (1939). Bauernregeln. *Hessische Blatter fur Volkskunde, 38,* pp 114–132.

Houghton, P. *A World of Proverbs.* Poole: Blandford.

Ichikawa, S., Mine, T., Inui, R., Kihara, K., & Takaha, S. (1964). *Kenkyusha Dictionary of English Idioms.* Tokyo: Kenkyusha.

Jente, R. (1931–32). The American Proverb. *American Speech, 7,* 342–348.

Jorgensen, P. A. (1976). Valor's Better Parts: Backgrounds and Meanings of Shakespeare's Most Difficult Proverb. *Shakespeare Studies, 9,* pp 141–158.

Kirshenblatt-Gimblett, B. (1973a). A Playful Note: The Good Old Game of Proverbs. *Proverbium, 22,* 860–861.

Kirshenblatt-Gimblett, B. (1937b). Toward a Theory of Proverb Meaning. *Proverbium, 22,* 821–827.

Kittredge, G. L. (1893–1984). To Take Time By The Forelock. *Modern Language Notes, 8 and 9*, Vol 8: Cols 459–469 Vol 9: Cols 189–90.

Krueger, D. W. (1978). The Differential Diagnosis of Proverb Interpretation. In W. E. Fann, I. Karacan, A. D. Pokorny, & R. L. Williams (Eds.), *Phenomenology and Treatment of Schizophrenia* (pp 193–201). New York: Spectrum.

Legros, E. (1972). A propos de dictons météorologiques. *Enquêtes du Musée de la Vie Wallone*, pp 17–46.

Lehman, E. (1960). The Monster Test. *Archives of General Psychiatry, 3*, 535–544.

Luce, L. F. (1977). The Mask of Language in Alfred de Musset's 'Proverbes'. *Romance Notes, 17*, pp 272–280.

Lundberg, G. A. (1958). The Semantics of Proverbs. *ETC: A Review of General Semantics, 15*, pp 215–217.

Maloux, M. (1971). *Dictionnaire des Proverbes, Sentences et Maximes* (2nd ed.). Paris: Larousse.

Matzke, J. E. (1893). On the Source of Italian and English Idioms Meaning 'To Take Time by the Forelock' with Special Reference to Bojardo's 'Orlando Innamorato', Book II, Cantos VII–IX. *Publications of the Modern Language Association, 8*, pp 303–334.

Maw, W. H., & Maw, E. W. (1975). Contrasting Proverbs as a Measure of Attitudes of College Students Towards Curiosity-Related Behaviours. *Psychological Reports, 37*, pp 1085–1086.

Mieder, W. (1982). *International Proverb Scholarship: An Annotated Bibliography*. New York: Garland.

Mieder, W. (1990). *International Proverb Scholarship: An Annotated Bibliography. Supplement 1 (1800–1981)*. New York: Garland.

Morby, E. S. (1954–55). Proverbs in 'La Dorotea'. *Romance Philology, 8*, 243–259.

Nares, R. (1822). *Glossary of Words, Phrases, Names and Allusions, particularly of Shakespeare*. London: Routledge.

Ojoade, J. O. (1978–79). When in Rome do as the Romans do: African Parallels. *Midwestern Language & Folklore Newsletter, 1–2*, pp 13–18.

Palmer, A. S. (1907). *Some Curios from a Word-Collector's Cabinet*. London & New York.

Perry, A. M. (1934–35). Pearls before Swine. *Expository Times, 46*, pp 381–382.

Peterson, G. (1969). *Proverbs to live by*. London: Roger Schlesinger.

Picherit, K. (1893). On the Source of Italian and English Idioms Meaning 'To Take Time by the Forelock'. *Modern Language Notes, 8*, Cols. 469–475.

Pigler, A. (1956). *Barockthemen Eine Auswahl von Verzeichnissen zur Ikonographie des 17 und 18 Jahrhunderts.* Budapest: Verlag der Ungarischen Akademie der Wissenschaften.

Prins, A. A. (1948). On Two Proverbs in the 'Ancren Riwle'. *English Studies, 29,* pp 146–150.

Reich, J. H. (1981). Proverbs and the Modern Mental Status Examination. *Comprehensive Psychiatry, 22,* pp 528–531.

Reisner, R. (1971). *Graffiti. Two Thousand Years of Wall Writing.* New York: Cowles Book Company.

Ridout, R., & Witting, C. (1967). *English Proverbs Explained.* London: Heinemann.

Sackett, S. J. (1972). E. W. Howe as Proverb Maker. *Journal of American Folklore, 85,* pp 73–77.

Simpson, J. (1992). *The Concise Oxford Dictionary of Proverbs* (2nd ed.). London: Oxford University Press.

Skeat, W. W. (1910). *Early English proverbs . . . of the 13th and 14th Centuries with illustrative quotations.*

Stambaugh, R. (1970). Proverbial and Human Corruption and other Distortion of Popular Sayings. *Proverbium, 15,* pp 531–535.

Stevenson, B. (1947). *Book of Proverbs, Maxims and Familiar Phrases.*

Taylor, A. (1931). *The Proverb.* Cambridge, Massachusetts: Harvard University Press.

Taylor, A. (1958). 'All is Not Gold that Glitters' and 'Rolandslied'. *Romance Philology, 11,* pp 370–371.

Taylor, A. (1965–66). The Road to 'An Englishman's House . . .'. *Romance Philology, 19,* pp 279–285.

Taylor, A. (1967a). The Collection and Study of Proverbs. *Proverbium, 8,* pp 161–177.

Taylor, A. (1967b). Stolen Fruit is Always the Sweetest. *Proverbium, 7,* pp 145–149.

Taylor, A. (1968). A Place for Everything and Everything in Its Place. *Proverbium, 10,* pp 235–238.

Tilley, M. (1950). *A Dictionary of Proverbs in England in the 16th and 17th Centuries.* Ann Arbor: University of Michigan Press.

Trench, R. C. (1853). *Proverbs and their Lessons: being the substance of lectures delivered to young men's societies.* London: Kegan Paul.

Vinken, P. J. (1958). Some Observations on the Symbolism of 'The Broken Pot' in Art and Literature. *American Imago, 15,* pp 149–174.

Walsh, W. S. (1892). *Handy-Book of Literary Curiosities.* Philadelphia: Lippincott.

Woods, B. A. (1970). English Sayings in Brecht: An Addendum. *Proverbium, 15,* pp 545–547.

Wright, T. (1846). On Proverbs and Popular Sayings. In T. Wright (Eds.), *Essays on Subjects Connected with the Literature, Popular Superstitions, and History of England in the Middle Ages.* (pp 124–175). London: John Russell Smith.

Zick, G. (1969). Der zerbrochene Krug als Bildmotiv des 18 Jahrhunderts. *Wallraf-Richartz Jahrbuch,* 31, pp 149–204.

INDEX